THE TRIALS OF PORTNOY

Patrick Mullins is a Canberra-based academic and writer. He has a PhD from the University of Canberra, and his first book, *Tiberius with a Telephone*, a biography of former prime minister William McMahon, was published by Scribe in 2018.

The Trials of Portnoy

how Penguin brought down
Australia's censorship system

PATRICK MULLINS

SCRIBE
Melbourne • London

Scribe Publications

2 John St, Clerkenwell, London, WC1N 2ES, United Kingdom
18–20 Edward St, Brunswick, Victoria 3056, Australia
3754 Pleasant Ave, Suite 100, Minneapolis, Minnesota 55409, USA

First published by Scribe 2020

Typeset in 12/16 pt Adobe Caslon Pro by the publishers

Printed and bound in the UK by CPI Group (UK) Ltd,
Croydon CR0 4YY

Scribe Publications is committed to the sustainable use of
natural resources and the use of paper products made responsibly
from those resources.

9781913348175 (UK edition)
9781925849448 (US edition)
9781925938265 (ebook)

Catalogue records for this book are available from the
National Library of Australia and the British Library.

scribepublications.co.uk
scribepublications.com
scribepublications.com.au

Contents

CHAPTER I

Wrap and pay

A few minutes before noon on Monday 31 August 1970, two men alighted from a car parked on Castlereagh Street, Sydney, and crossed the road, heading toward the Angus & Robertson bookstore. A cool wind was curling through the city and the street around them was busy: cars and buses stopping and starting on the road, lunching city workers jostling with wandering shoppers on the footpath. But amid this, the two men noticed, was a hubbub of activity. Outside Angus & Robertson, a film crew and television presenter were speaking to people on the street, and those with time were stopping to watch. As the two men approached, they observed an elderly man waving a book and talking into a proffered microphone, attracting favourable murmurs from the gathered crowd.

The two men noted the book the man was waving, but did not stop to listen. They made their way through the throng and entered the bookstore so slightly apart that no one could tell if they were together. Neither entered Angus & Robertson with the look of openness and idleness with which many enter bookstores. Once inside, they did not look around to gather their bearings. They did not browse the shelves, nor approach an attendant for help. Strangers to the store, they knew very well what they were doing.

The older of the two men, Quill, began walking towards the back of the store. His companion, Mitchell, followed two steps behind him. Their destination was the paperback section — a vast part of the store that encompassed seven display cases, two swivel shelves, and a wall of books that extended almost to the high ceiling. On any given day there were nearly 1,500 titles on those shelves: a varied and immense library of novels, poetry, short-story collections, works of history, philosophy, science, geography, and biography.

As Quill and Mitchell entered that section, uninterested in the books and undaunted by their number, they took note of the people milling around the shelves and the neat young man who was standing behind a counter, serving customers. There was a long, thin sign above him that read 'Wrap and Pay', and beside him, helping to package books, was a young woman with long, dark hair. There was a queue circling from behind the counter to the front, and Mitchell, with a nod from Quill, joined it. He made a mental note of those in front of him: a young woman with straight brown hair and no makeup, dressed in a navy-blue uniform and carrying a brown Globite bag; a man in his twenties, bearded, wearing a shabby navy skivvy, jeans, and old brown sandals; a middle-aged woman with grey hair, wearing a yellow coat; and, in front of her and at the head of the queue, three middle-aged men, all in suits and ties and all marks of respectability.

With Mitchell in the queue, Quill positioned himself so that he could see the counter. Both watched what happened there. They saw people exchange money for a book, which was withdrawn from below the counter, slipped into a brown-and-green Angus & Robertson–branded paper bag, and then handed over. It was the everyday commerce of any bookshop, but Mitchell and Quill watched as if it was the most interesting thing they had ever seen.

One by one, the line advanced. The exchange was repeated. It was quickly done. Each person in the queue was at the counter for barely a minute. As other people joined the queue, Quill and Mitchell continued to observe the transactions. They watched the middle-aged woman ask in a timid voice for a book, then smile nervously when she received it. They watched the shabbily dressed man. They watched the young woman. The two men were especially interested in her: they noted that her purchase — bold, unabashed, even a little loud — occurred without so much as a batted eyelid.

Finally, Mitchell reached the front of the queue. Quill watched him approach the counter. He saw it almost as an animatronic sequence, of action and reaction and reaction again. He saw Mitchell speak, the man behind the counter nod, the girl reach down and withdraw a book, which she slipped into a brown-and-green bag. She handed it over; the man behind the counter spoke again; Mitchell handed him a $2 note and received change. Then it was over: Mitchell was off, making for the exit.

Quill followed. Outside the store, amid the wind and the people and the noise of the city, Mitchell opened the bag and withdrew the book. He and Quill looked at it. It was a small, unremarkable thing: a paperback with an orange spine and a plain black cover. The publisher's colophon was in the top-right corner — an ambling penguin, facing to the left. The title of the book was printed in graceful white text; the author's name appeared above it in thick block capitals of yellowing scarlet.

Quill and Mitchell nodded to one another, satisfied, as though they had been doubtful they would receive the real thing.

They did not know it at that time, but by their simple purchase these two men had helped to set in train events that would lead to the collapse of a system that was, for many Australians, a simple and immutable fact of life. The government apparatuses that enforced censorship in Australia would be left tottering when a decision to prosecute those who had published and sold this book provoked a legion of booksellers, publishers, authors, journalists, and academics to rise to its defence. Those coming to this book's defence believed that Australians had the right to read whatever they wanted; that censorship was stifling Australian intellectual and cultural life; that closed-minded wowsers were enforcing a system of morals that was hypocritical, outdated, and out of sync with the country that Australia was becoming. Many of these beliefs had been long-held — indeed, in the fights between censors and their opponents, these beliefs had regularly incited great passion and fine words.

But in two years' time the battles would be virtually over. The censorship system, as it existed, would be all but abolished. And the slim novel that now rested in Mitchell's hands would be at the heart of the reason why.

At that moment, on that cool day at the end of winter, as they stood on Castlereagh Street, neither man knew this. Neither Mitchell nor Quill had any inkling of what would eventuate from their visit to the Angus & Robertson bookstore. For them, this was simply routine, the banality of day-to-day police work.

They slipped the copy of *Portnoy's Complaint* back into its bag. Then they turned and began walking towards King Street, unremarkable and unnoticed among the crowds. There was another bookshop to visit.

CHAPTER 2

In the national interest

By the time Australia federated in 1901, there existed already a thicket of laws to prevent publication and dissemination of the indecent and the obscene.[1] Derived from English statutes and largely passed in the preceding quarter-century, when each of the states was a colony, these state-based laws constituted the first thorny element of Australia's censorship regime. The second element was introduced later that year, when the new Commonwealth adopted the *Customs Act* and the *Post and Telegraph Act*. The former gave unbridled power to the Department of Trade and Customs to control all imports to Australia; the latter empowered the Postmaster-General's Department to police the distribution of material through the postal system within Australia.

The powers exercised under these laws stemmed from the belief that censorship was protection: Australia was an outpost of the British Empire, and as susceptible to the contamination of impure literature as it was to foreign invasion. The vulnerable masses of the new nation had to be quarantined from material that would undermine character and moral virtue; where that material grew

5

indigenously, it needed to be rooted out like a weed.[2]

It was moral guardianship writ large, and the Commonwealth Government wasted no time in donning the mantle of protector. On 8 July 1901, before the *Customs Act* had even been proclaimed, officials in Melbourne seized a shipment of books imported by bookseller George Robertson & Co.[3] The two works that were the cause of ire were Honoré de Balzac's *Droll Stories* and Paul de Kock's *Monsieur Dupont*: bawdy, licentious, lively works of fiction, written in the realist style, about prostitutes, adulterers, violence, and poverty. To Customs officials, these French novels were dangerous and unacceptable works.

The trials of English bookseller Henry Vizetelly in 1888 and 1889, for publishing and selling translations of novels by Émile Zola, were catalysts for this panic and fear. British moralist Samuel Smith had claimed in the House of Commons that Zola's work was poisonous and corrupting. Look what such literature had done for France, he said. It had 'overspread that country like a torrent'. Its 'poison' was 'destroying the whole national life'. Was Westminster to wait until this 'deadly poison spread itself over English soil and killed the life of this great and noble people' as well?[4]

The wave of moral panic that Smith helped to whip up swept across the oceans and reached Australia.[5] Alfred Deakin, then the chief secretary in Victoria, ordered police to hunt in Melbourne's bookshops for copies of Vizetelly's translations; in 1889, his colleague the minister for customs, James Patterson, ordered prosecution of bookseller Edward Cole for importing a selection of French novels written in the same realist tradition. That prosecution had been widely applauded. 'Probably every sane person,' intoned *The Age*, 'agrees that Zola is not only filthy but [also] revolting.'[6] There were, moreover, calls for greater control over the books imported to Australia. As *The Daily Telegraph* asked, 'Are we prepared to allow the more subtle and deadly infection of French literary vice to be emptied upon our bookstalls, and into the imagination of our children?'[7]

The motivations for the 1901 prosecution of George Robertson & Co. were therefore well understood and the explanations familiar. In the hearings in the Melbourne City Court that September, the Crown argued that prosecution was 'in the interests of public morality'. Books by Balzac and de Kock were 'literary garbage of the worst order, not even possessing literary quality to redeem them.' The minister for trade and customs, South Australian MP Charles Kingston, had deemed the books 'debasing, demoralising, and indecent', and in the course of the trial the experts summoned by the prosecution hastened to agree.

But there was a strong undercurrent of ridicule and disapproval at the prosecution.[8] The defence pointed out that there had been no warning that a prosecution might be launched, and no consistency in its application — the same books having been imported in Sydney without incident by the same ship. These books had been imported for more than forty years without question, and the library at Parliament House held an illustrated edition of *Droll Stories*. Why had court action been taken?

As would become standard practice, the judiciary would not dissent from the moral mission of censorship. The magistrate 'regretted' that the action had been brought, but agreed that the books were indecent within the meaning of the act and that a penalty would have to be enforced. George Robertson & Co. was fined £100, mitigated to £25, without costs.[9]

Successful in name, the result was hardly auspicious for the new Customs administration. Widespread criticism followed, especially from those uneasy at the prospect of politicians and officials determining the moral character of Australia's citizens. But if the puritan, Irish-Catholic-dominated department was scalded by the public opprobrium it had attracted, it was not dissuaded from the righteousness of its mission.[10]

In 1904, when a New South Wales royal commission on the declining birth rate identified a link between morality in the community and the use of contraceptives, Customs reasserted itself with a vehemence that was striking. It acted immediately on the commission's recommendation that it prohibit and impede all 'goods, articles, contrivances or other things designed or intended for use for the prevention of conception in women'.[11]

With the fervent agreement of the state governments, it worked to expand obscenity from the English law definition — the Hicklin definition, in play since 1868, of the power to deprave or corrupt — to include the functions of the body. Works that discussed, described, or advertised birth control, in particular, were now obscene. And in spite of the legal precedent to the contrary, the effect was that such information was banned.[12] Similar revisions of what constituted obscenity and indecency would follow: ten years later, Customs would inform its officers that 'indecent' should be defined by what officers believed was 'contrary to what is fit and proper', and that they should be guided 'by their experience of what is usually considered unobjectionable in the household of the ordinary self-respecting citizen'.[13]

Customs did this in the shadows. Avoiding public court trials, the minister for trade and customs made use of his power under section 52c of the *Customs Act* to ban by proclamation the import of any work deemed by him to be obscene, indecent, or blasphemous. Lists of the banned or restricted works — what David Marr would later call the 'index of Australia's innocence' — were themselves kept secret.[14] Aided by close relationships with the British government, which sent warnings of suspect publications, Customs officials inspected imported books on the wharves and runways, and seized questionable material from travellers' suitcases almost unfettered; clerks in far-flung offices screened parcels and letters sent via the post, and Vice Squad officers inspected bookshops for illicit material. State laws on obscenity and indecency — now compounded by legislation for public health, crimes, advertising, defamation, commerce, and gaming, among other areas — allowed material to be seized and destroyed by fiat.

Societal good was the aim and the defence. Customs 'would not hesitate to push the law to its utmost extent, in the public interest', said H.N.P. Wollaston, the comptroller-general of customs, in 1907.[15] Nor would it allow its standards to drop. When it came time, in 1910, to ratify an agreement with the British on obscene publications, Australia's government hesitated. Its censorship system and policies were pervasive and effective — more effective, even, than the British system that had been Australia's model. The discrepancy was such that, as the historian Deana Heath would argue, Australia now regarded the imperial metropole with deep concern: it was a threat to the purity that Australian censorship had done so much to foster and protect.[16]

* * *

The outbreak of the Great War allowed the censorship regime to widen its ambit to include explicitly political work. At the behest of the government of Billy Hughes, parliament passed the *War Precautions Act* in 1915. As its drafter, Sir Robert Garran, was to say, the act 'suspended' Magna Carta and gave to Hughes and Garran 'full and unquestionable powers over the liberties of every subject'.[17] The intention of that act was to restrict distribution of seditious literature — but, in the view of a government grappling with staggering casualties and, from 1916 on, controversial plans to introduce conscription, this came to include an enormous amount of material, benign or otherwise. Moreover, loath to surrender these powers at war's end, the Hughes government maintained them until 1921, whereupon it issued Proclamation 24, drawn from section 52g of the *Customs Act*, which all but duplicated those powers.[18]

   While aiming to check the spread of communist, anarchist, and fascist thought in Australia, the proclamation widened the scope for the seizure and destruction of material far beyond the stated purpose. Magazines ranging from *Harper's Bazaar* to *Cosmopolitan* were banned; works on the 1916 Easter Rising in

Ireland were seized; even important works of fiction, such as Ernest Hemingway's *A Farewell to Arms* and Erich Maria Remarque's *All Quiet on the Western Front*, were prohibited. The Scullin government revised the proclamation in 1929, but it was restored to its prior scope when the United Australia Party, led by Joseph Lyons, came to the government benches in 1932.

The following year saw the appointment of T.W. 'Tommy' White as minister for trade and customs. Son-in-law of Alfred Deakin and a decorated veteran of the Great War, White was a fervent anti-communist, a determined advocate for the military, and a pugnacious, even combative, politician. As minister for customs, he became closely identified with a resurgence of censorship. In 1935, he accused the Scullin government of allowing into Australia 'scores of publications previously banned as seditious', and he increased the number of bans on seditious works, targeting leftist publications about communism.[19]

But a crucial factor in the growth and consolidation of censorship in Australia was changing.[20] Banning pamphlets by small socialist organisations was one thing: they would rarely attract widespread and sustained attention. Banning works of fiction that were famous and acclaimed was different. And famous and acclaimed works of modernism — which sought a deliberate break from the empirical, the civilised, and the hierarchical, and prized instead the relentlessly new, the subjective, the chaotic, and the taboo — presented an impossible challenge for the censors. Bans placed on James Joyce's *Ulysses*, in 1929, Norman Lindsay's *Redheap*, in 1930, and Aldous Huxley's *Brave New World*, in 1933, were extensively reported and aroused considerable public criticism. The ban on *Redheap* caused Lindsay to scoff that censorship was as effective as banning air. 'Do they really think they can keep this country as an ignominious little mental slum, isolated from the world of serious intellectual values?' he asked. 'Do they think that an ostrich policy of sticking their own silly heads in the sand is going to save them from exposure elsewhere?'[21] For their part, booksellers were stunned by the *volte-face* that had rendered their stock a liability. 'The ban is utterly stupid,' said an employee of Melbourne bookseller Robertson & Mullens, of the ban on *Brave New World*. 'It will make us appear ridiculous to the English people … It is about time that the people knew who makes these decisions.'[22]

Calls for public attention and scrutiny cut through. Newspapers took up the cause. 'Whatever one believes,' the Adelaide-based *News* editorialised, 'he [or she] will hardly agree that the present system of censorship, under which a Minister of the Federal Government is the final arbiter of what Australians shall read, is anywhere near ideal.'[23]

The glare of public scrutiny was anathema to censorship: it required secrecy and shadows. This attention from newspapers and the public was crucial to forcing change in censorship practices. For White, it was galling. A month after *Brave New World* was banned, he said that 'the irritating critics' should fight the ban or be quiet. They should order a copy from London; tell Customs so that it could be seized; and then sue for its return. The courts could decide. 'I will meet the critics on their own ground,' he promised.[24]

But the government wished to shut the debate down. In May 1933, it created the Book Censorship Board, an honorary body composed of three qualified and interested persons who would recommend whether a work should be banned.[25] Designed to defuse criticisms of the lack of expert judgement and to defer responsibility for decisions from the minister, the committee's lack of remit and the secrecy surrounding its work demonstrated that its establishment was largely for show. The committee did not consider seditious works; White could override its recommendations; and the mechanism by which it considered works meant that it only ever followed in the department's footsteps.

White made clear his expectation that little would change. 'Fine writing by prominent writers will not save them if their work is tinged with obscenity,' he said. 'My idea is that authors like

[Richard] Aldington and Huxley should not escape the provisions of the law.'[26] Moreover, the lists of banned publications — works deemed obscene, blasphemous, seditious, or likely to deprave by an undue emphasis on sex or crime — only ever continued to grow during White's tenure. Records indicate that in December 1933 there were sixty-six publications that had been deemed seditious and remained banned; eighteen months later, that list had grown to 157 publications.[27]

The founding of the Book Censorship Abolition League in 1934 was the inevitable consequence of these continued controversies. Driven by University of Melbourne academic William Macmahon Ball and bookseller Roy Rawson, the league initially sought abolition of all censorship by means of public campaigns and legal challenges.[28] It was clear from the beginning that the league's ideological poles would affect how it pursued this: Ball, a liberal political philosopher interested in education, was spurred to action after Customs seized six books on communism and the Soviet government that he had ordered for a course he was teaching. Rawson, meanwhile, was a socialist and radical who papered the back wall of his store with Customs confiscation notices.[29]

Barely three months passed between the league's founding, in November 1934, and the first outbreak of dissent, with questions over whether abolition of *all* censorship was practical or even politically feasible. Ball himself wrote to *The Age* in February 1935 to call complete abolition 'an extreme view'. 'It is not the policy of the League,' he went on, 'and not a policy which would win any public support.'[30]

That month, the league presented a petition signed by 20,000 people calling for return to Scullin government–era censorship policy and release of all books that freely circulated in England. White was unmoved: 'The Cabinet is not taking the slightest interest.' There were political grounds to explain White's scorn: despite its popularity, the league had struggled to extend its influence beyond Victoria, and the presence of socialist and communist elements suggested that the league was a less liberal body than Ball's advocacy suggested. Moreover, White was aware that censorship enjoyed considerable support around the country. Letters from church groups and community organisations poured into his office and fortified White's resolve. 'I am quite sure that the majority of people appreciate what is being done in carrying out the laws of the country regarding the exclusion of indecent or seditious literature,' he wrote to one supporter.[31] Criticism levelled at him in the press, which he regarded as overtly personal, did much to reinforce White's view that he was in the right.[32]

Increasingly of the view that compromise with White was impossible, the league sought to circumvent him. Its opportunity came in December 1935, when the minister for industry and the attorney-general, Robert Menzies, returned to Australia. Then aged forty-one, Menzies was a former barrister who had served as deputy premier of Victoria until his election in 1934 to the federal seat of Kooyong. A man of spritely intelligence, with a fine speaking manner and a talent for debate, Menzies' skills were too many to be left unused on the backbench. Joseph Lyons, the prime minister, therefore elevated him immediately to the ministry and, almost as quickly, took him to London to participate in trade talks and celebrations for the silver jubilee of King George V.

Menzies' absence from Australia had allowed White to expand his control of censorship policy. The attorney-general's department was supposed to determine whether a seditious work should be banned or released — not Customs. But, late in 1933, when it started to approve for release works of communist and socialist literature, White countermanded convention by allowing his department to ban books without referring them to the attorney-general's department.

Menzies' return, therefore, was important. His mind was stricter on questions of the law than was White's, and his rapport with Ball — whom he had known since late in the 1920s — was considerably warmer than with his colleague. Moreover, usually unnoticed but important was Menzies' streak of quiet bohemianism: a willingness to be entertained by bawdy comedy, literary drama, and artistic whimsy. In response to representations from Ball, Menzies saw to it that responsibility for determining whether a publication was seditious was returned to the attorney-general's department, and he responded favourably to lobbying about specific books. 'Neither of us has time to waste,' Menzies replied, to one instance of Ball's lobbying. 'The banned books to which you refer will be unbanned in the morning.'[33]

* * *

That small victory set in motion the demise of the Book Censorship Abolition League, but the public opposition to censorship it had fomented continued to percolate. Prime Minister Joseph Lyons seemed to respond to this in 1936 when he answered a question on notice, in *Hansard*, stating that interpretation of censorship policy would be 'in a spirit consonant with the established British principle of the freedom of the press'.[34]

That hint of a change found form the following year, when the Book Censorship Board was reconfigured as the Literature Censorship Board, with formalised, regulatory duties, and an avenue for appealing board recommendations.[35] But, again, belying the extent of actual change — bans on *A Farewell to Arms, Brave New World*, and *Ulysses* were rescinded, and censorship of works of communist and socialist thought was relaxed, for example — the overarching powers of the government to reassert its control of censorship remained undiminished. It would delegate powers to mollify criticism and then retrieve them as it wished. This was particularly evident in the aftermath of the recission of the ban on *Ulysses*.

In September 1941 — six months after James Joyce's death, two years after the onset of World War II, and four years after the ban on *Ulysses* had been removed — the president of the Catholic Evidence Guild complained to Eric Harrison, minister for trade and customs in the perilously poised Fadden government, that Joyce's maze of a novel was 'blasphemous, indecent, and obscene, almost from cover to cover'. Harrison flicked the matter to his department. A senior clerk obtained a copy of the book, and, citing passages on fifteen pages, reported that its supposed literary merit could not justify its unrestricted circulation in Australia. He claimed, inaccurately, that *Ulysses* was banned in the United Kingdom and Canada.[36]

That clerk's superiors backed him up. 'In my opinion,' wrote A.H. Wilson, acting assistant comptroller-general, 'the book reeks with indecency, obscenity, and blasphemy and should be prohibited.' And yet there was a note of hesitancy. Reasserting a ban could be logistically difficult and would certainly be embarrassing.[37] Harrison — a man who saw black and white, and nothing in between — had no such hesitation.[38] On 16 September, he ordered the department to reclassify *Ulysses* as fit only for 'restricted circulation'.[39]

The decision brought immediate controversy. Criticism of inconsistency and the sidelining of the board filled the newspapers, which carried additional reports of bookshops being rushed for copies. Amid the hoopla were some who simply wanted to know what the fuss was about. Former prime minister Billy Hughes went to the Parliamentary Library to borrow a copy of *Ulysses*, but found that too many others had been there before him: there were none left to borrow. So he tried *Finnegans Wake*. 'This man is an Irishman,' said a boggled Hughes — a Welshman — afterwards. 'If Irishmen talk like him I don't wonder that Ireland has her troubles. I couldn't read that sort of stuff.'[40]

Harrison refused to back down. 'This [book],' he said, 'is crude and vulgar in every possible way, and can only pander to pornographic minds.' *Ulysses* was simply indecent: 'Why, there is hardly a page that is fit to read!' The book had made his hair stand on end, he said, and he had banned it in order to preserve 'clean and decent literature'. *Ulysses* scorned 'the highest principles on which civilisation was founded. It held up to ridicule the Creator, the Church, and the whole of moral standards of civilisation, citizenship, and decency.' Harrison made clear that he thought the matter at an end: 'My decision is final. There can be no appeal, and I hope no attempts in this direction are made.'[41]

Harrison would strain to ensure this remained true. Two weeks later, the Fadden government lost a vital budgetary vote in the House of Representatives, and Fadden was forced to return his commission to the governor-general. Four days after that, on 7 October, the Labor Party's John Curtin was sworn in as prime minister. From the opposition benches, Harrison lobbied his successor as minister for trade and customs, Senator Richard Keane, to maintain the ban. 'I have no doubt that the press will be approaching you with regard to the lifting of the ban on *Ulysses*,' he wrote to Keane on 13 October. 'Therefore I feel you would be fortified in any decision you may make by having before you copies of communication that I have received.' Those communications were almost entirely from church groups — who had written, Harrison neglected to say, in response to extracts of *Ulysses* that Harrison himself had sent them. 'I can assure you,' Harrison finished, 'my fan mail in this regard is of some dimension.'[42]

Amazed that the press could be fixated on a novel when a war was underway, and regarding the ban as a matter of neither 'great national interest' nor urgency, Keane was content to leave well alone. *Ulysses* remained banned.

* * *

At almost every turn the censorship system had a backstop. But for the High Court's ruling against efforts to enforce censorship of the press during World War II, the government, bureaucracy, and judiciary were in lockstep. The state governments were zealous prosecutors of a swathe of writers, publishers, and booksellers in the immediate post-war years. Max Harris, the precocious, young

South Australian poet and editor of the modernist art journal *Angry Penguins*, was prosecuted and found guilty of publishing obscene and indecent works in 1944, after rushing to print the poems of the fictional Ern Malley. Bookseller Angus & Robertson was prosecuted in New South Wales for selling Lawson Glassop's war novel about Tobruk, *We Were the Rats*. Agreement from the prosecutor and trial judge that it was a novel 'true to life' did not save it: Angus & Robertson was found guilty.

Perhaps the most controversial prosecution was that of Melbourne writer Robert Close, in 1945, for using *rutting* as a substitute for *fucking* in his novel *Love Me Sailor*. Close was sentenced to three months' jail. An appeal to the Victorian Supreme Court saw the sentence quashed, but the conviction was affirmed and the justification of literary merit seemingly scotched. Justice Wilfred Fullagar admitted to a belief that there was a 'general instinctive sense' in the community of what was decent and indecent — a forerunner of the justification of community standards — but declared nonetheless that objectionable passages in literary works were not redeemed by the skill that had been used to write them. Likening such works to a drunk yelling in the street, Fullagar wrote that 'the general sense of a civilised community condemns both, and the instinct which condemns them is thoroughly sound and far more realistic than any sophistic doctrine which would find something praiseworthy in either'.[43]

As exemptions were made for works that were of clear literary merit, as the New South Wales government did in 1946, laws for censorship continued to proliferate. Moral panics sparked by the popularity of film, pulp magazines, lowbrow genre fiction, and comics intended for children and adolescents spurred a burst of legislation between 1953 and 1955, creating extra offences and more efficient machinery for suppressing obscene and indecent material.[44] The governments of Victoria and New South Wales introduced licensing and registration schemes for publishers in 1954 and 1955 as way to regulate and control their output;

in 1951, the New South Wales government added 'any matter which emphasised unduly matters of sex, crimes of violence, gross cruelty or horror' to its definition of obscenity. In Victoria, the defence of literary merit would not be admitted; in 1954, the Queensland government introduced its own censorship board, the Queensland Literature Board of Review, with the power to ban domestically produced and imported publications that it deemed obscene, irrespective of whether they had been refused or allowed into the country and other states. Tasmania mimicked the move that year by establishing its Publications Board of Review, but raised its status by removing any provision for appeal of the board's decisions.

This consolidation continued to be driven by a fear of contaminating international influences. In May 1945, Customs requested that the Literature Censorship Board review American writer Kathleen Winsor's novel *Forever Amber*. The department was concerned that a film adaptation and British edition of the book might excite Australian interests, hence the 'urgency' of its request.[45] The board set to examining the 900-page bestseller, which would be acclaimed for inaugurating the modern romance genre. But, with the scathing dismissal that 'popularity is no sure guarantee of worth', chairman Leslie Allen declared that its 'crude and obvious appeal to the sexual instinct' made its popularity fatal: the book posed a danger to Australian readers. Two other board members, neither of whom had read the whole book, agreed. Customs minister Senator Richard Keane, who had also not read the book, announced a ban on *Forever Amber* on 6 June with an invocation of providence and moral purpose: 'The Almighty did not give people eyes to read that kind of rubbish.'[46]

Censorship went on almost irrespective of who was in power. The Labor government of Ben Chifley did not see fit to alter it materially; nor did the Liberal–Country Party coalition government of Robert Menzies, which won office in 1949. The Department of Trade and Customs continued its work in much the same way as it had for the previous forty years: with citations of its righteous mission and intimations of ruin if it were stopped. 'The Department has a definite duty to protect the morals of the community by exercising censorship,' wrote comptroller-general J.J. Kennedy in 1946, '... and after 40 years' experience in the Department I would say that the need is as great today as ever.'[47] Ministers were happy to let this be. Recalling the impossible flood of 'paperback junk' into Australia during his short tenure as customs minister in 1955–56, Fred Osborne said later that 'one had to rely on the good sense of Customs officers in applying the taste of the time'.[48]

For its advocates, censorship was necessary for protecting the standards and morals of the community; for its opponents, censorship was stultifying and a much-abused inhibition on freedom. A notorious case in the 1950s concerned a series of popular romance comics banned by the Queensland Literature Board of Review on grounds that they would be 'injurious to [the] morality' of the 'unstable adolescents' who would read them — namely, girls and young women. At a Supreme Court hearing over the ban, a matron from a Salvation Army girls home was summoned to condemn the comics for the effect they would have on the girls in her charge: 'The love scenes would excite them and retard their rehabilitation and the pictures of "pick-ups" would do particular harm.' Was this really true? Could it really be accepted as fact? The Supreme Court was of a mind to accept it, but the High Court would not. Setting aside the ban in 1956, it ruled that its disapproval of the American-influenced passionate love portrayed in these comics was outweighed by the sound morality of their stories: 'The theme of them all nearly is love, courtship, and marriage. Virtue never falters and right triumphs. Matrimony is the proper end.'[49]

Booksellers were intimidated into cooperating with Customs officials. The penalty for not doing so, as one bookseller wrote, was to be raided and searched, and have stock seized and staff surveiled. 'All this may be done, and has been done, not unostentatiously,' he wrote, 'but by a large squad of officers while a shop is actually trading, with customers present.'[50]

Opposing censorship was difficult. Its effects could not easily be documented or protested. It was 'a fog on the wharf', as Nettie Palmer said; it removed any sense of clarity for writers, publishers, printers, and readers.

West Australian writer Peter Cowan, whose poems had been found indecent in the prosecution of Max Harris, recalled that censorship left writers and readers inhibited: 'You didn't know about these [banned] books because they never came in and nobody ever said anything about them.' Moreover, if you wanted to write, he said, 'what you did really was to accept that there were certain things that you would not be able to say in any straightforward way … You still had to keep off certain things, and editors were uneasy, and what you developed, I suppose, was a way of writing around these subjects that were forbidden.'[51]

Dymphna Cusack, co-author of *Come in Spinner*, spoke from firsthand experience of the timidity and conservatism that censorship fostered in Australia: *Spinner* had been ruthlessly edited before publication in 1951. 'In Australia, we're basically wowsers,' she said. 'Reviewers aren't very enlightened, [and] consequently you get a backlash. Most of them haven't read a great deal of literature, particularly foreign literature. They would accept in London, Paris or Berlin what they wouldn't take here.'[52]

* * *

For all the efforts to quarantine Australia from those foreign influences, change abroad would force change to censorship. In the United States and the United Kingdom, censorship policies suffered severe setbacks in the 1950s and 1960s, including the increasingly accepted argument that the existence of literary or artistic merit in a work mitigated its obscenity. The fact that the Literature Censorship Board appeared to accept that, recommending release of works that would otherwise have been banned, caused considerable dismay within the renamed Department of Customs and Excise. In May 1957, comptroller-general F.A. Meere called for his minister, Tasmanian senator Denham Henty, to overrule the board's recommendations on three titles, and argued that if there were a lack of confidence in the board then 'action should be taken at the first appropriate occasion to change' the board.[53] Meere's view steadily hardened, and he pressed the point repeatedly. 'My view is that the Board, on a number of occasions,' he wrote, a few months later, 'has given undue weight to literary merit and in doing so condoned the presence therein of blasphemous, indecent, or obscene matter.'[54] Henty agreed to some of these moves, but the influence of a liberalisation worldwide could hardly be stopped.

What would force change was public scrutiny of censorship policy. This occurred next in 1957, when a ban placed on J.D. Salinger's 1951 novel, *The Catcher in the Rye*, caught press attention.[55] Widely regarded as the inaugurating work of the young adult genre, *Catcher* had been published to acclaim and controversy, and been banned in Australia in August 1956 by Customs officials within the department. Despite this, American ambassadors to Australia had frequently donated copies to school and public libraries, on the basis that it was an excellent example of modern American literature. Geoffrey Dutton, an elegant and well-connected Adelaide-based writer, thought the ban on *Catcher* particularly dumb, and criticised Henty for maintaining it. He was surprised to receive a letter proposing a meeting, where Henty said he would explain the ban. But their meeting only exposed the ban as a farce: Henty said that *Catcher* had been banned for its portrayal of male vice, and pointed Dutton to a passage where the narrator indicts his brother for 'prostituting' himself as a hack screenwriter in Hollywood. Dutton could only laugh.[56]

Criticism of the ban on *Catcher* became especially loud in September, when the parliamentary librarian removed a copy from the Parliamentary Library. It was the third mishap in an embarrassing week for the censorship regime: Leslie Allen, chairman of the Literature Censorship Board, had stepped down from his post, and the early stirrings of a campaign to see the ban on *Redheap* rescinded were reported with glee in the *Sun* newspaper. As a *Sydney Morning Herald* editorial argued, the secrecy over censorship had to end. There were laws aplenty in the country, should anyone feel that censorship was still necessary. 'No further "protection" — especially by anonymous Customs clerk[s] — is needed,' the editorial argued. 'Commonwealth censorship is superfluous, and should be abolished.'[57] Henty sought to defuse the criticism by moving to have the board assess *Catcher* — which it did, recommending release early in October — but the unabating scrutiny meant that pressure for wider change continued to build.

It was too much for Henty, who gave way yet again. On 25 October, he announced that officials within the Department of Customs would no longer make decisions on what was banned: the Literature Censorship Board would decide that. To help prevent delays, the board would be split into two committees that would rule on individual works. Moreover, the board would 'overhaul the present list of books that have been banned'.[58]

The result, by April 1958, was a considerably whittled-down list of banned books.[59] Works that had attracted attention for being banned — Lindsay's *Redheap* and Winsor's *Forever Amber* among them — were now permitted. There were still 178 titles remaining on the list, but any additions or deletions to the list would now be published in the *Commonwealth Government Gazette*, thereby becoming publicly available. Second, the list would be reviewed at five-yearly intervals.

This was, for some, a victory. Journalist Peter Coleman, who would soon begin to research the history of censorship in Australia, argued that it marked the start of a 'period of qualified liberalism' in Australia.[60] Others took a different view. As the University of Melbourne academic Stephen Murray-Smith would argue, these changes marked the movement of censorship as a political issue from the fringe to the mainstream. Confrontation — between those who wished to maintain it and those who wished to see it gone — was imminent.[61]

CHAPTER 3

Another country

Henty's changes had the desired effect: public attention turned from censorship to other matters; and, in its absence, briefly, Customs reverted to form. It banned Ian Fleming's *The Spy Who Loved Me*. It banned James Jones's *The Thin Red Line*. It banned William Burroughs' *Naked Lunch*. The public seemed to pay no attention.

What changed that was the banning of James Baldwin's *Another Country*.[1] A study of interracial love, homosexuality, racism, and masculinity, *Another Country* had been unofficially banned after its publication in 1962, with a formal ban in place by the following year.[2] That ban was not absolute — the novel was made available for the 'serious minded student or reader' — but the fact it had been instituted at all provoked enormous controversy. The Literature Censorship Board had cautioned that acute sensitivity and political heat over race could cause a ban on *Another Country* to be 'associated with Australia's misunderstood "White Australia policy" and her refusal to support UN condemnation of South African apartheid'.[3] But that caution was ignored — and, when the ban was announced, writers Geoffrey Dutton, Rosemary Wighton, and Max Harris wrote an open letter calling for Henty to overturn the ban for precisely those reasons.

'The banning of *Another Country* is very likely to be interpreted as an act of colour and racial prejudice on the part of Australia,' they wrote, 'and to be interpreted in an anti-Australian way by Asian students and newspapers, by communist powers, and by liberal racial forces in the USA.'[4] The impact on Australia's reputation internationally was another point of criticism. As Dutton, Wighton, and Harris added, Australia had joined Ireland as the only English-speaking nation that had banned *Another Country*. A reputation as a conservative, puritanical backwater was being consolidated by the continuing intransigence and narrow-mindedness of the censorship regime.

The fresh attention that *Another Country* drew to censorship did not abate. Further controversy spread to the ban in place on Vladimir Nabokov's *Lolita*, which narrated the grooming, rape, and sustained abuse of a teenage girl by the adult Humbert Humbert, who delusionally viewed this as part of a great romantic affair. Then there was controversy over *The Group*. An account of the lives of eight young American women after their graduation from Vasser College, Mary McCarthy's novel was contentious for its candid depiction of sex, breastfeeding, contraceptives, and the characters' experiences of sexism and autonomy. It had been banned in Ireland and Italy — but, in a small victory, had been cleared for publication and dissemination in Australia. Yet in March 1964, in an act that would thrust him into the centre of the censorship battles, Arthur Rylah — deputy premier, attorney-general, and chief secretary in Victoria — ordered that everything be done to see *The Group* removed from sale in his state.

A fifty-five-year-old solicitor who had enjoyed a stunning rise through the Liberal Party — becoming its deputy leader a mere six years after entering the state parliament — Rylah was a man of prodigious stamina and will whose qualities of character seemed to manifest themselves in his appearance. To Rylah's complaint that standard shirt sizes never seemed to fit him, an exasperated tailor once replied, 'When you've got a bull neck, a pigeon chest, and a scholar's stoop, what else do you expect?'[5]

Rylah's record of reform would be laudable and immense, but in retirement he would argue that nothing he had done had been so subject to distortion as his involvement in the censorship fights. Believing that there was no support in the community for the complete cessation of censorship, Rylah thought the only matter of contention should be where the line was drawn on what to censor and what to allow to go free. Yet this, too, was a distortion: Rylah's obstinacy and conservatism led him to resist all attempts to redraw that line. In the 1960s, he became a bulwark against liberalisation of the censorship regime. He saw moves abroad to liberalise censorship as evidence of lowered standards and something to be deplored. 'Do we want the youth in our community to be depraved and corrupted by this filth?' he said. 'I say firmly we do not. And I say with calm and resolution, despite the criticism and excesses of the current campaign, the government will not yield on this issue.'[6]

Not yielding would require Rylah to exercise his powers and influence with considerable force. His opposition to *The Group* — not followed by any other state or territory — became one of the most notable attempts to forestall change in censorship in Australia. It also prompted opposition, most notably in the formation of the Freedom to Read committee, which criticised Rylah's method for preventing sale of *The Group* in Victoria. Instead of declaring it obscene, which could be fought in court, the committee pointed out, Rylah had ordered police to warn booksellers they *could* be prosecuted under Victoria's *Police Act*. To this effective threat, the booksellers responded as Rylah hoped. They were too terrified to stock the book.[7]

The continuing controversy led to a debate on the ABC's current affairs program *Four Corners* in March 1964 between Rylah and Freedom to Read chair Hector Monro. In the course of that debate, Rylah stated that he had read *The Group* and 'would not like it to be in the hands of my teenage son and daughter'.

Neither of his children were then teenagers. Emblematic of the censorship regime's unabashed paternalism and capriciousness, the remark became notorious.

* * *

Remarks like Rylah's, and the attitudes to which they spoke, sparked the involvement of most relentless opponents in the fights against censorship, most of whom emerged from the alternative and student press. These underground and campus-based magazines — produced in straitened circumstances via cold type and photo offset printing, published on irregular schedules, advertised by word of mouth, and sold on street corners or in pubs — were a self-conscious alternative to the newspapers and magazines produced by Fairfax, Australian Consolidated Press, and News Ltd: a fifth estate that was willing to experiment and to publish frank and controversial material.[8] Amid the great flowering of student activism in the 1960s — in campaigns over the White Australia policy, military involvement in Vietnam, women's rights, sexual freedom, and Indigenous rights — those involved in these presses agitated for change and freedom. As historian Barbara Sullivan later wrote, the 'thoroughgoing cultural freedom' these activists sought could only follow from freedom from censorship.[9]

One of the most notable publications was *Oz*, based in Sydney and founded by former student editors Richard Neville, Richard Walsh, and Peter Grose. Featuring an eclectic roster of contributors and a distinctive look, thanks to the efforts of art director Martin Sharp, *Oz* immediately caught the ire of authorities with its mocking, satirical coverage of government and Australian culture. After the restrictions of writing for student publications, Walsh said later, 'we wanted something that left us free to write whatever nonsense that we wanted … We set it up to amuse ourselves and other people.'[10] Grose recalled the origins similarly: *Oz* was inspired by the potent satire of Lenny Bruce, Mort Sahl, Bob Newhart, and institutions such as *Private Eye* and *That Was the Week That Was*. 'We had no intention of challenging censorship,' he explained later, 'only of challenging pomposity and hypocrisy through the medium of satire.'[11]

Calling itself both 'a stand-out sophisticated magazine' and 'a real epigram of depravity', *Oz* took a simple stance on offence and censorship: 'If you are offended by *Oz*, don't buy it,' Walsh wrote, in 1963. 'There is no justification in the world for censoring "offensive" material, unless the offended are forced to read or view it.'[12]

Their first number, published on 1 April 1963, seemed designed to provoke a reaction. It contained extracts of a fake diary kept by the Queen, a history of chastity belts, and an interview with an abortionist.[13] At a time when abortion was illegal in New South Wales, this last piece was particularly provocative. And yet, as Walsh argued later, the editors had not 'set out deliberately' to be so.

> We were not really aware of how out-of-step with the community we were. Nor, as it turned out, were the authorities. Society was on the move. The conservative values that we were protesting against were not in sync with the rest of the community. The new generation that was coming along did not accept the values and ideas of the 1950s.[14]

As further issues were published, the gaps between *Oz*, the community, and the authorities became chasms. Advertisers fled, and the editors were kicked out of the offices they had leased. The state government 'went into a tailspin', and moved to shut the magazine down.[15] In June 1963, it brought obscenity charges against Neville, Walsh, and Grose. Walsh's family solicitor advised the three to plead guilty, on grounds that, as first-time offenders, they would be treated leniently. They might even escape a conviction, the reasoning went. The price, however, was giving up their right to appeal and guaranteeing a severe sentence should they reoffend.[16] 'Soft-pedalling' their intentions and stating they had no plans to 'sail so close again' to the wind, the three pleaded guilty early in September, and were fined £20 apiece.[17] Grose, who had decided to leave, dissociated himself from the magazine, and his solicitor told the court that that he had 'searched his soul and found *Oz* to be utterly worthless'. But Neville and Walsh were unrepentant about what they had produced.[18] Outside the court, they repeated their belief that nothing in the magazine was obscene and that they were not worried about further prosecutions.[19] 'Most people agree that *Oz* improves each month,' they said, 'and our aim has always been the publication of a satirical, rather than smuttish, magazine.'[20]

The February 1964 issue caused another uproar. The front cover, featuring a photograph of three men appearing to urinate on a sculpture set into the wall of the Sydney offices of P&O Shipping, was made all the worse by the note that the building had been opened by Prime Minister Sir Robert Menzies.[21] Court action again followed — and, this time, the mistake of pleading guilty the year before became acute. Justice Gerald Locke disparaged evidence tendered on the merits of the satire in *Oz* as 'an affront to the intelligence of the court'. He rubbished the magazine and its readers: 'In my opinion, the publication would deprave young people or unhealthy minded adults so injudicious as to fancy it as literature and so misguided as to cultivate the habit of reading it.'[22] Regarding them as unrepentant reoffenders, he sentenced Neville and Walsh to six months' hard labour, Sharp to four months', imposed a £100 fine on Oz Publications Ltd, and, for good measure, added a £50 fine on their printer.

The severity of that sentence prompted a considerable welling of support for the *Oz* team. Funded by donations, they lodged an appeal that was heard in December in the Sydney Quarter Sessions Court. This time, represented by future governor-general John Kerr QC, the *Oz* team saw its evidence and arguments accepted.

Literary experts testified with success. Justice Aaron Levine agreed with James McAuley's evidence, for example, that the magazine presented 'successful satire' and that exposure to it would not necessarily corrupt or deprave. Upholding the appeal, Levine also held that prosecutions for obscenity needed to point to real examples of people who would be corrupted or depraved. 'Not some mere theoretical, nebulous, or fanciful tendency to deprave,' he declared, 'but a real and practical tendency to deprave, not a theoretical group of unidentified persons, but persons or groups for whom the court in judgement can refer to as those likely to be affected.'

This was an important and overdue refining of the Hicklin test. Walsh had foreshadowed it in 1963 when he argued that actual corruption or depravity caused by a publication should be proven, not accepted as a potentiality of a publication.[23] But this standard would not stand long. Charges against the magazines *Censor* and *Obscenity* reached the High Court in 1968 and resulted in the ruling that there was no onus on the prosecution to prove the Hicklin test for corruption and depravity: 'It is assumed incontrovertibly by the common law that obscene writings do deprave and corrupt morals, by causing dirty-mindedness, by creating or pandering to a taste for the obscene.'[24]

There was change, however, at the state level. In May 1965, in response to controversy caused by the sentences given to the *Oz* team, the state Liberal Party opposition leader, Robin Askin, promised to introduce trial by jury in obscenity cases, should his party win that year's election. In 1967, it followed through, replacing the 'lottery of the magistrate' that had so markedly affected the outcomes of the *Oz* case. As new New South Wales chief secretary Eric Willis was to say, 'Matters relating to what is acceptable or otherwise in the community should be decided by a representative of the community.'[25]

Willis became another notable figure in the censorship fights.[26] Then aged forty-five, he had been in politics for more than fifteen years and, in that time, developed a reputation for mirthless efficiency. Like Rylah, his appearance — lacquered dark hair, a blue, clean-shaven jaw, heavy glasses, and narrow eyes — seemed to echo his qualities: an absolute professional who was diligent, stern, sharp, and somewhat cold. Deputy leader to Askin, Willis ruminated publicly about the 'serious conflict of principles' that censorship posed for 'true liberals' like himself:

> There is the thought in the minds of all responsible people that they must ever be anxious to remove any influence in the community that is liable to corrupt moral standards, particularly those of the more youthful members of the community. But at the same time there is a revulsion on the part of people reared in the British tradition against any curtailment of our inherent freedom … Somewhere between the two extremes of censorship and complete license, there is a point that the vast majority of the members of the public would regard as a satisfactory medium.[27]

But, over and over again, Willis established himself as another bulwark against liberalisation of censorship. Simultaneous to his introduction of jury trials in obscenity cases, he increased the penalties for those found to have published and sold obscene and indecent works, and he tried to stamp out the small magazines of the alternative presses by restricting the circumstances in which they could be sold.[28] Citing polling that showed continued majority community support for censorship, disavowing his own agency in censorship decisions, and spurred by the support of the League of Welfare and Decency, Willis proclaimed that he was doing his best to 'drive the smut pedlars from the street'.[29]

What most confirmed Willis's wowserish reputation were his attempts to stop performances of the third one-act instalment (titled 'Motel') of the play *America Hurrah*. The play had run for five weeks without incident at the New Theatre on Peter Street, Sydney, but one complaint from a grandmother disturbed by the profanities written on the walls of the set prompted a massive response. Police warned the cast and crew that they would serve summonses if performances went on unamended. Willis agreed, threatening prosecution under the *Theatre and Public Halls Act*. The only people who would object to this, he told the ABC, 'would be hippies and the lunatic fringe'. He scoffed at suggestions that he was impinging on cultural freedom: 'Just because pornography is on the stage, it is not culture.'[30]

The theatre agreed to rework the play, but defenders mobilised to organise to stage a free performance of the original version, hoping that they would evade the act by not charging for admission.[31] Willis responded by threatening to prosecute under the *Vagrancy Act*, which prohibited the writing, drawing, or utterance of obscene language in a public place. The organisers — including Russell Drysdale, Cyril Pearl, Tony Blackshield, Harry Seidler, and the youthful South Australian Labor leader Don Dunstan — were not cowed. Seidler told the press that prosecution 'would be worth it'.

Around 3,000 people showed up at the 500-seat theatre, with police mingling not-so-anonymously among them. The performance proceeded: two actors dressed as dolls simulated sex, wrecked the set, and drew on the walls the words *fuck, shit,* and *a big cock up my juicy cunt*. As police all over the theatre leapt to their feet, the actors jumped into the audience and made for the side doors. At this, play director John Trasker recalled, 'pandemonium broke out'. Audience members obstructed the police, and bought time for the actors to change out of their costumes and re-enter the theatre, where they were lost in the dispersing audience. Moreover, when police tried to seize the partitions on the set as proof that the obscenities had been written, the audience surged onto the stage and shredded them.[32]

Plays would remain contentious. Further performances of *America Hurrah* were curtailed. The one-act play *Norm and Ahmed,* by Australian playwright Alex Buzo, attracted police attention for the use of *fucking* in the script, and fines were levied on actors in performances in Victoria and Queensland. Perhaps most famously of all, *The Boys in the Band* — about a group of gay men in New York gathering for a birthday party — played for months in Sydney without incident. But when it moved to Melbourne in 1969, police decided that the line 'Who do I have to fuck to get a drink around here?' warranted prosecution, and successfully charged and prosecuted three of the principal actors.

* * *

Another of the most committed and pivotal protagonists in the censorship fights was Wendy Bacon.[33] A postgraduate student of sociology at the University of New South Wales, Bacon was twenty-four when she was elected as an editor of campus newspaper *Tharunka* in 1970. A loose affiliation with the clique of left-wing Sydney-based libertarian intellectuals called The Push gave Bacon and her fellow editors, Alan Rees and Val Hodgson, a serious intellectual basis for their agitation against censorship. As Bacon recalled, their opposition was prompted by the belief that the abolition of censorship would allow a broader debate about gender, sexuality, education, and power. 'This was a time of cultural foment,' she said later. 'The Pill had come out, there were protests, there were debates and big issues going on.'[34] To force those debates, they began publishing material that was edgy and confrontational: a guide to cannabis, criticism of the campus doctor for his issue of contraceptives, a review of Anne Koedt's 'The Myth of the Vaginal Orgasm'.[35] But it was the 18 March publication of a poem, 'The Ballad of Eskimo Nell', that catapulted *Tharunka* to the forefront of the censorship battles. The bawdy, ribald poem on the back cover — a staple of sporting teams in the locker room and at the bar — caused outrage:

> When a man grows old and his balls grow cold and the end of
>   his nob turns blue,

When it's bent in the middle like a one-string fiddle, he can tell
    a yarn or two.
So find me a seat and stand me a drink and a tale to you I'll tell,
Of Dead-Eye Dick and Mexico Pete and the gentle Eskimo
    Nell.[36]

The poem was accompanied by a declaration of serious intent. The question at stake in the censorship fights, the three editors argued, was freedom — freedom to think, read, write, and publish anything, irrespective of its obscenity or quality. Defending a work for its literary or artistic merit was simply a way to change the issue: obscenity itself was a legitimate expression, and the public should be free to use it.[37] 'We thought the literary merit [justification] was a distraction and elitist,' Bacon said later.[38]

Bacon, Rees, and Hogson also promised more. A newspaper was a vehicle for 'direct action' against censorship, the editors declared, and the time was right to use that vehicle. They laid out exactly how they would drive that vehicle and the strategy behind it: 'If the government prosecutes in all cases, it slows up the courts; if it picks and chooses, their ridiculous inconsistency will be even more apparent and underlined; if it prosecutes in no cases, at least there will be a temporary and minor victory against censorship and for freedom.'[39]

Bacon, Rees, and Hodgson therefore continued much in the same vein, publishing issues of *Tharunka* replete with four-letter words, frank depictions of sex and violence, and innumerable articles of satire. Although eventually forced to resign, the three editors found favour with their readers. They had distributed more than 17,000 copies of the 'Eskimo Nell' issue, and their efforts in spin-off titles, *Thorunka* and *Thor*, continued to command attention. Writers — including academics and journalists, some of whom were well beyond university age — were attracted by the force, creativity, and freedom that they found there. 'It was my first experience of illegal or "underground" journalism,' wrote Frank

Moorhouse, who became one of the paper's stalwart forces, 'and it was the first time in our lives that we had written for, or had available, an uncensored public outlet for our writing.'[40]

Amid rising fury from politicians and outraged community leaders, court summonses duly arrived. In August 1970, the director of student publications at the University of New South Wales, the printer of the June issue of *Tharunka*, and Hodgson appeared at the Sydney Central Court on obscenity charges — only to be eclipsed by Bacon, who protested outside wearing a nun's habit that had been embroidered with the phrase, *I have been fucked by God's steel prick*. She was arrested, charged with wearing an obscene publication, and released on $100 bail.[41] Arrested again two days later, Bacon was convicted in the Sydney Quarter Sessions Court the following February for a litany of charges relating to *Tharunka* and her wearing of the habit.[42] But Bacon and her fellow editors were not dissuaded from continuing their fight, even as further charges piled up, and punishments — such as the one-week prison sentence Bacon received — followed. By 1972, the promise of that early editorial in *Tharunka* had been fulfilled: charges were clogging the New South Wales court system. Eventually, when the Supreme Court overturned Bacon's conviction for obscenity, the exhausted and frustrated authorities gave it up.

But even this was not enough. Bacon would not desist from the campaign to see censorship ended. In March 1971 she promised to continue so long as censorship remained in place: 'I'm going to be really keen to keep doing it.'[43]

For those still pressing for the enforcement of censorship, messages of this kind were the last thing they wished to hear.

CHAPTER 4

The lady

The weeping sore in the censorship battles was *Lady Chatterley's Lover*. D.H. Lawrence's 1928 novel about a young married woman's affair with a gamekeeper had been banned in Australia since 1929, but by the 1960s it had become a totemic title in censorship struggles around the world.[1] In 1959, the US District Court of New York allowed the novel's free publication in America; in the following year, UK paperback publisher Penguin published the novel and successfully defended a prosecution brought against it in a six-day trial at the Old Bailey. The pressure was on Australian authorities to follow suit.

Penguin had approached the Commonwealth government to request a review of the ban on *Lady Chatterley* in February 1960. Citing the novel's age, fame, and the reputation of its author, the Literature Censorship Board recommended its release. But Denham Henty deferred a decision until proceedings in the UK had been resolved; then, after the trial, he referred the book back to the board, with the directive that it be reassessed as 'an isolated novel' — that is, with no consideration of its place in Lawrence's oeuvre, and with no regard for Lawrence's standing. Henty also sought advice on 'whether it would be in the best public interest to release a cheap paper-backed edition'. The board was unmoved: it recommended, again, that the book be released.

It was plain that the government wanted the ban to continue and — as ever — would disregard advice on censorship matters as it saw fit. It was a mark, however, of how seriously it took the matter that it went to cabinet on 16 February 1961. Henty noted the history of the book, Penguin's application, and the advice from the experts. 'They recommend to release,' he said, 'but in effect it was a contradictory report ... My own view is to ban.' He conceded that Penguin might take action in court against the government, but added, ominously, that failure to maintain the ban on *Lady Chatterley* 'might well be the end of any effective censorship of imported literature' in Australia.[2]

Cabinet was in no mood to disagree: it opted to maintain the ban.[3]

The reaction was hostile. Critics accused the government of allowing political factors to influence the decision, and the press asked the obvious question: why, when accounts of the British trial included lengthy discussions of the merit of *Lady Chatterley*, should the book be banned?[4] Were the witnesses who had testified so mistaken? Was the jury decision wrong? Moreover, why should English readers be able to read *Lady Chatterley*, but not Australians?

Almost immediately there came a new problem: Penguin's publication of a transcript of the *Lady Chatterley* trial. Edited by the pseudonymous C.H. Rolph, a writer and former police officer, *The Trial of Lady Chatterley* allowed a glimpse of the clash between 'the striped-trousered ones' ruling Britain, as Orwell called them, and the liberalising forces agitating for change. But Henty would not allow the book. Citing its inclusion of passages from *Lady Chatterley*, Henty added *Trial* to the banned list.

The reaction was as caustic as before. The court proceedings had been reported in Australian newspapers. Why should they now, when placed in a book, be unfit for publication? In June 1961, Sir Allen Lane, Penguin's founder and managing director, met Henty to discuss the ban. It was a 'pleasant interview', Henty commented afterwards, and Lane had 'agreed' that the prohibition of both *Lady Chatterley's Lover* and *The Trial of Lady Chatterley* would be reviewed in two years' time.[5]

What Lane could disagree with was never clear; nonetheless, *Trial* was duly sent for review early in 1964, and the appeals board recommended that it be released. But the new customs minister, New South Wales senator Kenneth Anderson, appointed in June, was unconvinced. Reporting to cabinet that the timing was 'inopportune', he opted to maintain the ban.[6]

Anderson had a gentlemanly personality, was a former POW at Changi, and had been a real estate agent before entering politics. Asked when he was appointed if he had any 'conscience problems' with censorship, Anderson said not — but, like so many before him, he soon discovered otherwise. He was happy to allow a pamphlet of ribald verse by Robert Burns: 'I'm the son of a Scot, my mother was the daughter of a Scot, I lived in a Scots home, and I'm not going to find my place in history as being the person who banned the immortal bard.' But works that dealt with sex were subject to different standards. 'Normal, healthy sex was one thing, that's life,' Anderson said later:

> But perverted sex was the thing that got in my gizzard: homosexuality, lesbianism, bestiality. Too often you'd find — this is where the rub came — a book of literary merit, unquestionably with literary merit, would have something in it which, in my judgement, wasn't normal, healthy, human behaviour ... When it got into that other area — I had a blind spot, I suppose — but I could never stomach it.[7]

But Anderson would be made to, thanks to the actions of Leon Fink, Alex Sheppard, and Ken Buckley. Fink, a

twenty-eight-year-old Sydney-based entrepreneur and businessman, professed utter disdain for the censorship regime: he thought
it self-defeating and stifling. Buckley, an economic history lecturer
at the University of Sydney and secretary of the New South Wales
branch of the Council for Civil Liberties, was certainly no fan;
and Sheppard — a bookseller, a tenant in one of Fink's properties,
and a decorated veteran of World War II — was no different.[8]
A plump man with thinning silver hair, a small moustache, and
horn-rimmed glasses, Sheppard was embarrassed by censorship.
While attending a PEN International gathering in London in
April 1964, he had been stung to overhear the historian Dame
Veronica Wedgwood mocking the 'big, brawny Australians' who
had acquiesced so meekly to the ban on *Trial*.[9]

During a meeting afterwards, Fink, Buckley, and Sheppard
bemoaned censorship, and canvassed ways to force change. It
did not take them long to alight on the idea of publishing *Trial*
themselves, in Australia. It would evade the federal government's
authority, embarrass them, draw attention to censorship, place
the onus on state governments to respond — and, perhaps, force
change.

The three made plans to make the idea a reality. Fink offered
to provide the money for publishing the book. Buckley agreed to
involve the Council for Civil Liberties: 'Alright,' he said, 'you do
it, and, if you're prosecuted, we'll find a lawyer to defend you at no
cost.'[10] Sheppard volunteered to approach Allen Lane to obtain
permission for an Australian edition. Since he had been unable
to find an Australian printer willing to take the job, Lane was
happy to allow Sheppard his head. He licensed the copyright for
six months, to begin from 15 April 1965, for a sixpence-per-copy
royalty. 'We did it with the full support of the Penguin group,' Fink
recalled. 'They were happy for us to take it on.'[11]

Next, Fink tasked a UK-based friend with buying a copy of
Trial, tearing it into swatches, folding those into letters, and sending them, addressed to various friends of Fink and Sheppard, to

Australia via airmail. Those letters were collected and the pages passed on to Fink and Sheppard, who now sought a printer. There were precious few willing to run the risk of prosecution and, for a time, it seemed the whole project would fall through. Sheppard had to write to Allen Lane to plead for his forbearance. Eventually, Sydney printer Edwards & Shaw took the job, on condition that none of their employees did the typesetting. 'They [Richard Edwards and Roderick Shaw, the owners] said they would only do it if they could typeset it themselves,' Fink recalled. 'They didn't want their employees to be liable to prosecution.'

Fink and Sheppard were similarly cautious. They destroyed the smuggled pages of *Trial* as they were typeset, and split up the typeset pages, so that no person could be caught with a complete copy of the book. There could be no mistakes in this: as Sheppard wrote, everything they did was geared towards throwing a 'probing light on the present censorship laws'.[12]

By April 1965, they had printed 10,000 copies of *The Trial of Lady Chatterley* and distributed them to bookshops in Sydney, Melbourne, and Brisbane.[13] Unveiled on 15 April amid a flurry of headlines about the possibility of court action and proud statements from Sheppard and Fink of their willingness to go to court, the book sold briskly. It was a stunt, a show — and at it, Stephen Murray-Smith recalled, 'the whole of literate Sydney smiled with delight'.[14]

Fink and Sheppard sent copies to state and federal authorities, with letters inviting prosecution. They did not regard *Trial* as being 'in the slightest degree offensive', they wrote, but the lack of certainty of whether its publication broke 'any law that has been decided or tested' was not sustainable in the long term. 'Therefore, one of the purposes of this letter is to ask that you permit this book to be put on sale and, if you wish to launch a prosecution, this should be launched against Minderon Pty Limited [the company Fink had set up for publishing the book] and not against an individual bookseller.'[15] The bravado was no affectation: 'I *wanted* to go to jail for obscenity!' Fink said later. 'I suppose that I was cavalier about it — but it was the right thing to do.'

The letter sent to Kenneth Anderson, however, was geared towards finding an acceptable resolution. Assuring the Customs minister that no court would convict them for publishing *Trial*, Sheppard argued that any charges would put Anderson's department 'in a bad light'. He suggested that the minister immediately lift the ban and, importantly, gave him some inducement to do so. 'If then the ban were lifted,' Sheppard explained, 'Mr Fink and I would be losers financially because our edition would not sell against the much-lower priced Penguin edition which would be available.'[16]

For several days, Fink and Sheppard heard applause from the public and silence from the censors. Unwilling to rescind the ban and unable to intervene, Anderson ruefully announced that the onus was on the states to deal with the matter. But the Queensland government did nothing, and the New South Wales authorities shied away entirely, pursuing a policy that *The Sydney Morning Herald* called 'masterly procrastination'.[17] It was not accidental. 'You must think I'm a fool,' said the state's chief secretary, Labor Party politician Gus Kelly, when presented with Sheppard's letter. Pointing to the postscript, which contained a not-too-subtle reminder of Sheppard's military rank and service, Kelly added, 'You think we'll prosecute *this* man?'[18]

Victoria, however, was another matter. At Rylah's direction, police raided bookshops and seized copies. But instead of prosecuting Sheppard or Fink, the Victorians elected to pursue the booksellers who had stocked it, issuing summons to Austral bookshop proprietor Paul Flesch and Toorak newsagent John Petty, and instigating charges based on offences to the *Judicial Proceedings Publication Act*.[19] Sheppard reacted with outrage, but Flesch privately pleaded with him to tone it down. His solicitors, he told Sheppard, had stressed that any inflammatory criticisms would only antagonise the authorities. For Flesch's sake, Sheppard should be careful — and, preferably, say nothing.[20]

Sheppard resisted this. 'We will meet your wishes as far as possible,' he replied, 'provided this does not clash too much with our objective — which is to force some changes in the censorship laws. We, also, have some good legal advisors here as well.' Flesch's solicitors, he pointed out, were looking out for Flesch; and, fairly, the best course for Flesch was that he was never prosecuted. But, from Sheppard's point of view, the best outcome was the opposite: 'We must somehow force the government to have the law and their powers tested by a competent court — that is the whole object of the exercise.'[21]

But events were moving fast. Simultaneous with the fight Fink and Sheppard had sought to bring on, the Council for Civil Liberties had opened another front. They announced their intention to challenge the 1964 ban on *The Quest for Love*, a psychoanalytic study of sex and love by British scholar David Holbrook, which had been banned for its use of passages from *Lady Chatterley*.

It was with this promise at front of mind, with defiance in the air, inaction rife, and the ground giving way beneath them, that cabinet met on 13 May. By now, Customs had given way: it recommended that the bans on *Trial* and *Quest* be rescinded. Anderson, grudgingly, echoed this.[22] But, he added, doing so was likely to demolish the government's rationale for maintaining the ban on *Lady Chatterley's Lover*. 'It would and without doubt,' Menzies said to this.

Frustration with the situation was palpable. 'Why do we make life so complicated for ourselves?' treasurer Harold Holt demanded to know. Pointing out that the government had established the Literature Censorship Board precisely so as to take decisions of censorship out of the government's hands, Holt lamented the lack of an agreement between the states for uniform censorship: 'We're only busybodying in trying to knit [the] states together.' David Fairbairn, the minister for the air, wondered if the decision to rescind the ban on *Trial* and *Quest* would backfire: 'If we yield on this,' he said, '[it] will encourage further stunts.'

Menzies was frustrated but also realistic. 'We're getting into, or [are] in, a state of farce,' he said. 'Books [are] coming in page for page by post and [are] published here ... Perhaps our error, in retrospect, was not to accept [the] Board's recommendation to release *Chatterley*.' There was much to be said for Holt's view and, in the future, for abiding by the decisions of the board. 'The trouble is that we have to eat [our] words,' Menzies added. 'But we've done that before!'[23]

Cabinet agreed that the bans on *The Trial of Lady Chatterley* and *The Quest for Love* would be rescinded. Within days, the Victorian government dropped the charges against Flesch and Petty, and other banned books, including *Lady Chatterley's Lover*, were referred to the board and cleared for release. By July, Lawrence's novel was available in bookshops across the country — except in Victoria, where Rylah mounted a rearguard action to keep the novel out.[24] Bookshops in other states had no problems with mailing copies to paying readers: thus, in effect, the most storied title in the censorship fights was finally free. Sheppard thought it amusing. 'Obscene one day in June 1965, and no longer obscene the next,' he wrote. '... Perhaps we Australians had grown adult in the interim.'[25]

But the overarching fight was not over. The *Lady Chatterley* affair had exposed crucial flaws in the censorship system. The federal government's inability to prosecute individuals for domestically produced editions of banned works, and the inconsistency of state government prosecutions of those individuals, had emboldened the anti-censorship campaigners. A uniform approach, to ensure that censorship was maintained from harbour port to bookstore, was necessary if the system was to maintain any kind of consistency and respectability.

* * *

The embarrassment that Fink, Sheppard, and Buckley had caused heralded an apparent retreat on the part of the Customs department in the second half of the 1960s. The ban on *Lolita* was removed in 1965. The ban on Gore Vidal's novel *The City and the Pillar* was removed in 1966. The two-year-old ban on G.M. Glaskin's novel *No End to the Way* — subsequently recognised as Australia's first gay novel — was removed in 1966. The ban on J.P. Donleavy's *The Ginger Man* — a comic, manic novel about an American GI who goes from bender to bed and back again — was rescinded in 1967.[26]

For some, this was cause for alarm. One Brisbane dentist wrote a public telegram to Canberra expressing his outrage at the 'fall from grace' implicit in the release of *Lady Chatterley*. 'Your government's astounding release of four sex-soaked books constitutes [a] major contribution to potential cases of delinquency both juvenile and adult,' he declared. '… If Australia's moral decline is to be halted, the present malfunctioning censorship machinery operated by four intellectuals — most academics — must be replaced by a commonsense down to earth body drawn from average homes.'[27]

But, at the same time, progress on a uniform censorship policy began to gather pace. It was a decided change from the past, where progress had been halting and usually prompted only by embarrassment or scandal. When federal and state ministers met in 1961 to discuss the prospect of an agreement, there was no movement on the idea. Nor could agreement be found at a meeting in April 1964. That September, Anderson therefore took to cabinet a proposal to establish either a federal judicial body that would centralise determinations of whether a publication was obscene, or an advisory body that would reach a decision and seek to bind the states to its recommendations.[28]

But cabinet would have none of it. Menzies rubbished the proposal, and minister for external affairs Paul Hasluck argued that it would be the 'worst' idea to centralise responsibility for censorship. 'If there is a need for uniformity — and I don't accept there is,' he said, 'it is for uniformity in the *law* relating to obscenity.' That point carried the day. Cabinet agreed that at the next meeting of federal and state ministers, there should be discussion of reaching uniformity across the states on what constituted obscenity. 'The present system of difference between the states is ludicrous,' said Menzies. 'As of now, it promotes the sale of pornography rather than blocks it.' What the government needed, he argued, was 'some co-operative system of consultation in order to arrive at a uniformity of interpretation'.[29]

The meeting that followed again failed to produce a consensus, prompting Holt's lament during the *Lady Chatterley* mess that the federal government's involvement was 'busybodying'. But it was the pain and embarrassment of *Lady Chatterley* that finally made the states recognise the need for uniform censorship. Thus it took them only six months to agree to a plan for uniform censorship of literary works; over the next two years, they worked to institute that plan.

Amid a host of amendments to the *Customs Act*, the National Literature Board of Review was established on 1 January 1968, replacing the Literature Censorship Board, and tasked with considering books of 'literary, artistic, or scientific merit'. It would consider imported and domestically produced titles; it would tender judgements that were understood to be binding; and a book's contravention of federal or state law on obscenity could be tested in a court of law.

From far away it sounded fine. On close inspection, however, the new system was beset by inconsistencies and problems. They mattered nought for the government: it expressed its 'pious hope' that the new system would last.[30]

* * *

The first test of the new system came that year, when University of Sydney lecturer Dennis Altman, on a trip to the US, posted a trunk of books to his address back in Australia. Customs opened the trunk and seized copies of the novels *Myra Breckinridge*, by

Gore Vidal, and *Totempole,* by Sanford Friedman.[31]

Released in February 1968, *Breckinridge* had become a bestseller in the US. Shocking, absurd, buoyed by Vidal's fizzing intelligence and wit, the American edition of *Breckinridge* had been banned from import to Australia in September. The UK edition, from which Vidal had removed some words and lines 'in deference to the high moral climate' of the UK, had been permitted. *Totempole,* meanwhile, which depicted a homosexual Jewish man's coming of age, had been banned since 1966.

Returning home, Altman realised that the revised *Customs Act* offered an opportunity to challenge Customs' seizure of his books. Poet and academic Stephen Murray-Smith had considered doing so when Customs seized his copy of *Borstal Boy,* but was dissuaded when he found that he could be liable for costs.[32] The newest changes to the *Customs Act,* however, had removed this possibility: a plaintiff could only be liable for costs if the goods that had been seized were worth more than $200.

The Council for Civil Liberties agreed that the opportunity was worth pursuing and, when the case came up for hearing in December 1969, approached George Masterman to represent Altman *pro bono.*

Then aged forty-one, Masterman was a barrister of patrician manner and fierce integrity. His schooling and his training were of a sterling pedigree: the King's School, Oxford, the University of Sydney, and articles at the establishment law firm Allen Allen & Hemsley. Masterman went to the Bar in 1956, a year after his admission as a solicitor, took rooms on the progressive eleventh floor of Wentworth Chambers, and developed a broad and sweeping practice. Later the New South Wales ombudsman, Masterman co-authored a textbook on the *Trades Practices Act 1965,* edited the conference proceedings of the Australian Institute of Political Science (for which he was also a director), and for a spell edited its journal, *Australian Quarterly.* Masterman's political outlook was liberal and, considering his education, fittingly cultured. He delighted in representing the nudist sunbathers of Lady Jane Bay, pointing out to sceptics their good behaviour and respectability, and was a happy volunteer for the Council for Civil Liberties. 'He was driven and he was so idealistic,' said his wife, Joan Masterman. 'He was always putting his hand up to be involved in causes.'[33]

The case he could present for Altman, however, was straitened. There was limited opportunity to extract a win in the small pea-green courtrooms in Queen's Square, Sydney. Masterman was not permitted to quote reviews of either book to prove their literary merit. He was not allowed to produce any evidence of community standards that could show the books were inoffensive. He could not even cite from the expurgated edition of *Myra Breckinridge*, which had been published in Australia with passages that the prosecution now cited as examples of the book's obscenity. All that Masterman could argue was that the literary merit of both books trumped their supposed obscenity. It was a thin case to make, although Masterman fortified it with far greater elegance than did the prosecution.

Justice Levine — the same judge who had ruled in the *Oz* case — announced his decision six weeks later. *Totempole* did not offend community standards, and should be returned to Altman, he ruled, but *Myra Breckinridge* was most certainly objectionable. 'The author has spelled out, as it were,' Levine said, 'physical details as to permit the reader to form only mental pictures which the words *filthy, bawdy, lewd,* and *disgusting* aptly describe.'

One book in; one book out: Altman called it a draw. But, as he was to argue, the fight made it clear that the censorship regime was not wholly based — as its reputation in the community suggested — on preventing the import and dissemination of sex-based obscene material. The censorship was political. 'Under the guise of preventing obscenity we in fact ban material of a political nature,' Altman wrote. '... As political and cultural radicalism increasingly coalesce, and radicalism is expressed in attacks on traditional moral virtues, censorship acts not only to preserve "good taste", but also to exclude radical critiques.'[34]

Cases like this prompted Geoffrey Dutton and Max Harris to solicit essays for their book *Australia's Censorship Crisis*. Published in February 1970 with strident criticism of the censorship regime from a host of eminences, the book included lengthy extracts from various banned works, including *Myra Breckinridge*, Henry Miller's *Tropic of Capricorn*, and Steven Marcus's *The Other Victorians*. 'We certainly have rendered ourselves liable to prosecution by publishing the banned stuff,' Dutton said. 'But we are hoping the basic seriousness of the book will be obvious to any unbiased reader.'[35]

No charges would result, but the book contributed to the growing foment in literary circles over censorship, which had been punctuated by a burst of critical coverage in the Melbourne-based literary magazine *Meanjin*. One of the most notable instalments came from Arthur Angell Phillips, the longtime English master at Wesley College, coiner of the term 'cultural cringe', and a former censor of nine years' service on the Customs censorship boards. Phillips agreed that any decision to ban a book was 'almost always an act of exceptional repression by international standards', but, perceptively, attributed this to Australia's 'cultural geography' and the self-perpetuating existence of the censorship regime. The existence of the board, he argued, could only be asserted by drawing a line on what should be censored. 'If in practice they were never to draw the line at all, they would feel intolerably pointless. It's a dog's life for a watch-dog if there are never any trespassers to bark at — so the postman gets harried.'

Moreover, Phillips identified what might be considered the most insidious effect of censorship. With no clarity on whether a work might be prosecuted, publishers and traders 'have to draw the line well on the windy side of the law'. Thus, Phillips argued, the main effect of censorship was not the 'sentence of execution' that censors imposed, but the 'literary onanisms and abortions for which they are directly responsible': the stories never written, the books never published, the voices never heard.[36]

For the censorship regime to be truly made to totter and fall, writers, publishers, and sellers would need to be willing to face those sentences — and to defy them.

CHAPTER 5

A literary onanism

Defying censorship would require courage, boldness, and skill —
and a good bit of ammunition. The American writer Philip Roth
possessed all of these qualities in spades, and would also, at the
crucial time, supply that vital ammunition — what might also
be called, if with a rather different meaning to what Phillips had
suggested, a 'literary onanism'.

Born in 1933 in Newark, New Jersey, the second son of an insurance salesman and a devoted housewife, Roth was a third-generation
American Jew. His first experience of public opprobrium came in
1959, when he was twenty-six years old, following publication
in the *New Yorker* of his short story 'Defender of the Faith'. The
story centres on a war-wearied Jewish-American sergeant named
Marx, who, on the basis of their shared Judaism, gives successive
breaks to conniving nineteen-year-old draftee Sheldon Grossbart.
Marx allows Grossbart an exemption for the Sabbath; lobbies on
Grossbart's behalf about the food; and allows Grossbart and some
friends to visit an aunt for Seder. Then Grossbart pleads for Marx
to get him out of a posting to the Pacific, where war still rages.

Marx, who discovers that Grossbart has lied about visiting his aunt, refuses, disgusted by Grossbart's lies and abuse of their shared faith. When he discovers that Grossbart has pulled another string to get him out of that posting, Marx decides that Grossbart will go — and pulls his own string to guarantee it. Grossbart confronts Marx and again invokes their faith — this time to accuse Marx of disloyalty to it: 'There is no limit to your anti-Semitism, is there?' But the faith that Grossbart invokes is trumped by Marx's awareness of another: 'For each other we have to learn to watch out, Sheldon.' The faith that Marx defends is one of shared loyalty, of a duty not merely between one Jew and another, but one that is 'for all of us'.[1]

Roth's portrayal of Grossbart offended Jewish leaders in the US, who, only fourteen years since World War II and the Holocaust, were sensitive to negative portrayals of Judaism. A New York rabbi sent an open letter to the Anti-Defamation League of B'nai B'rith in this vein, but with a censorious note. 'What is being done to silence this man?' he demanded to know, referring to Roth. 'Medieval Jews would have known what to do with him.'

The demand for Roth's silence stunned the young author. 'Defender of the Faith' was no more or less offensive — if at all — than any of his other short stories. 'The Conversion of the Jews', about a thirteen-year-old schoolboy who threatens to jump from the roof of his local synagogue unless his mother, his rabbi, and all those watching kneel and say that they believe in Jesus, had aroused comment but nothing of this sort of outrage. 'Epstein', about a middle-aged Jew whose affliction by a rash and then a heart attack reveals that he has had an affair, was irreverent but, again, had caused nothing like this kind of scandal. Most of Roth's stories had been published in small journals such as *Partisan Review* and *Commentary*. Publication in one of these, or, indeed, in an Israeli newspaper, Roth was told privately, would have ensured that 'Defender of the Faith' was judged 'exclusively from a literary point of view'. Its publication in the *New Yorker*, however, was tantamount to an act of 'informing'.

It was a serious charge to level. In the months that followed, the accusation once thrown at Marx was thrown at Roth. 'You have done as much harm as all the organised anti-Semitic organisations have done to make people believe that all Jews are cheats, liars, connivers,' ran one letter. 'We have discussed this story from every possible angle and we cannot escape the conclusion that it will do irreparable damage to the Jewish people,' ran another.[2] 'The only logical conclusion that any intelligent reader could draw from [Roth's] stories or books,' wrote Rabbi Theodore Lewis, 'is that this country — nay the world — would be a much better and happier place without Jews.'[3] Roth described his supposed crime in a straightforward way: 'I had told the Gentiles what apparently it would otherwise have been possible to keep secret from them: that the perils of human nature afflict the members of our minority.'[4]

Roth would have no truck with it. As a writer, he had the freedom to depict characters as he wished. To depict those characters as philandering or conniving was no more to say that all Jews were so than it was to say that all French and Russian women, like Emma Bovary and Anna Karenina, were adulterous. Moreover, the kind of saintly depiction of Jews that Roth's critics might wish for was mistaken. To refrain from writing about Jews in the same vein as 'Defender of the Faith' because anti-Semites might use that writing would only *empower* those anti-Semites, by submitting to them.[5]

Roth was convinced that he was in the right; that time would prove he was in the right; and that if he explained why he thought so, people would understand. The first belief would never be shaken, but events would shake the latter two certainties. Two months after 'Defender of the Faith' appeared, Roth's first book — a collection of his short stories and a novella that gave the book its name, *Goodbye, Columbus* — was published to glowing reviews and acclaim that culminated, in 1960, in the National Book Award and the Daroff Award of the Jewish Book Council of America. But Roth continued to attract criticism, notably from Leon Uris, who had won the Daroff Award in 1959. 'There is a whole school of Jewish American writers,' Uris said, 'who spend their time damning their fathers, hating their mothers, wringing their hands, and wondering why they were born. This isn't art or literature. It's psychiatry. These writers are professional apologists. Every year you find one of their works on the bestseller lists. Their work is so obnoxious and makes me sick to my stomach.'

Roth heard this criticism again when he accepted an invitation to speak at Yeshiva University, in New York, in 1962. While appearing alongside Italian author Pietro di Donato and Ralph Ellison, author of *Invisible Man*, it was clear that Roth was the main attraction — even the target — of the event. After each had spoken on the 'crisis of conscience in minority writers of fiction', the moderator turned to Roth and asked, 'Mr Roth, would you write the same stories you've written if you were living in Nazi Germany?'

What followed seemed, to Roth, a 'trial'. He was grilled, berated, and interrogated, and no response that he gave seemed to satisfy the audience: 'I realised that I was not just opposed but hated.' Ellison, whose work had attracted similar charges within the African-American community, came to Roth's defence, but even that seemed only to pause the deluge. When the symposium was over, antagonistic students surrounded Roth as he sought to leave, accusing him of anti-Semitism and shaking their fists in his face. Afterwards, a shaken Roth vowed, 'I'll never write about Jews again.'

And yet, as he would admit, the affair left him in 'thralldom' to Jewish characters. He believed in the merits of his work, and saw untilled soil in which to work. But he would resist the lure of Jewish characters for some time. His first novel, *Letting Go*, was published a few months after the Yeshiva affair; it concerned Jewish characters, but its fine plotting and formal polish pointed to the influence of Henry James. His next book, *When She Was Good*, published in 1967, eschewed Jewish characters in favour of Midwest Americana.

Both novels were influenced by Roth's then-wife, Margaret Martinson Williams. Four years older than Roth, Williams was a divorcée and the mother of two children, who were in the care of her ex-husband. Feeling free, young, and accomplished, yet also searching for something challenging, Roth idealised Williams and her troubled background: for having survived it, she seemed to him a woman of courage and strength. But his infatuation was short-lived. They took up together, split up, got back together again, and split up again. Roth moved to New York, went to Europe, and — as a gesture of both his guilt and his goodwill — got Williams a job at *Esquire* while he was away. But after his return she knocked on his door with a suitcase in hand. Beholden to a sense of duty that he would later rue, he took her in.

She claimed to be pregnant. He was certain this was a lie, but when she came to him with the results of a pregnancy test, he agreed to marry her — on condition that she have an abortion. She agreed, went, and returned in tears with details of how it had happened. They married on 22 February 1959, a few days before 'Defender of the Faith' was published and the heavens came down upon him.

The marriage was fraught. There were constant fights, and Roth was unfaithful. In 1962, threats from Williams that she would suicide angered Roth so much that he left; then they frightened him so much that he returned — at which point, while he was helping Williams to regurgitate the sleeping pills and whisky she had taken, she told him that there had never been a baby. She had purchased the urine from a pregnant woman in a park, substituted it for her own when it came time to take the pregnancy test, and used the money Roth gave her for the abortion to go to a movie. It was downhill from there.

Letting Go had been dedicated to Williams, and *When She Was Good* was about her. By the time it was published, Roth was as far from her as he could be. She had rebuffed his efforts to obtain a divorce, and he had been forced to agree to a legal separation that entailed paying her around half of his income for the rest of his life, unless she remarried. He was furious about the deception she had practised on him, and bitter about the pull she had exerted on his promising trajectory as a writer. Hoping to work through this, in 1962 Roth began seeing Dr Hans Kleinschmidt, a New York–based psychiatrist well known for treating artists and writers. Unbeknownst to Roth, Kleinschmidt authored a thinly disguised account of their sessions in 1967, identifying Roth's mother as his real problem:

> His main problem was his castration anxiety vis-à-vis a phallic mother figure. He was six when he threatened to leave his home because of his displeasure with his mother's discipline. He remembers that, at one point, his mother packed a little bag for him, told him to go ahead and leave the house, as he had said he would, but then he suddenly found himself outside the locked door, while trying in vain to get back inside by hammering at the door and crying to be permitted to come back … He may have been eight or nine years old when he still fantasied that his teachers were really his mother in disguise who in some very clever magic way would get home quickly and be there by the time he returned from school … He was eleven years old when he went with his mother to a store to buy a bathing suit. While trying on several of them, he voiced his desire for bathing trunks with a jock strap. To his great embarrassment his mother said in the presence of the saleslady: 'You don't need one. You have such a little one that it makes no difference.' He felt ashamed, angry, betrayed, and utterly helpless … Submission seems to be the price for love both vis-à-vis his mother and his wife.[6]

According to Kleinschmidt, to avoid confrontation with 'emotional reality' and feelings of pain, Roth's solution 'has always been to libidinise both anger and anxiety'.

Roth was infuriated by the betrayal of his privacy. He was

already sceptical of his sessions, particularly after Kleinschmidt persisted in making outlandish diagnoses. When Roth became ill while attending a party for the writer William Styron, Kleinschmidt said he was envious of Styron's success. When Roth objected that he had felt ill even before the party, Kleinschmidt said it was his anticipation of the envy. The problem turned out to be physical: a ruptured appendix that required immediate surgery. Peritonitis had killed two of Roth's uncles, almost killed his father, and kept Roth confined to a hospital for almost a month. He emerged from it, therefore, feeling as though he had cheated death — and that his time with Kleinschmidt was perhaps at its end.

But the time spent in analysis had sparked ideas, of form and character, and brought Roth back under that earlier 'thralldom' of Jewish characters. Teaching at the University of Iowa, Roth had noticed similarities in material written by three of his students: an overbearing mother, and a yearning for sexual experience. Then, in four different drafted works, Roth explored facets of the same idea. In *The Jewboy*, he explored growing up in Newark as a 'species of folklore'. In *The Nice Jewish Boy*, a playscript read at the American Place Theatre in 1964, with Dustin Hoffman in the title role, he treated *The Jewboy* material more realistically and harshly. In a scatological and spirited spoof lecture on the genitalia of various eminences, he toyed with ideas of obscenity and fame. And, finally, in an autobiographical novel with the working title *Portrait of the Artist*, Roth found some room for invention. Over time, ideas and themes from these works began to coalesce and resurface in new material.[7]

In April 1967 — a month before the publication of *When She Was Good* — Roth began publishing short stories from this new material. 'A Jewish Patient Begins His Analysis', published in *Esquire*, was first. A first-person monologue about an overbearing mother and ineffectual father, it began with an incident that Kleinschmidt had recorded from his sessions with Roth: 'So deeply imbedded was she in my consciousness that for the first few years of school I believed that each of my teachers was actually my mother in disguise.'[8] The sensational 'Whacking Off' came in August. Published in that 'Mecca of modernism' the *Partisan Review*, it opened:

> Then came the years when half my waking life was spent locked behind the bathroom door, firing my wad down the toilet, or into the soiled clothes of the laundry hamper, or with a thick splat, up against the medicine chest mirror, before which I stood in my dropped drawers to see how it looked coming out. Or else I was doubled up over my flying fist, eyes closed but mouth wide open, to take that sticky sauce of buttermilk and Clorox on my own tongue and teeth — though not infrequently, in my blindness and ecstasy, I got it all in the pompadour, like a blast of Wildroot Cream Oil.[9]

Another instalment, 'The Jewish Blues', appeared a month later in *New American Review*. Another, 'Civilisation and Its Discontents', followed in another issue of *Partisan Review*. To each, there was a tremendous response: laughter, praise, interest. Roth felt that he was on the cusp of something good. His editors wanted more. And so did Maggie Williams, who now began to make noises about getting an increase in alimony. If there was anything that could stop Roth writing, it was this. To Roth, the marriage, which had lasted barely four years, had not resulted in any children, and yet had indebted him for life, was nothing less than court-ordered robbery.

And then he received a telephone call. Williams was dead, killed in a car accident. Roth was shocked, but not entirely sorry: 'She died and you didn't,' he told himself.[10] He organised the funeral, and then left for the verdant artist's colony of Yaddo, near Saratoga Springs. In a burst of intense work, he finished writing the book that the earlier instalments had heralded: *Portnoy's Complaint*.

* * *

An epigraph introduces the fictional medical condition that gives the book its title. 'Portnoy's Complaint', it declares, is 'a disorder in which strongly felt ethical and altruistic impulses are perpetually warring with extreme sexual longings, often of a perverse nature'.[11] Succinctly introduced is the key character, thirty-three-year-old lawyer Alexander Portnoy; his central problem and the novel's theme; and, implicitly, the 'silent ear' of Dr Spielvogel, who listens to the monologue that constitutes the novel — the psychoanalytic session in which Alexander Portnoy is on the couch.

There is no traditional linear plot in *Portnoy's Complaint*. Portnoy's monologue moves backward and forward in time, digressing and leaping between events and subjects, sometimes without an apparent link or cause. Everything is mercurial. Portnoy on the couch is literate, manic, profane, mean, funny, touching, ashamed, abusive, euphoric, and vulnerable. He details his childhood and adolescence, and narrates the formative influence of his parents. His father, Jack Portnoy, is an insurance salesman who is as oppressed by his work as he is by his body and his spouse. Chewing dried fruit and taking suppositories to relieve his ever-present constipation, he is dominated by Sophie Portnoy, the omnipresent gorgonic force who smothers her son with love, surveillance, threats, and put-downs: 'Who is Mommy's good little boy?'[12]

The relationship between Portnoy and his parents is the cause of his adolescent compulsion to masturbate: it becomes his private rebellion from the suffocating drama in which they make him a central player. In what was to become one of the novel's most famous scenes, Portnoy masturbates in the bathroom as his mother and father hammer on the door to be let in. Portnoy screams that he has diarrhoea, and pleads to be left alone. But his mother does not believe him:

> 'Alex, I want an answer from you. Did you eat French fries after school? Is that why you're sick like this?'
> 'Nuhhh, nuhhh.'

'Alex, are you in pain? Do you want me to call the doctor? Are you in pain, or aren't you? I want to know exactly where it hurts. *Answer me.*'

'Yuhh, yuhhh —'

'Alex, I don't want you to flush the toilet,' says my mother sternly. 'I want to see what you've done in there. I don't like the sound of this at all.'

'And me,' says my father, touched as he always was by my accomplishments — as much awe as envy — 'I haven't moved my bowels in a week,' just as I lurch from my perch on the toilet seat, and with the whimper of a whipped animal, deliver three drops of something barely viscous into the tiny piece of cloth where my flat-chested eighteen-year-old sister has laid her nipples, such as they are. It is my fourth orgasm of the day. When will I begin to come blood?[13]

The central issues of the book are always present: the constant interference by Portnoy's parents; the dichotomy between Portnoy's Jewish heritage and America; and his penchant for comic exaggeration. He declares himself 'the Raskolnikov of jerking off'; prompted by the discovery of a freckle on his penis, he believes that he has cancer and will soon die; he ejaculates accidentally into his eye, and fears he will go blind; he describes masturbating into a 'maddened piece of liver' behind a billboard on the way to a bar mitzvah lesson.[14] This is the second time he has used liver in this way. On the first occasion, that used liver became part of a meal. 'So,' Portnoy tells Spielvogel. 'Now you know the worst thing I have ever done. I fucked my own family's dinner.'[15]

Is it, though? As the novel progresses — narrating Portnoy's intergenerational conflict, and his increasingly taboo-breaking sexual experiences — this declaration comes into question. Portnoy describes the way that Jewish clannishness and hyper-protection rule him in ways that are comedic and desperate. 'YOU FUCKING JEWISH MOTHERS ARE JUST TOO FUCKING MUCH

TO BEAR!' he screams, at one point. But there are occasions where this becomes brutal. The most notable is the story Portnoy relates of his uncle Hymie, who discovers that his son Heshie intends to marry a gentile. Hymie meets with the girl and, telling her that Heshie has an incurable disease and can never marry, pays her to leave him. When an outraged and heartbroken Heshie confronts his father, Hymie wrestles him to the floor and cruelly forces his physical surrender. Of this, Portnoy remarks, 'We are not a family that takes defections lightly.'[16]

Portnoy's awareness of the difficulties of defection is ironic, for every action he takes to try to break free only ever ends up binding him more closely. The worst thing that he does will always be trumped by another worst thing. Even as Portnoy deliberately chases '*shikse* cunt' — arguing that, 'through fucking, I will discover America', and thereby escape his family — he castigates himself for failing to put down roots and marry, which in turn leads him to even further transgressions. Taking up with the Monkey — his nickname for the woman he will not marry, but who fulfils his 'most lascivious adolescent dreams' — Portnoy has a *ménage à trois* with a prostitute in Rome, but afterwards finds that disgust and pity overwhelm him. It is a recurrent experience. He cannot escape the force of his heritage and his family — his fate, even:

> Doctor Spielvogel, this is my life, my only life, and I'm living it in the middle of a Jewish joke! I am the son in the Jewish joke — *only it ain't no joke!* Please, who crippled us like this? Who made us so morbid and hysterical and weak? Why, why are they screaming still, 'Watch out! Don't do it! Alex — *no!*' and why, alone on my bed in New York, why am I still hopelessly beating my meat? Doctor, what do you call this sickness I have? Is this the Jewish suffering I used to hear so much about? Is this what has come down to me from the pogroms and the persecution? From the mockery and abuse bestowed by the *goyim* over these two thousand lovely years? Oh my secrets, my shame, my

palpitations, my flushes, my sweats! The way I respond to the simple vicissitudes of human life! Doctor, I can't stand any more being frightened like this over nothing! Bless me with manhood! Make me brave! Make me strong! Make me *whole*! Enough being a nice Jewish boy, publicly pleasing my parents while privately pulling my putz! Enough![17]

Towards the end of the novel, Portnoy travels to Israel and attempts to seduce a Jewish-American woman named Naomi, who has been working in a team to clear volcanic boulders from a mountain overlooking the Syrian border. In no small part because she also resembles his mother, Portnoy has deluded himself that Naomi is his 'salvation'. But she has no interest in him in that way. 'You seem to take some special pleasure, some pride, in making yourself the butt of your own peculiar sense of humour,' she tells him. 'I don't believe you actually want to improve your life. Everything you say is somehow always twisted, some way or another, to come out "funny".' Portnoy deflects this, and tries to force himself upon her — only to find himself impotent. 'Another joke?' she asks, when he titters at this.[18]

The novel is awash in comedy and shards of icy pain. Both are present in every new transgression, amid Portnoy's despair, and immediately counter the heated declarations of his desires. Derived from the schtick of Roth's dinnertime playacting and conversation with friends, the duelling forces were also, Roth said later, drawn from Kafka. 'It was all so *funny*, this morbid preoccupation with punishment and guilt,' he explained later. 'Hideous, but funny.'[19] They punctuate the novel's conclusion. As Portnoy — tormented, wracked, and self-flagellating — bursts into a scream of inarticulate agony, Spielvogel finally speaks. 'So,' he says. 'Now vee may perhaps to begin. Yes?'[20]

Portnoy's Complaint was both an abrupt departure from Roth's earlier work and a radical piece of literature. It drew together the stream-of-consciousness method of narration pioneered by

Virginia Woolf and James Joyce, the bodily focus of Joyce and Henry Miller, the shock and vigour of D.H. Lawrence, the force and mania of comedians such as Lenny Bruce, the morbid preoccupations of Kafka, and the ideas of Freud. Delivered in a voice so natural-seeming that Roth's craft and skill were invisible, the novel belied its intricate construction and brimmed with ideas and energy. As the literary scholar David Braudel later wrote, *Portnoy's Complaint* was 'both the culmination of a certain tradition of Jewish American fiction, and its death-knell'.[21]

* * *

Roth emerged from Yaddo elated and relieved. As he was to recall, he had survived Williams, had survived the Roth family menace — peritonitis — and the book that he had written was unlike any other.[22] He felt triumphant, that he had come into his own. He presented the manuscript to his publisher, Random House; within days, chairman Bennett Cerf was presenting him with a contract and a $250,000 advance.[23]

This was not all. The paperback rights to *Portnoy* were sold to Bantam for $350,000, and the film rights to Warner Bros. for $250,000. The incredible sums of money, and the notoriety of the chapters that had already appeared, ensured that *Portnoy's* publication was widely anticipated. *The New York Times Book Review* said there was no question that it would be 'one of the most talked about books of the winter'; *Time* declared that it had the biggest prepublication fanfare since William Manchester's account of the assassination of US president John F. Kennedy; and *Newsweek* noted that excitement in the literary world over the novel was 'intense'.[24] In February 1969, the month that *Portnoy's Complaint* was published, *Life* decided that it was going to be 'a major event in American culture'.

For once, magazine hyperbole turned out to be true. *Portnoy's Complaint* all but flew off the shelves. It sold 210,000 copies in hardback in ten weeks, and more than 400,000 by the year's end

— more than Mario Puzo's *The Godfather*. It was, recalled Cerf, 'an immediate sensation and one of the fastest-selling novels in the history of Random House'.[25] The simple, lurid yellow cover that Paul Bacon designed for the Random House edition, with the title and Roth's name rendered in swash script, avoided any kind of sensationalist image that might undermine the novel's literary merit — appropriate, Bacon said later, for this 'enormously complicated' book.[26] Especially important for publicity, the cover ensured that the book was distinctive and memorable.

The critical reception to the book was effusive. In *The New York Times Book Review*, Josh Greenfeld lauded Roth's decision to pair tropes of American Jewish literature and culture — in particular, 'the mother lode of guilt' that the American Jewish character could neither live with nor without — with the psychoanalysis-spurred monologue. 'The result is not only one of those bullseye hits in the ever-darkening field of humour, a novel that is playfully and painfully moving, but also a work that is certainly catholic in appeal, potentially monumental in effect — and, perhaps more important, a deliciously funny book, absurd and exuberant, wild and uproarious.' For all the apparent digression and circuitous plotting, Greenfield argued, the book was intricately constructed: 'every curlicue is a real clue'.[27] Critic Alfred Kazin, one of the 'tigers' of Jewish-American literature, wrote that Roth was 'vibrantly talented, an original, as marvellous a mimic and fantasist as has been produced', and that *Portnoy* was 'touching as well as hilariously lewd'.[28] *Time*, meanwhile, called it a 'dazzling performance', and lauded Roth's writing. The novel was skilfully paced, layered, with characters that were 'super-stereotypes', and absurdly funny: 'It is a work of farce that exaggerates and then destroys its content.'[29]

The praise was not confined to America. When Jonathan Cape published its hardcover edition in the UK, critic Tony Tanner called it 'compulsive reading' for anyone who could recall 'the awesome mystery and humiliating farce called growing up'. *Portnoy* broke its own mould, he argued, and exhausted its genre: 'And it is, blessedly, extremely funny.'[30] *Guardian* critic Christopher Wordsworth got squarely at the near-dichotomous facets of the book:

> It is the most scabrous and disgraceful piece of living tissue since Henry Miller, and just possibly the most outrageously funny book about sex yet written. Also and curiously, far from being offensive it is positively and humanly endearing. It should be suspended by a hair, preferably pubic, as a warning, over the desks of those novelists who brandish their current sex-license like a rattle. Rather than toil in Roth's wake they might be persuaded to reapply their talents and leave sex to a master of the field.[31]

But the old charges of anti-Semitism returned, with a vehemence and passion that would have been comedic had they not been so extreme. As Bernard Avishai would joke, 'American Jews thought they had earned a kind moral intermission.'[32] Yet here was Roth, again, tweaking the nose of the sacred cow, brutally exploring the fallacies, contradictions, and failings of Jewish characters. The response was extreme, and the most notable was that authored by German-born Israeli philosopher and critic Gershom Scholem. In the Israeli newspaper *Haaretz,* Scholem declared that Roth was perverted, that *Portnoy* was 'the book for which all anti-Semites have been praying', that it would be more disastrous than *The Protocols of the Elders of Zion,* and that the Jewish people were 'going to pay a price' for it. *Portnoy's Complaint,* he intoned, would make all Jews 'defendants at court':

> This book will be quoted to us — and how it will be quoted! …
> I wonder what price k'lal yisrael [the Jewish community] — and there is such an entity in the eyes of the Gentiles — is going to pay for this book. Woe to us on that day of reckoning![33]

Others believed that the novel was evidence of the decline in standards of public decency. On 1 April, *The New York Times* wrote of a 'best-seller hailed as a masterpiece which, wallowing in a self-indulgent public psychoanalysis, drowns its literary merits in revolting sex excesses', and lamented the failure of the court system to arrest such 'descents into degeneracy'. That this anguished editorial appeared opposite an enormous advertisement for the novel was, to say the least, ironic; nonetheless, the plentiful obscenities and the relish with which *Portnoy* smacked taboos aside did become notorious. Thinking *Portnoy* a confession masquerading as a novel, people conflated Roth with Portnoy himself — to the point that they would accost him in the street, call him Portnoy, and tell him to 'leave *it* alone'. *Valley of the Dolls* author Jacqueline Susann spoke to this when she declared on Johnny Carson's *Tonight Show* that, while she would much like to meet Roth, she would not wish to shake his hand.

Roth was not shy about responding. As he told George Plimpton, 'Obscenity as a usable and valuable vocabulary, and sexuality as a subject, have been available to us since Joyce, Henry Miller, and Lawrence ... In my writing lifetime the use of obscenity has, by and large, been governed by literary taste and tact and not by the mores of the audience.'[34] But the notoriety of obscenity, Roth argued, should not overshadow the fact that obscenity itself was, in many ways, the subject of his book. Obscenity was the issue itself: Portnoy was 'obscene because he wants to be saved'. His pain, Roth argued, arose 'out of his refusal to be bound any longer by taboos which, rightly or wrongly, *he* experiences as diminishing and unmanning'. There was a joke to this, however: breaking the taboo was as 'unmanning' for Portnoy as honouring it might have been. Added Roth: 'Some joke.'[35]

What was not a joke was the impact the novel made in popular culture. *Portnoy's Complaint* spread like the cold. It was shocking. It was sensational. It was funny. It did things that no novel before seemed to have done. When young British writer Salman Rushdie read *Portnoy*, he thought that 'the cobwebs had been blown away' from the novel as a literary form. Here, he thought, was a harbinger:

'Something very new was being born.'[36] The writer James Atlas recalled it in similar terms: the book upended all he was being taught about literature at college. 'An entire expressive medium had been instantaneously transformed,' he said later. 'Had a fire broken out in the hallway of my dorm, I wouldn't have noticed.'[37] There were some who were uneasy: Saul Bellow said later that he 'wasn't *down* on it', and Gore Vidal, after *Portnoy*'s sales overtook those of *Myra Breckinridge*, said that it was 'the greatest blow for masturbation I've ever read'. But more lauded the freedom with which *Portnoy* had approached sex and praised its breaking of the mould.[38] The writer Anthony Burgess declared that *Portnoy* had done for masturbation what 'Melville did for the whale'.[39]

The book spoke to a broad cultural moment. The 'most important book of my generation', as the *Washington Post* called it, the 'autobiography of America', as the *Village Voice* decided, it reached for readers in a way that no other novel in this time did. In retrospect, Claudia Roth Pierpont would argue, *Portnoy's Complaint* was one of the 'signal subversive acts of a subversive age', the detonated charge of a turbulent decade and the start of a new one:

> Along with rock concerts and protest marches — with which it seemed to have more in common than with other books — it spoke to the generation-wide rejection of long unquestioned and nonsensical rules, to the repudiation of powerful authorities, and to the larger struggle for personal and political freedom.[40]

It was for reasons such as this that *Portnoy's Complaint* would become a battering ram in the battles to defeat censorship in Australia.

CHAPTER 6

Regulation 4A

It was of little surprise that *Portnoy's Complaint* ran afoul of Australia's censors. Its force and its skill counted for nothing with them; all the overseas praise and excitement that the book had generated meant little. The censors looked for sex and four-letter words — and, when Jonathan Cape sent a copy of the book as part of its application for approval to export it to Australia in March 1969, they found them in abundance.

'This is a bound copy set for publication in April,' wrote the Customs officer tasked with assessing the novel. 'Whilst of some merit, there is an over frankness in the attitude toward sex.' The officer duly noted instances of sex and crude language, and recommended that the book be prohibited. But, with an eye to the considerable publicity that surrounded the novel, he sent the decision up the chain for review.[1]

Another official looked the book over. 'Jewish lawyer with chip on his shoulder tells of his life and upbringing with particular emphasis on his sexual exploits,' ran his assessment. That official made the same recommendation, but was similarly unnerved by *Portnoy's* fame and acclaim.[2] Citing the publicity that it had attracted, Customs officials suggested sending the book to the National Literature Board of Review, where the decision could be made and owned by experts.[3]

Thus the request to the board: was *Portnoy's Complaint* possessed of literary, artistic, or scientific merit? Was it blasphemous, indecent, or obscene? Did it unduly emphasise sex, horror, violence, or crime? Was it likely to encourage depravity?[4]

The board had doubts and expressed internal differences.[5] Una Mulholland thought the language repetitive, the story slight, the satire ineffective, the sex tedious — but admitted a scruple: 'I am not completely sure that it could [do] harm to a mature person.' H.C. Chipman identified literary merit and thought the book 'an excellent satire', but regarded the focus on sexual issues so narrowing as to render it 'spurious'. Marie Neale anguished over whether the 'obscenity and vulgarity' was outweighed by the 'literary merit' of the novel's themes, plot, and character. 'I am most perplexed as to how to make a recommendation,' she wrote, 'which takes account of the merit and the excesses of abnormal reaction to love and other accepted modes of behaviour in personal encounter[s] in our society.' Board deputy chairman Lloyd O'Neil thought it 'a brilliant and witty novel of high literary standard', but argued that its frankness when dealing with sexual matters meant that 'it must be considered obscene'.

On the vital question — should *Portnoy's Complaint* be allowed into Australia? — all four concurred: the book should be prohibited.[6] The decision was made. On 11 June, the first assistant comptroller-general, R.M. Keogh, wrote to the new customs minister, West Australian senator Malcolm Scott: 'I submit that the Board's recommendation be accepted and that *Portnoy's Complaint* be prohibited in terms of regulation 4A.'[7] Five days later, with Scott's assent, the telegrams went out to all of the Customs offices and state governments: 'PORTNOY'S COMPLAINT BY PHILIP ROTH PROHIBITED REG. 4A.'[8]

Jonathan Cape was stung by the decision. The publisher had made hopeful plans to ship *Portnoy* to Australia by air as soon as Customs gave its approval; with those plans shattered, it turned critical. Tom Maschler, Cape's literary director, lambasted Australia's censors and pointed out their isolation. 'I'm not wildly surprised that the book has been banned,' he said. 'It's just one of the more absurd cases I've heard of. Obviously we will appeal, but one thing I flatly refuse to do is produce an Australian edition. That would be acknowledging censorship, and I am opposed to it absolutely.' The book's literary merit was beyond dispute, he said. 'This is clear from a literary point of view — and almost universally acknowledged to be — one of the most important literary works we have published in the last ten years.'[9]

The charismatic Maschler attracted the first headlines, but it was his colleague, managing director Graham C. Greene, who would be pivotal thereafter. Then thirty-three years old, Greene was a genial, bookish, bespectacled man with a round, usually beaming face. The son of BBC director-general Hugh Carleton Greene, and a nephew of the famed British novelist who was his namesake (hence his use of the differentiating initial), Greene was diligent and self-effacing, and prized literature for its role in shaping culture. He had been an unsuccessful, if naïve, advocate for *Lolita* when the UK rights were in the offing; had been instrumental, along with Maschler, in founding the Booker Prize the previous year; and would become the implacable advocate of publishing the diaries of former British cabinet minister Richard Crossman, despite considerable pressure from the British government.[10] Greene was quiet, liberal, and cautious, but when set upon a cause he was unswerving in his pursuit of it. When he learned of the ban on *Portnoy*, he became determined to see it published in Australia.

Prompted by a suggestion that he 'protest and scream blue murder' about it, Greene wrote to Malcolm Scott on 4 July to echo Maschler's astonishment.[11] 'I cannot believe,' he wrote, 'that it can be the intention of your department to use the Customs Regulations to prevent Australians from reading a work of serious literature which freely circulates elsewhere and I would, therefore, request you to give this book your personal and immediate consideration.'[12]

Scott's 'consideration' extended to referring *Portnoy* back to the National Literature Board of Review for a review.[13] There was no urgency attached to the matter, and Greene would be kept waiting. The board did not meet until 22 August, and did not see fit to communicate its decision until 10 September.

'There was understandably some regret amongst members that a novel by a well-known contemporary author in America that had been widely commented on by overseas reviewers should come within the scope of the Australian system of controls,' wrote board chairman E.R. Bryan. This regret was window-dressing, nothing more. With a shrug of his shoulders, Bryan claimed that 'it was seen that Australia on the one hand, and the USA and UK on the other, were just not of the same mind on the subject of permissiveness'. Therefore, he went on, 'in Australia, at least for [the] time being, a holding operation was necessary'.

The board did not believe that *Portnoy* had much merit. Its success was due to the 'skillful promotion' of its publisher and author, and Roth had departed from his 'earlier standards' in his use of a 'shock technique' that consisted only of frankness in treatments of 'obsessive sex'. 'The view was expressed that to release the novel,' wrote Bryan, 'would imply the virtual abandonment of controls over literature in this country.'[14]

The appeal was disallowed. Greene was informed, in a perfunctory letter, on 18 September, that the ban on *Portnoy* would be maintained. 'I find this an astonishing decision,' he replied, 'and naturally will now have to take legal advice.'[15]

There was considerable consternation over it. Geoffrey Dutton wrote to Greene in July to beg him to fight the ban. Publishing an Australian edition of *Portnoy*, he wrote, 'is the *only* way of freeing ourselves from these absurd restrictions, by forcing a major public issue'. Suggesting that Sun Books might be prepared to take the risk of prosecution, he asked Greene to consider granting it the rights to publish *Portnoy* in Australia. 'Our associate Max Harris had the impression after visiting you that you would like to put a bomb under Australian censorship,' Dutton went on. '*This* is the best way to do it.'[16] Greene deflected the proposal while he waited to hear from Scott about the appeal, but he began searching for clarification about the situation. *What were the regulations?* he asked friends in Australia. *Was Customs really able to stop a book, even though it had literary merit?*

He was quickly enlightened. Arthur Harrap, of the Australasian Publishing Company, was forthright about the facts of *Portnoy*'s situation and the suggestions Greene was receiving. 'I can only say rather them than me,' he said of Dutton's proposal. '… In publishing this book out here they would run the risk of possible legal action and costs in each and every state and it would only want one state to actually take action against them and the legal costs involved could well put the whole operation in the red.'[17]

There were some willing to run the risk. Towards the end of August, Greene received an approach from the left-leaning businessman Patrick Sayers. Writing on behalf of a group that included the Council for Civil Liberties, Sayers requested the publishing rights expressly so as to use the book in the censorship fight. He noted, coyly, that an underground group was planning to print an illegal edition, without any kind of payment for rights or royalties, and that if Cape granted him the rights he might be able to dissuade that group. Would he do so?[18] Again, however, Greene held off, hoping that the government would see sense and rescind the ban.[19]

Protests against the decision to ban *Portnoy* echoed Greene's astonishment. One correspondent wrote to Canberra to ask when Australia would be allowed to join the rest of the world and read books like *Portnoy*.[20] Novelist G.M. Glaskin — author of the banned novel *No End to the Way* — protested the confiscation of his copy with an indignant 5,000-word letter to officials in the federal and state governments.[21] When his copy of *Portnoy* was seized, a social psychology academic protested to his local MP, Andrew Peacock. Likening the situation to that in the Soviet Union, he declared that he was 'the best judge' of whether reading any book would do him harm, not government officials.[22] Another correspondent was scathing of Customs and the government: 'I deplore your holier-than-thou attitude and I feel that if your authoritarian approach is typical of your party's approach to democracy, [then] perhaps we should ask for an alterative in the next election.'[23]

But there was support in the community for the government's actions. Congratulations on the ban did come in equal fervour, if not in as great a number. 'The majority of people support your action,' one solicitor told Scott. 'Do not give way to the noisy minority who would abolish reasonable censorship.'[24] Ninety per cent of the community supported Scott, wrote another correspondent, and 'those who do no[t] agree are the irresponsible, the alcoholics, perverts, and morons, and of course vested interests'.[25] Those who wrote to support the ban emphasised that they were ordinary folk, and did not hesitate to label their opponents as morally bankrupt. As one North Strathfield pharmacist was to write:

> As a young family man with two children, I am becoming increasingly disturbed at the growing permissiveness of our so-called 'adult' society. Particularly disturbing is the increasing popular acceptance of thinly disguised anti-censorship ridicule promulgated by the profiteers of pornography. I am no saint, am not particularly religious, and unless coming from a happy home and having had a G.P.S. education labels me a 'wowser' neither am I one of those. Australia is a great country and any genuine attempt to limit the production and/or distribution of anything designed to undermine marriage, morality, family life, and religion is to be applauded. To be one of only a handful of

countries to condemn *Portnoy's Complaint* and other deviously worthless verbiage should indeed be a singular compliment to your Department. Your task is obviously a thankless one, but I do hope that my few words (and I can assure you they are supported by countless others) will help you to continue to carry out your work with courage and diligence in spite of the vocal minority.[26]

Whatever the truth of claims to community support, *Portnoy's Complaint* had caught the attention and unsettled the views of people throughout Australia. The novel's frank treatment of sex could, for any two people, be attractive or repulsive; its profane language could be familiar or disturbing; its merit could be obvious or non-existent. There was no denying the novel's ability to provoke. Enthusiasm and outrage trailed it like the detritus of a comet.

It was for this reason that Greene continued to hope. During a visit to Australia in October 1969, he repeatedly criticised the ban. 'It is ridiculous,' Greene told the *Sunday Observer*. 'Practically everybody else in the world has been able to read the book. It is not as if it is some cheap "girlie" magazine. It is published by a well-known literary publisher.' Greene said he was amazed at the willingness of Australians to put up with censorship: 'The censorship laws in this country are a fantastic infringement of individual liberty. Australians don't seem to care that much. In England, with a similar situation, there would be an enormous outcry.'

Most sensationally, Greene let it be known that his company would publish the book, come what may. Likely derived from a flare of hope sent up during a lunch with George Ferguson, the publishing director at Angus & Robertson, Greene talked about smuggling *Portnoy* into the country and printing it in New South Wales. Of the obstacles and legal risks, Greene said nothing. He sounded brazen and determined. 'We will have no problems getting the book in,' he declared. 'Even a naval blockade would not stop us.'[27]

* * *

Greene's comments were overshadowed by the 1969 federal election. Prime Minister John Gorton, elected in January 1968 after Harold Holt's disappearance in the waters off Cheviot Beach, had had a turbulent time in office. There had been concerns over his personal conduct; problems with the state premiers; issues with defence policy; and internal divisions and personal tensions. All of these problems were compounded by the professional campaign of a resurgent Labor Party led by Gough Whitlam. The tall, imperious, and urbane Whitlam had unveiled a suite of policies in areas designed to appeal to Australia's emerging middle classes: in education, urban development, and healthcare, among others. Of most interest to Australia's literary community was the promise to reform censorship.

Following successful moves at Labor's federal conference to have this made part of the party platform, the promise was also the culmination of a long-running campaign, led by Senator Lionel Murphy, Labor's leader in the Senate, to emphasise social justice and civil liberties. Murphy argued that there had been a 'great mass of day-by-day repression' of fundamental rights in Australia. The promise to reform censorship law was as much a part of lifting this repression as it was a recognition that the environment in which censorship had taken root was now profoundly changed. It was not the 1920s anymore, Murphy argued. Australia was on the cusp of a new decade, and Australians deserved to live 'freely'.[28] They should be able to use their own judgement when deciding what to read.

As former premier and then-leader of the opposition in South Australia Don Dunstan put it, the individual's judgement should be central: 'Not Arthur Rylah's, not some tribunal's, not some academic's, and not some Customs officer's.'[29]

Thus Whitlam's promise on 1 October 1969: 'The censorship laws will be altered to conform with the general principles that adults be entitled to read, hear, and view what they wish in private or public and that persons and those in their care be protected from exposure to unsolicited material offensive to them.'Whitlam promised to establish a judicial tribunal to hold public hearings on proposed bans, and undertook to reform federal law on imported books, records, and films to align with those principles.[30]

Voters responded to Whitlam's proposals. On 25 October — the day before Greene's comments about an illegal edition of *Portnoy* appeared — the election left Gorton wounded and Whitlam agonisingly close to triumph. The Liberal–Country Party government suffered a 6.6 per cent swing and the loss of sixteen seats in the House of Representatives. The result prompted challenges to Gorton's leadership from treasurer William McMahon and minister for national development David Fairbairn. Gorton survived, but it was clear that there would be trouble ahead for the government and that changes would need to be made.

Among those changes was Gorton's removal of Malcolm Scott from the Customs portfolio. Scott had been 'just dreadful' in the portfolio, Gorton told the governor-general, Paul Hasluck: he 'dribbled sounds when he was supposed to be answering a question'.[31] Scott's replacement was a Victorian MP, Don Chipp. A sportsman in his youth and 'management consultant' before entering politics, Chipp was decidedly younger than his predecessors; with his dark, crinkled hair, automatic white smile, and permanent tan, he was certainly smoother than them. He was no believer in the virtues of censorship: he was doubtful about its justification, utility, and consistency, and he let this be known. Early in his tenure, Chipp showed a journalist two pornographic magazines and a collection of historical erotic postcards. 'Now, here's the problem,' said Chipp, pointing to the material. 'We ask ourselves, *what is obscene?* You'll agree there's no question that *this* is obscene, and there's no question about *this* sort of rubbish. But what about a book like *this?* ... Now, look *here*. I suppose most of these pictures are pretty harmless, but then you get to a photo like *that*! Now, do I let that through?'

But Chipp also believed that a debate on censorship needed to be handled with care. Any liberalisation needed to be gradual. He believed that he had a responsibility to be cautious. 'Remember, I have to decide the things I want to fight on,' Chipp said. 'Do I fight on a book like *this*, which has no real literary merit? Or do I fight on something that has obvious literary merit, a novel perhaps, that has been acclaimed overseas?'

Chipp stressed the exacting questions that censorship should answer: 'We need extremely good reasons to prohibit anybody from seeing or hearing anything he wants,' he said. 'But we must accept that in our present cultural and social climate, the majority of people want censorship in some form. The third thing is that while censorship is inherently undesirable and illogical and cannot be justified in a perfect society, we do not live in a perfect society. And my fourth rule is that all censorship must be done as openly as possible.'[32]

Sentiments like this gave hope to those pressing for the release of *Portnoy's Complaint*. 'It might be worthwhile having a go at him,' Arthur Harrap wrote to Greene, on 19 November.[33] Greene wrote to Chipp a few days later, asking that he 'personally review' the ban on *Portnoy*. Enclosing extracts of reviews of the book, Greene stressed its merit and Cape's reputation as a publisher of 'literary distinction'. 'I would not trouble you personally if I did not feel that this is an unusual case,' wrote Greene, 'where an important book has been prohibited in error.'[34]

Chipp had the documents and the reports sent to his office. He studied them. The reviews were many; the praise laudatory. But then he read the board's reports. At the end of the month, Chipp wrote to disappoint Greene once again:

At no time has the book been considered to be lacking in literary merit. In fact, the submission of the book to the Board is recognition of its literary qualities and an acknowledgement that expert advice is required before a decision is made. I have examined the novel and considered the reports submitted by the Board. However, in light of current Australian community standards, the criterion by which all publications are reviewed, I consider that the work contravenes the provisions of the Customs (Prohibited Imports) Regulations.[35]

Greene was 'glad' to have Chipp's assurance about *Portnoy*'s literary merit, but his suggestion of surprise at reaffirmation of the ban could hardly have been true.[36] At every turn, Australia's censors had delivered the same verdict: the book should not be allowed.

Where *Portnoy* managed to get into Australia, it was seized. In November, a few West Australian booksellers obtained copies, but they were quickly found out. Arthur Williams, of the In Bookshop in Perth and secretary of the state's Civil Liberties Association, opened his store on 24 November and was immediately brushed aside by Customs officials. 'They asked me if I knew anyone in England,' Williams wrote that evening. 'I said I knew Her Majesty [and] Mr Wilson (I met him when he was on a visit here last year). They said they were not the ones they were after.' The officials were not to be dissuaded by Williams's humour or his dissembling:

> One 'goon' asked me if I had ordered that Book. I said good heavens no, it must be an X-mas present. They were furious. They said they had seized them. They will not charge me if I did not solicit them. I rang my solicitor after they left. He said it would be expensive to order them to return them.[37]

Another bookshop, the Terrace Arcade, tried to post a copy to a customer, but it too was seized. 'Thanks for trying,' that customer wrote back. 'At least I have the consolation of remaining uncorrupted.'[38]

Letters of protest continued to arrive in Canberra. A longtime Liberal voter demanded to know if his MP would liberalise the censorship regime and lift the ban on *Portnoy*; the chairman of the

Liberal Party's Darling Downs area executive — who had stood unsuccessfully in the 1969 Queensland state election — was staggered when a copy of *Portnoy*, a birthday present from his daughter, was seized. 'I have a complaint,' he wrote to Chipp:

> I would be interested to know, firstly, if I am going to get the book, and, secondly, if I am not, what the situation is about lifting of the ridiculous ban thereon. I have no doubt that you would agree with me, personally, that the censorship ban, and the censorship which allows such a ban, is, at the very most, pettifogging, obscurantist, and achieving nothing.

Exasperation and immoderation were palpable in his postscript: 'What next — brain washing or book burning?'[39]

Greene would not stop pushing to get *Portnoy's Complaint* into Australia. 'We are determined to try and find a way to do the book,' he told one intimate.[40] He wrote to Lloyd O'Neil, asking him to review the ban, but O'Neil would not budge.[41] He wondered about George Ferguson, and whether he might still be willing to take the novel on, but Arthur Harrap sent the sad news in January 1970: Angus & Robertson would not do it.[42] Greene had taken care to follow up Geoffrey Dutton's offer to have Sun Books publish *Portnoy* by lunching, during an October 1969 visit to Australia, with Brian Stonier, who since taken Sun Books into the Cheshire publishing group. Stonier had mentioned publishing *Portnoy*, but since then Greene had heard nothing. He wrote in March 1970: would Stonier consider it?

Stonier would, but with a heavy heart and considerable caution. 'After a great deal of thought, discussion, and more market investigation than we have ever given any other book,' he wrote back, in June 1970, 'it is with great regret and some feelings of cowardice that we have come to the conclusion that it is not yet possible to publish *Portnoy's Complaint* in Australia.' The chief problem, Stonier explained, was the business dimension: the ongoing prosecutions for censorship in New South Wales and Victoria were a guarantee that a costly prosecution and legal action would follow any move to publish an Australian *Portnoy*. But there were also — forebodingly — problems of support, as Stonier outlined:

> A number of leading Melbourne booksellers who are particularly sympathetically inclined, have stated that they just would not stock the book, and our other line of contact has been newspaper editors anxious to start an anti-censorship move. The chief editor of the *Age* [Graham Perkin] is in this class, but has stated that the Board would not support any move to print excerpts from Portnoy's and they are certainly the most likely to support the cause.[43]

There was not yet the support that could make it work, he finished. It was just too early.

* * *

It all came back to the system. Customs had examined *Portnoy*; the National Literature Board of Review had scrutinised it; the minister had appraised it; there had been a verdict; there had been appeals that had been disallowed; and there had been reports and reviews. The ban had been reaffirmed at every step, and there was no reason to overturn it. And though some copies of the novel were available for import by particular individuals — psychologists, in the main, working at universities — the restriction remained. *Portnoy's Complaint* could not be imported into Australia. The government would not allow it to be published in Australia.

Chipp kept the door shut and barricaded. He would not rescind the ban. There were plenty of opportunities for him to do so, but he refused them all. At every moment, he reaffirmed it. It was perplexing. He was making no secret of his unease with censorship, was expressing the same arguments against censorship as his correspondents, and seemed intent on showing people how flawed the system was.

In April 1970, he screened a selection of pornographic and violent film clips for 150 selected MPs, journalists, religious figures, and academics, stating that his aim was to show the necessity of censorship and the absurdities of judging depictions of sex and violence without considering their context. It was not wholly persuasive, as no one was arguing about those aims. The issue in contention was critically acclaimed works that more than adequately justified their inclusion of depictions of sex or violence. Should those works be censored? Chipp would not say. 'There is a case of for censorship for the protection of the young,' wrote one reporter, after the April screening. 'There is a case for saying … that today's permissive standards in art and entertainment are injurious to the quality of art itself. There may even be a case for censorship in its present form, but Mr Chipp's exhibition — interesting though it was — did nothing to prove it.'[44]

Chipp's intransigence on *Portnoy* stemmed from his desire to maintain a balance: to reassure those who believed in censorship, and to encourage those who wanted it gone. By standing firm on the high-profile, controversial *Portnoy,* he placated the former, and in so doing had room to push for change within the censorship system that could satisfy the latter. In 1970, this did appear to bear fruit. In a ministerial statement on censorship in June — the first such statement since the 1930s — Chipp announced that the government had abandoned, as a test of what should be censored, the tendency of a work to encourage depravity. That test remained in legislation and regulation, but at a practical level Chipp said that it was no longer the determining question. 'Community standards' — which he defined as the level of sexual behaviour, bodily exposure, or violence that the community was prepared to tolerate — would now guide decisions.

The second of Chipp's changes was the introduction of R and X rating certificates for film. If implemented correctly, and with the cooperation of the state governments, these certificates would prevent children and young people from accessing inappropriate films while preserving the rights of adults to do so. These changes, Chipp hoped, would satisfy censorship's supporters and its opponents.

But consternation over the ban on *Portnoy* continued. In March 1970, student editors at Macquarie University printed a 'lifted, stolen, appropriated' extract of the novel in the campus newspaper *Arena*. 'You should be able to see what has been banned,' they wrote. '… If you find this subject distasteful or depraved, don't read it, but see a psychiatrist instead. For those other free souls, read on and laugh.'[45] One Liberal Party MLA in New South Wales complained about their 'flagrant contempt for the law of the land and the moral standards of the people', but the editors were unapologetic.[46] In the next issue, they called the extracts 'shock therapy', and printed more.[47]

As 1970 wore on, the controversy became a weeping sore for the federal government. Letters continued to stream in, protesting the ban. 'I do not see why anyone living in this country should be denied access to a book judged important in a civilised country,' wrote one woman.[48] A mature-age student studying literature was bewildered when copies of *Portnoy* and Norman Mailer's *Why Are We in Vietnam?* were seized: 'At my age — 60! — am I likely to be corrupted?'[49] A South Yarra man made a similar point when his copy was seized: 'I would point out that at my age, 66 years, I would stand little chance of being corrupted by reading it.'[50]

By July, Chipp had heard it all. He had put up with it for months. There was nothing new to be heard, said, or done. Then, on 19 July, he received a telegram:

WE HOLD AUSTRALIAN RIGHTS PHILLIP ROTH NOVEL PORTMOYS COMPLAINTS [SIC]. PROPOSE PUBLISHING THIS WORK IN AUSTRALIA IN THE NEAR FUTURE. IN VIEW OF YOUR OFFER OF PRIOR CONSULTATIONS ON MATTERS OF CENSORSHIP

HAVE BEEN ANXIOUS TO DISCUSS THIS MATTER WITH YOU
BEFORE PROCEEDING.[51]

Chipp could have been forgiven for feeling blindsided.
Nonetheless, his reply was remarkable for its equanimity. 'I am
agreeable to a meeting as suggested,' he cabled back. 'Please contact
my secretary in Melbourne … with a view to arranging a suitable
time.'[52]

CHAPTER 7

Straws in the wind

The telegram had come from John Michie, managing director of Penguin Books Australia. A laconic and somewhat austere man, Michie had been raised on the sparsely populated King Island, in Bass Strait, and educated in the bosom of the establishment: Melbourne Grammar and the University of Melbourne. He knew money and its manners, and was interested in the arts. He loved Melville and *Moby-Dick*; read Waugh, Conrad, Dostoevsky, and the English naturalist poets; listened to Bach, Mahler, Stockhausen, and Sibelius; and possessed an enduring love of the sea and sailing, to the point that once, after sailing single-handed to New Zealand, he remarked that it had been 'Sibelius all the way'. Thirty-four years old, he was tall, lean, stern, and handsome — a striking man with dark hair and keen blue eyes. Charming when he wanted, ruthless when it suited, Michie was intelligent, by instinct independent, and immensely canny.[1]

He had displayed all of these qualities in his work as managing director. In the previous decade, the modest, post-war beginnings of the Australian branch of Penguin — as a distribution centre for the paperback books that its British parent was famous for — had been left behind. Thriving in a prosperous period of Australian publishing, Penguin had cornered the market for inexpensive, quality books from the UK. It was building a small Australian list by taking over titles available only in hardcover and republishing them in paperback. It had paid attention, with lucrative results, to the needs of the education sector. And it had lately won grudging acquiescence from its parent company to begin building a program of original Australian titles that were culturally engaged and critically astute. Donald Horne's *The Lucky Country* (1964) was one of the most famous examples; another was Robert Hughes's *The Art of Australia* (1966).

Michie had joined Penguin right at the cusp of some of its greatest success. Hired in 1965 as a sales manager, he was given an early opportunity to demonstrate his talents when Brian Stonier, Geoffrey Dutton, and Max Harris — who had started the domestic publishing program — left to found Sun Books. Within six months, Michie had been promoted to manage promotions and distribution; by 1968, his abilities were in such evident abundance that the managing director was shown the door and Michie was appointed in his place.

Michie came to the job with especially noteworthy ambitions. In his view, the days where Australians read what publishers in England wanted should end.[2] The domestic publishing program that Stonier, Dutton, and Harris had begun was instrumental in presenting to Australian readers their own voices and perspectives. Michie wanted to build on it, to increase it, to make it sustainable; in doing so, Penguin could shape Australian culture and life, present new ideas, expose old canards, question orthodoxies, and pose alternatives. There was an idealistic, even outsized, dimension to this — the belief that Penguin could even play a role in shaping the region around Australia, too. A nationalism that by its vehemence could be heard as Anglophobic ran through this mission: to make Penguin Australia an international publishing house, publishing

Australian and international books, for Australia and the region.[3]

But this could only happen if Penguin continued to be commercially successful. Aware that the 'takeovers' that constituted Penguin's easy source of profit was soon to dry up, Michie sought to hone Penguin's competitive advantages. The main way he sought to do this was by overhauling the company's distribution system. 'When I took over Penguin,' he said later, 'it had a small but flourishing local publishing program instituted by Brian Stonier, but the actual machinery of the operation — the distribution and so on — was in some disarray.'[4]

To repair this, Michie drew on the talents of Peter Froelich, a fellow commerce graduate of the University of Melbourne and an accountant who had joined Penguin in 1964 at the age of twenty-eight. A keen sportsman who wore pinstripe suits to work and was thought a Menzies man by his colleagues, Froelich too believed in the cultural mission of publishing.[5] But, like Michie, he also believed that that cultural mission needed to be accompanied by constant improvements in the company's bottom line.[6]

One of the most pressing improvements needed to be in tracking sales and processing. The tabulating machine in use, which required an operator to punch holes in a series of forty- or eighty-column cards that would be fed into a primitive computer that would spit out a list of sales, was too slow for the voluminous business Penguin was now engaged in. Froelich persuaded the board to lease, and then to buy, a GE-115 computer, which replaced the tab-card system with large, plate-sized discs, each of which could hold the content of 25,000 cards.[7] The improved processing and tracking it afforded allowed Penguin to order timely and better-sized print runs. The constant problem of any publisher — of ensuring the minimum of stock necessary to maintain sales, without an oversupply of stock that would have to be written down — became easier and easier to manage. Money lost because of exhausted stock was reduced to between two and three per cent of Penguin's yearly earnings. The computer, recalled Hilary McPhee, who joined Penguin as an editor in 1968, aged twenty-six, 'revolutionised Penguin's efficiency. Everything was efficient in a way that no other publisher was.'[8]

Getting books to booksellers quickly was another area that needed changing. The system for packing orders was inefficient: taking orders via a phone in the warehouse, packers would fill them individually, doubling back and forth through the warehouse and shelves, slowing down distribution. The computer improved this process significantly. 'Because we could now update the stock dynamically,' Froelich said, 'we could, when the orders came in, have the data-processing staff process the order. They could prepare the invoice, and a copy of the invoice could go to the warehouse, and it would be set out in the same order as the warehouse was laid out. It would be quicker. Then we installed a conveyor belt to help streamline that, too. It helped make it quick and more efficient.'

Michie and Froelich also sought to gain more control of how books were ordered and shipped. In the past, booksellers had been able to order titles in paltry numbers, and Penguin would ship them at a loss. Froelich changed that by putting a floor on the number of books that a seller could order. When booksellers objected, he pointed out that it was unsustainable for Penguin to persist with the current system, and that without change Penguin would need to start passing on the costs, thereby increasing prices for everyone. The discontent continued, but Froelich and Michie managed to bring opponents around by explaining the benefits that this efficiency would bring. 'In effect,' Froelich said, 'we were saying that booksellers needed to smarten up their logistics, too.'

Such improvements would always be in-progress, never finished, but they spoke to Penguin's determination to innovate. 'I managed to crank up that distribution system,' Froelich said later. 'That was my baby.' It would not have been possible to do this without the goodwill and opportunity that Michie and other Penguin staff offered, he added. 'Michie saw that he needed someone with skills other than what he had. That was the catalyst for it. He used to trust me and give me free rein. It was also an environment where people were objective about stuff. They were open to it.' Bob Sessions, who joined Penguin in September 1970, was in no doubt about the effect and the credit of these changes: 'As a team, he [Michie] and Peter Froelich built on the good things that been done before them, and made sure that the company became computerised and the warehouse worked and the accounts system was brought up to date.'[9]

All this markedly improved Penguin Australia's financial position in the immediate years before 1970. The company became cash rich, to the point that it could meet the demands for regular infusions of money from its British parent company, which began to suffer a series of cashflow crises late in the 1960s. These demands would have been impossible to meet had Penguin Australia's position not been strengthened by its changes to operations.

The economic growth was accompanied by an increasingly vibrant non-fiction list that was invigorated by John Hooker, a New Zealand–born editor who joined Penguin in September 1969.[10] Literate and creative, a self-proclaimed 'ideas man' who lived by his 'publishing wits', Hooker brimmed with projects that he would pitch to promising writers.[11] He was interested in politics and social issues, and was unfazed about taking on the risky or unlikely. He offered Anne Summers, then a PhD student, a contract for the book that would become *Damned Whores and God's Police* (1975); he published Humphrey McQueen's seminal New Left history, *A New Britannia* (1970); and he commissioned Aboriginal writer and artist Kevin Gilbert to write *Living Black* (1977), which would win the National Book Council Award in 1978.

Lean and tousle-haired, with a finely boned face and penchant for cigarettes and long lunches, the thirty-seven-year-old Hooker was a novelist in his spare time and a sharp-tongued rebel.[12] This could have made for a hard fit with Michie: at a philosophical level, Hooker acknowledged later, they were 'poles apart'.[13] But the distance between those poles did not prevent the two from striking up a rapport. In Hooker, Michie found someone with a similar grandness of vision for Australian publishing, who wanted to produce books that were culturally engaged, new, and exciting.

This was a notable point. Penguin's engagement with Australian culture, through its domestic and original publishing list, was opportune. The war in Vietnam, the advent of the women's movement, the increasing knowledge of Indigenous discrimination, and uncertainty about Australia's place in the world meant that there was a literate population yearning for works that addressed these issues. 'These were exciting and heady times,' Hooker said later. '... It was a publisher's paradise.'[14] McPhee echoed this. The politics and cultural shifts, the burgeoning arts and theatre scenes, and the emergence of new and interesting writers, she recalled, were sustenance for a publisher looking to engage: 'It was a heady time.'[15]

It was also a happy, successful period. Tensions with the British Penguin offices were assuaged by transfusions of cash. The independent directors who sat on the board were kept docile by the company's ever-stronger financial position. The staff at Penguin Australia were idealistic and young. They were passionate about the cultural mission of their work. McPhee recalled being 'starry-eyed': 'There was always a real energy in the place,' she said later.[16] Conversation was about expansion, about reshaping the publishing world, about illuminating Australian life, showing that Penguin Australia's books were not for Australia alone but for the world as well: thus McPhee's successful argument that they should remove from the colophon the boomerangs that marked their books as Australian Penguins only. Penguin published serious works, some of them original, some of them takeovers, all of them intended for the whole world — not just Australia.

And at the top of the company were the three men, Michie, Hooker, and Froelich: working at the frontier, willing to challenge outdated assumptions and ideas, to push for more, and to pursue the big picture they saw.

* * *

There were frequent conversations. Over lunches that lasted late into the day and dinners that drifted late into the night, whether at the office or at Jimmy Watson's in Carlton, the staff at Penguin often talked about the problems afflicting publishing and literature in Australia. Sessions recalled the passion that Michie and Hooker, in particular, brought to these conversations. 'We used to sit around the common room after work, and chew the fat and have a drink,' he said. 'Out of the conversations we had there developed a certain rebelliousness. "Why are they doing this? Why are they doing that? Why can't we do this?" They were all questions we were asking.'[17] Amid Michie's ambitions and Penguin's engagement with culture and politics, it was not surprising that censorship was a regular topic. 'We'd had issues with it before, in minor ways,' Froelich recalled, 'and when we'd have drinks we'd say, "It's wrong! How can we fix it? What can we do? How do we bring it to people's attention, so that it can be changed?"'

There were constant spurs for the sentiments expressed over meals and drink to become action. The trials of Wendy Bacon and the travails of Arthur Rylah and Don Chipp were always in the news. But the most instrumental was the publication of Dutton and Harris's *Australia's Censorship Crisis* — for among the extracts from banned works it included was one from *Portnoy's Complaint*.

It stood out immediately. It was frank, funny, profane, biting, riven with bitterness and bursting with colour. It was justifiably famous, a bestseller the world over, of well-discussed literary merit. If there was a work that deserved publication, this was it. Why should it stay banned? All three — who had read the book in toto — thought highly of it for its skill, humour, and the compassion that informed its treatment of the taboo. 'I was brought up in the era where you were taught that if you masturbated then you went blind. That was normal,' Froelich said. 'So, to actually read about it was perhaps to see that it was not so abnormal or strange. To me, that was a good part of it.'[18]

Importantly, publication of *Australia's Censorship Crisis* revealed that Tom Maschler's flat refusal to allow an 'Australian' edition of the novel, made after *Portnoy* had been banned in 1969, was not so clear-cut as it seemed.[19] A letter from Greene to Dutton, quoted in the book, suggested that Maschler's refusal referred only to an expurgated edition. 'It is a reflection of the current censorship situation in Australia and the rest of the world's attitude to it,' wrote Greene, 'that "Australian edition" has become shorthand for "expurgated edition."'[20]

Cape's willingness to allow *Portnoy's Complaint* to be published in Australia, so long as it was unexpurgated, meant that it could become a potent weapon with which to take on the censorship regime. It was perfect for the cause. The combination of merit and unshying, expletive-ridden depictions of sex pointed to all the problems and failures of Australia's censorship system. Hooker was immediately convinced. 'Jack,' he said to Michie, 'we ought to really publish *Portnoy's Complaint* and give them one in the eye.'

It was a bold idea. Certainly, there was no other publisher better placed in Australia to take *Portnoy* on and use it against the censorship regime. With its reputation, contacts, and resources, Penguin could make the novel a hit and, simultaneously, deliver a body blow to the censorship system. But however compelling the idea might be over lunch, and however attractive it was at those late-night dinners, Michie knew that, in the light of day, it required serious thought. He would not take the decision lightly. He knew that it needed to be thought through: the risks needed to be assessed; the logistics needed to be planned; success needed to be defined and a path to it mapped out. But he came on board early. Michie's attention to the business side of publishing, his passion for its cultural value, and his awareness of the conservatism that censorship fostered made for a neat marriage: he was in favour of publishing *Portnoy*. As Hooker put it later, 'John offered to smash the whole thing down.'[21]

The two approached Froelich. 'Where are you in this?' they asked. 'What do you think?'

Froelich was as cautious as Michie, but, ultimately, agreeable to the idea: 'Well, okay, if you want to.'

Initially, they kept the idea quiet. 'I said that we needed to talk to some legal people about it,' Froelich recalled. 'We did that. We went through it. We documented the risks in order to see it clearly and assess it.' The obstacles and dangers were considerable. Publishing the novel would not be easy. Nor would it be without risk to Penguin. Fines could undo all the work of the previous decade. Criminal charges were in prospect for them, personally, with jail time a distinct possibility. Booksellers could refuse to stock the novel. The public, too, might stay away: as repeated polls purported to show, there was strong support for censorship in the community.[22] Was it worth all the risks? Were they willing to accept the potential consequences? What would they do if everything went wrong? 'As we worked through all that,' Froelich recalled, 'we kept coming back to the key point: why are we doing this? We're taking on the censorship laws.'

One dimension to the decision was the parallel with Penguin's publication of *Lady Chatterley's Lover*. Michie, Froelich, and Hooker were aware that Penguin took considerable pride in its actions then; indeed, it still glowed from the accolades it received for the successful defence it had put forward during the trial in 1960. 'That was one of the things that helped us with the decision,' Froelich said later. 'We thought, *This is what happened with Lady Chatterley. It is a parallel. We would be doing the same thing here.* There was the excitement of repeating that exercise.'

This aided the case that Michie put to the Australian and UK boards. He did this alone. Intent on ensuring that whatever adverse consequences eventuated fell on him and him alone, Michie took the lead and the responsibility. He put the case for publishing *Portnoy* in Australia.

The independent directors on the Australian board were

initially ill disposed to the idea. 'There was not a total comfort level from them,' recalled Froelich. But Michie's arguments and personal stake assuaged their concerns. Telling Michie and Froelich (by then on the board) that they trusted them, the directors said that the decision was a matter for their judgement. The UK board, early on, was also hesitant. Bereft of the galvanising influence of Allen Lane, ailing and soon to die, and concerned by the risk to the revenue it enjoyed and was coming to need, the UK board equivocated. It would take until late June, until almost the final moment, for it to send its assent.

* * *

Plans quickly became action. Hooker telephoned Graham C. Greene on 8 June, offering to pay $5,000 for the Australian paperback rights to *Portnoy* for three years, with a 12.5 per cent royalty on a likely print run of 30,000 copies.[23]

But Greene did not control the paperback rights in Australia: Cape had sold these to UK paperback publisher Corgi for £7,500. Notwithstanding that, owing to the ban, it was hesitant to exercise these rights, Greene told Hooker the next day that Corgi was 'not at all keen' on allowing Penguin to produce an edition. He suggested Penguin produce a hardcover edition instead. Hooker demurred, and ruled the idea out a day later. Penguin's distribution system was set up for a paperback edition only, he explained; moreover, were the ban on *Portnoy* suddenly rescinded — as Customs had done with *Another Country*, when Alex Sheppard was preparing to publish an illegal edition — Penguin would doubtless be undercut by an inexpensive paperback edition from Corgi.

Hooker decided to remind Greene of the larger cause that Penguin was pursuing. Don Chipp's early signals of an increased liberalism in censorship matters, Hooker wrote, were 'mere straws in the wind'. Chipp had neither reformed legislation nor cleared up the muddle of state and federal responsibilities. In the absence of any change, he argued, repression would continue. Censorship was as pressing an issue as it ever was. But there was a solution, Hooker said:

> If we were to print and publish *Portnoy* here as a paperback and have it distributed literally overnight in bookshops and wholesalers throughout Australia, it would be a massive blow against the State and Federal censorship ... It is only by this kind of distribution that we can force both State and Federal governments to change their present repressive attitudes.[24]

To this, Greene seemed sympathetic. But Corgi, still hoping to get the book into Australia, continued to resist giving up the rights.[25] Hooker proposed three options for a deal: Penguin could pay Corgi a $5,000 advance with a 15 per cent royalty for a three-year licence; it could make the same deal, but in association with Corgi; or both companies could publish and share the risks equally. The last two options were non-starters for Corgi, which believed that prosecution would be all the more certain if it were involved in an Australian edition.[26]

But even as it ruled out these options, Corgi was urgently contacting its Australian distributors for information. The publisher quickly realised that the situation with *Portnoy* was dire. Word arrived that their distributors would not cooperate with any move to publish *Portnoy* in Australia illegally. Police action was a certainty. Legal action was inevitable. No distributor was willing to risk the legal fees, let alone the penalties. In the face of this, Corgi began to rethink its position. Admitting that it was losing money every day it did not publish *Portnoy* in Australia, Corgi contacted Cape on 22 June to say that it would do a deal. 'They [Corgi's distributors] still decline to distribute *Portnoy*, so it's all clear for Penguin,' ran the memo.[27]

With Corgi giving way, matters moved quickly. Within a few days, Greene had given Penguin permission to use, for no fee, the Cape edition and its artwork as basis for Penguin's paperback edition. Penguin would sell the book for $1.35, reserving some of that money for legal costs, and would pay royalties to Cape on its sales: 7.5 per cent for up to 25,000 copies; 10 per cent for up to 50,000 copies, and 12.5 per cent thereafter. Penguin would also pay $10,000 to Corgi — in effect, reimbursing the £7,500 Corgi had spent — for the rights.[28] It struck an agreement with Corgi for the rights in an Australian paperback edition for three years, with the catch that Penguin had to publish within twelve weeks of 1 July 1970.

Thus, from the beginning, speed and secrecy were the order of the day. Penguin was 'insistent' there should be no leak before publication. 'They want copies distributed all over Australia by the time the first case is brought against them,' Greene wrote. Not even Philip Roth would be informed about what was afoot. Roth's British agent, Deborah Rogers, had his American agent approve the deal on Roth's behalf: 'So he won't know until everything is signed,' Greene recorded, 'which will probably be about the same time as publication.'[29] The secrecy extended to material placed in the post: letters, contracts, cover art, galleys. Should Customs open the wrong parcel, the jig would be up.[30]

Among the most important decisions to be made was the number of copies Penguin would print. The plan that Michie, Hooker, and Froelich had hatched called for Penguin to go big on *Portnoy*. 'We had to print lots of copies, and we had to distribute them quickly and to a lot of places,' Froelich recalled. 'We needed the big bang. There was no other way. It would be a waste of time if we didn't go big.'

Printing a lot of copies was not unusual: when Penguin published *Lady Chatterley's Lover* in the UK in 1960, it abandoned 'arithmetical niceties' and printed more than 200,000 copies.[31] But Michie, Hooker, and Froelich were aware that they could not simply print a lot of copies, and then — as Penguin UK did — refrain from selling them until proceedings were over. The set-up of Australia's censorship system could have seen the entirety of the *Portnoy* stock seized and the case buried. It was essential to have both a large print run and countrywide distribution. If this were done right, police would be unable to seize all the copies, and it would be impossible for the state governments to bury the case. There would have to be court action in every single state. There would be headlines in newspapers, and bulletins on television and radio across the country. There would be public attention. There would be public demand. There would be public accountability for the censorship laws. 'We thought our big hope was that the press picked it up, and showed people how ridiculous censorship was,' Froelich said. '... We wanted to draw attention to the censorship laws.'

Michie, Froelich, and Hooker decided that they should print 75,000 copies of *Portnoy's Complaint*. It would be enough to make a splash, and then — if all went as planned — to sell out, creating more demand as the inevitable court cases made their way through the legal system. But there was, almost immediately, a hiccup.

Griffin Press, located in South Australia, was Penguin's printer of choice. Aware, however, that the manager director, Bryan Price, would be wary of printing *Portnoy*, Michie promised that Penguin would shoulder any financial losses that might arise from a prosecution. Price weighed this, and approached the new South Australian Labor government for advice. Led by Don Dunstan, who had been returned to the premier's office after the 30 May state election, the government was progressive and libertarian, particularly in matters of censorship, as Dunstan's support for *America Hurrah* had suggested. But Dunstan's attorney-general, Len King, QC, was less than comfortable with this and mindful of the agreement for uniform censorship. When Price came to see him, King was clear: decline the job. If Price accepted it, King would ensure there was a prosecution. Price was hardly in a position to argue. The threat was too real to ignore. He turned Michie down.

'Right, that's the end of Griffin,' Michie said, when he was told. 'No more work for them.' These were not idle words. Michie was furious with the company. In light of the surety that he and Penguin were going to be prosecuted, with all the might that the state governments could bring, Michie believed that Price's decision was a betrayal. 'They had let us down,' Sessions said, later.

But Michie was determined to press on. 'We have had some difficulty with the printers and this has mean't [sic] a delay,' Hooker wrote to Greene on 29 June. But, he added, production would be underway soon. There would not be any further delay.[32] Michie was approaching other printers, among them Halstead Press, based in Sydney and owned by Angus & Robertson. He did not consider it a likely candidate for the job: Halstead had high prices and was thought conservative. But, to the surprise of everyone at Penguin, Halstead seemed receptive, to the point that it sought advice from Angus & Robertson's lawyers at Allen Allen & Hemsley, whose senior partner, Sir Norman Cowper, was, until the end of that month, also the chairman of Angus & Robertson.

Then aged seventy-one and only a few days from retirement, Cowper was an establishment figure through and through. He had attended Sydney Grammar School and the University of Sydney; had been involved in non-Labor politics; and was a member of the Australian Club and the University Club. He was also a liberal and cultured man: he wrote articles for *Australian Quarterly*, encouraged law clerks to think for themselves, and was married to Dorothea McCrae, daughter of the poet Hugh McCrae. 'He had a bit of the literary glow about him,' one colleague recalled.[33]

Between his legal skills and his literary pedigree, Cowper was well placed to offer advice on *Portnoy*. But there are some indications that he may have provided advice for Graham C. Greene during his earlier efforts to get *Portnoy* into Australia. According to Reginald Barrett, then a solicitor with Allen Allen & Hemsley, at some point late in 1969 or the first half of 1970, the firm was asked by a London client for advice on the likelihood of a successful prosecution of *Portnoy*. Barrett, aged twenty-five, was given a copy of the Jonathan Cape edition and directed to prepare a draft for Cowper. 'Relying on the then-recent High Court decision in *Crowe v Graham*,' Barrett recalled, 'I concluded that there was a significant risk of a successful prosecution under the New South Wales obscenity law.'

Cowper then read the book and settled the advice. According to Barrett, it was 'generally cautionary'. 'His personal view, expressed to me,' added Barrett, 'was that it was a "silly book."'[34]

Whether this advice was recycled in June 1970 or was wholly new is unclear. But colleagues at Allens would later recall that the firm tendered advice on *Portnoy* to Angus & Robertson, and attributed authorship to Cowper. Concise, clear, and with a judicious amount of wriggle room, the letter was two paragraphs long. The last was key: 'I've read this book. It's a book about a neurotic New York man who seems to have a series of erotic adventures. Some of it's quite disgusting. But no jury, properly instructed, could convict on any charge of obscenity.'[35]

The proposal to print *Portnoy*, along with this advice, was referred to Angus & Robertson's board early in July. It was a precipitous meeting. The company — a prestigious publisher of many Australian novels and a well-regarded bookseller — had just been taken over by Gordon Barton, a young, enterprising, and controversial businessman who had begun his career smuggling onions and potatoes across state borders in the 1940s as a way of circumventing trading laws. Barton had made a fortune through his parcel-delivery service, IPEC, but his business now lay in buying failing companies, stripping them of assets, and selling them at a profit as lean and efficient operations. Buying into Angus & Robertson — which, for all its prestige, was ailing and unable to respond to the pressure of competitors — seemed an odd decision for Barton. Profit margins in publishing were thin; Halstead Press was leaking money, thanks to the proliferation of cheaper printers, particularly in Asia; and though Angus & Robertson had assets in property, those assets were integral to its bookselling operations. Why do it?

The choice was understandable once Barton's passions for culture and society were understood. He had founded and bank-rolled two newspapers, and had emerged as a political player by criticising the federal government for its two-airlines policy and its military commitment to Vietnam. During US president Lyndon Johnson's visit to Australia in October 1966, Barton had written an open letter that criticised the Vietnam War as a 'dirty war'.[36] He had resigned from the Liberal Party, formed the 'Liberal Reform Group', and run candidates against the government at the 1966 election. All had been unsuccessful, but Barton's boldness remained undiminished. By 1970, he was forty-one years old, charming, handsome, obliged to no one, and still determined to make his mark. Hence his willingness, when he took over Angus & Robertson, to revitalise the company and honour its traditions.

At the meeting of the Angus & Robertson board early in July, Barton came out in favour of printing *Portnoy's Complaint* and, moreover, stocking the book in Angus & Robertson's stores.[37] Some board members were nervous, and argued that prosecution was likely and that Angus & Robertson's reputation would suffer. Barton agreed with the first proposition and emphatically agreed with the second, but for different reasons. It would be a poor reflection on Angus & Robertson's reputation, he argued, if it allowed the police to determine what it published and sold. Between this and the advice provided by Allen Allen & Hemsley, the new chairman carried the day. Halstead was told to take the job.[38]

Penguin had its printer. On 24 July, copies of the Cape edition of *Portnoy's Complaint* that had been smuggled into Australia were delivered to Halstead for reproduction, via photo offset, in the Penguin edition. Aubrey Cousins, Halstead Press's managing director, began the job immediately. 'Work is proceeding,' Michie wrote to Greene that day. '… Barring mishaps, we hope to publish in Australia on September 2nd.'[39]

There were two main mishaps that might occur: first, word might leak; second, the distribution might go awry. 'I am concerned that the job is not intercepted by the New South Wales police while it is on the machines,' wrote Michie, 'and for this reason we are keeping as quiet as possible for the time being.' Secrecy was paramount, but the success of the distribution and logistics of publication were going to be vital. 'Everyone knew that the success of it was going to come down to logistics,' Sessions said later. 'It needed to be a smooth operation.' Here, then, was the payoff for Froelich's changes to Penguin's ordering, packing, and distribution systems. Froelich, said Sessions, 'took the whole thing on with some relish. He saw it as a challenge to be overcome.' Froelich planned to take orders from wholesalers who could distribute the book efficiently. With great secrecy, he leased a warehouse in Sydney, near Halstead, from which a substantial consignment of the printed copies of *Portnoy* could be shipped to wholesalers, thereby avoiding the delays that would result from bringing the books to Melbourne, and minimising the risks of police confiscation.

With great care, Michie now began to let Penguin's sales staff in on the secret and to enlist wholesalers and booksellers to take *Portnoy* on. It took all his charm to bring Penguin's sales staff onside. They had to be persuaded that it was a good thing to do, recalled Hilary McPhee. 'John had to explain why Penguin was doing it, and why they should be involved.'[40] Then he had to persuade booksellers and wholesalers. It was testament to his powers of persuasion, the respect in which he was held, and the loyalty that he had engendered that Michie could make headway where Brian Stonier and Corgi had each been blocked. One by one, booksellers came on board. 'We've got Robertson & Mullens!' Michie announced when he scored an agreement from the long-time establishment bookstore in Elizabeth Street, Melbourne. Every bookseller who agreed to take a carton, every wholesaler who agreed to take a shipment, boosted Penguin's confidence and fed into its preparations. Everything was carefully, even minutely, planned. Success, Hooker said later, was 'quite impossible without the distribution machine. It was like the Germans going into

Poland in 1939.'[41] Everybody involved knew that the stakes were high. 'Look,' Froelich said to Hooker, at one point, 'we can't afford to muck this operation up.'[42]

With events in motion, Michie decided to warn the federal government. Thus his telegram to Chipp on 19 July, announcing that Penguin Books held the rights to *Portnoy*, wished to exercise them, and wanted a meeting. 'The matter is, of course, now outside his province,' Michie wrote to Greene, 'but I have a feeling that he would have liked to release the book.'[43]

Chipp's staff hastened to set the meeting up; meanwhile, the department prepared to guide its minister to the correct view and to predict what would happen. 'In view of Clause 20 and the spirit of uniform action which has strengthened since 1968,' wrote first assistant comptroller-general R. M. Keogh, 'I am certain that the States ... would act against the publication and distribution of *Portnoy's Complaint* in Australia in the absence of a full Board recommendation for release.' There was also an unsubtle attempt to lock Chipp in and prevent him from overriding the board: 'The release of *Portnoy's Complaint* would be of profound significance in terms of standards and, in effect, would mean that most books of the type now referred to the Board would no longer be detained for censorship examination. Another consequence would be that the majority of titles now contained in the gazetted list would have to be released.'

'In these circumstances,' finished Keogh, 'it is recommended that you inform Mr Michie at your meeting that you propose to maintain the prohibition on *Portnoy's Complaint* and that you subsequently inform the State Ministers of the proposed publication of the book in Australia and send them a copy for their information.'[44]

Chipp did exactly that. On 29 July, he told Michie that *Portnoy's Complaint* had been banned and that he had no intention of changing that ruling. The spirit of the agreement between the federal and state governments ensured that the responsible ministers would act in concert on censorship matters. Any copy of *Portnoy's Complaint* that Penguin might possess was prohibited and could be seized. In possessing a copy, furthermore, Penguin was liable to prosecution under the *Customs Act*. 'Should it come to my notice that there are such prohibited copies in Australia,' ran a heavily underlined section of Chipp's notes, 'I will have to consider what action I shall take (seizure and/or prosecution for possession).' Implying the threat was not enough for Chipp. As Michie related to Graham C. Greene, Chipp 'tried very hard to cut the project off at the ankles by talking about all the penalties we run the risk of incurring and even offered to fine me $1,000 if he could locate a copy of the bound edition in my possession!'[45] Chipp also made a promise: he leaned across his desk, looked the publisher in the eye, and told him, 'I'll see you in jail for this, Michie.'[46]

But Chipp's threat was hollow. 'I also advised Mr Michie that in view of the provisions of the States' legislation relating to the publication and distribution of literature in Australia,' he wrote afterwards, 'the matter of publishing *Portnoy's Complaint* is one he should discuss with the State Governments.' In effect, Chipp had admitted that Michie's problems would not be with him — they would be with the state governments. The states, alone, had the power to launch prosecutions over the novel's publication, distribution, and sale.

Michie understood that. He had expected anger, and he had expected threats. They altered nothing. Aware that the Halstead Press had been printing copies of *Portnoy* for five days already, he had known before walking into the meeting that there was no turning back.[47]

He told Chipp that Penguin would persist. It would publish *Portnoy's Complaint*.[48]

Halstead finished printing just over three weeks later. Forty thousand copies were delivered to the warehouse Froelich had leased in Sydney, and were dispatched from there to wholesalers and distributors. The remaining 35,000 copies were delivered to

Penguin's warehouse in Ringwood, in outer Melbourne, on 27 August. Orders were phoned into the office that afternoon; the invoices were prepared that evening; by the next morning the books had been packed and dispatched. They had not even been there for twenty-four hours.

CHAPTER 8

An endemic complaint

Penguin had done its work well. In that final week of August 1970, as its agents and managers continued to approach booksellers, and the surreptitiously printed copies were transported around the country, word leaked that they were publishing *Portnoy's Complaint*. The response gave Penguin great heart: booksellers were supportive, even enthusiastic. 'I said, "Yeah, too right,"' recalled Bob Gould, of the Third World Bookstore in Sydney.[1] But all were surprised by the speed with which the publisher was moving, shocked that the book had already been printed, and stunned that it would be delivered within the week. 'Usually there are whispers when something is likely to happen in the trade,' said one bookseller. 'This time there hasn't been a murmur. We were utterly taken aback.'

Publicly, Penguin continued to be tight-lipped. When approached by reporters, Sydney sales manager Bill Snodgrass denied any knowledge of an imminent publication, and declined to make any further comment. 'You seem to have all the facts,' he told one journalist, 'so I'd better not say anything more.'[2]

The state governments were forewarned. Worried booksellers

had informed them, and Chipp had alerted them, that an Australian *Portnoy* was on its way. In Queensland, Victoria, and New South Wales, the censors tried intimidation, and blustered about criminal action. In New South Wales, Eric Willis warned that anyone involved in printing, publishing, or selling the book in his state could expect a fine of $250 or six months' imprisonment.[3]

Few were deterred by the noise. Advice from the Booksellers' Association that month did not suggest that its members should refrain from stocking *Portnoy* — only that they should not display it or sell it to minors. Some accepted this; others preferred to be forthright. One Sydney bookseller who had agreed to take a consignment placed a sign in his window: 'Get your copy while stocks last.'

News finally broke on Sunday 30 August that Penguin had printed *Portnoy's Complaint*. Michie held a press conference at his home in Mont Albert on the Sunday evening. He told journalists that the book was an internationally acclaimed masterpiece and should be available to read in Australia.[4] Penguin was distributing copies to more than 2,000 booksellers throughout the country. The book would be available in every state on the first day of spring. He was not afraid or nervous of the likely prosecutions. He was defiant about it all: 'We are prepared to take the matter to the High Court.'[5]

The bureaucracy was swinging into action. On the Friday, the New South Wales undersecretary for justice wrote to the commissioner of police requesting he 'take any action necessary' to deal with the imminent publication.[6] On the Monday, with Michie's announcement in the newspapers, detectives from the New South Wales Vice Squad received instructions to visit bookshops around Sydney, purchase copies of *Portnoy*, and take note of anyone they saw buying the book. Two detectives, Mitchell and Quill, received additional instructions to visit Halstead Press and find out how it had happened. They collared Aubrey Cousins on the doorstep, and interviewed him for half an hour in his office to get what they wanted. Then they told him that he could be prosecuted. 'Yes,' Cousins replied, 'but we have acted for a reputable firm — and we are not censors. So, how are we to know?'

Meanwhile, the book was arriving in bookshops. In Melbourne, at around mid-morning, a crowd of 600 surged into Robertson & Mullens and overturned a counter, knocking down the store's assistant manager and nearly trampling him in their rush to get copies.[7] 'I expected some sort of rush this morning — but nothing like this,' the store's managing director said. 'It was a stampede.' The store sold out almost immediately; when it received 200 copies more that afternoon, it sold them all in eighteen minutes.[8] The demand was huge. Cheshire's Bookshop, on Little Collins Street, received 500 copies at 12.30 pm — and had sold out by five o'clock.

In Sydney, Angus & Robertson's paperback manager, Paul Grainger, told his staff that *Portnoy* would be coming and that they needed to be vigilant about who they sold the book to. 'The biggest risk that Angus & Robertson and the individual staff were running was in selling the book to a minor,' he said later. '… I knew that it was one of the most fatal mistakes we could possibly make. So, I made it clear to my staff that if they had any doubts as to the age of the person trying to buy the book they should ask for ID — and if the customer had any arguments about that, they should talk to me.' Word had spread that Angus & Robertson would be selling the book. Even before it was delivered, people were queuing up to ask for it, wanting to know when it would come in. When it did finally arrive, at 11.30 am, there was a rush. 'We virtually didn't have time to unpack it,' Grainger recalled. 'People were already there and wanting to buy it.'[9] Copies of the book had to be kept behind the counter, in their cartons, to be plucked out and slipped into bags as people purchased them. There was no time to do any-thing else.

The queues never seemed to shorten. Customers continued to arrive and to line up. Some bought one copy only; others took a stack. The cartons soon began to empty. The 500 copies that had arrived that morning were gone by two o'clock. The arrival of another delivery, at 4.45 pm, saw Angus & Robertson sell 100 copies more before the store closed at 5.30 pm. Said Grainger, laconically: 'The book sold fast.'

Grainger was vigilant throughout the day: keeping an eye on the people queuing, and, if anyone appeared underage, informing them that they could not purchase a copy from Angus & Robertson. 'I was aware that this book should not be sold to people under eighteen,' Grainger said. 'Penguin mentioned that the book should not be sold to people under eighteen … I followed that advice.' So, too, did his staff: 'I have no doubts that no one sold a copy to a minor.'

They did, however, sell a copy to police officers Mitchell and Quill. Minutes after midday, the two arrived in the shop, joined the queue, and purchased a copy. They did not reveal that they were police officers and did not speak to anyone — but they did note who was buying the book. Then they went around the block to 137a King Street, where James Thorburn's Pocket Bookshop was also selling copies. Thorburn, an amiable, bearded Scotsman with a marked intolerance for censorship, was there, but was soon to leave for Eric Willis's office. Later claiming that Penguin had asked him to give — not to sell — a copy of *Portnoy's Complaint* to Willis directly, Thorburn nonetheless settled for meeting with Willis's assistant. He handed over a copy of *Portnoy*, gave his name, address, and business details, and was undeterred when informed that by giving the copy to the assistant he was 'virtually publishing the book', and could be liable to prosecution. He was aware, he said.

The press was on to it. A photographer from *The Sydney Morning Herald* was waiting outside the room and, when Thorburn left, tried to take a picture. Willis's assistant refused to allow photographs, but Thorburn was happy to pose and to talk. He was proud of his actions. 'I'm not worried now about a possible six months' imprisonment, [or] a possible $250 fine,' he said outside, in his soft burr. '… To ban the book these people must have read it. I can't see any justification for one person deciding what another should read. By what standards do they play God, to think they are immune from things that others are not?'[10]

There was support in the community for *Portnoy*. In Thorburn's store, customers said they were buying the book 'on principle'. The Australian Society of Authors gave its 'unqualified approval' to Penguin's decision to publish the novel, and argued that the principle of how obscenity was established was crucial. 'It is important that ideas about obscenity should be tested before the court,' a spokesperson said, 'and not always decided by ministerial direction or customs officials.'

There were those in the community who disagreed. A man whose son was employed at Halstead had telephoned the chief secretary's department on 28 August to provide details of the book's printing and to express his outrage. Saying that *Portnoy*'s price was 'quite wrong', as it was affordable for young people, the man complained that he could not stop his son from reading the book at work, and was 'not at all happy about the situation'.[11] On the Monday, a magazine editor wrote to Willis to congratulate him on his 'vigorous stand against pornography in New South Wales'; on the Wednesday, a scandalised woman from Homebush called to report that she had seen schoolchildren browsing the book in a newsagency.[12]

Police and politicians used missives like these to justify themselves. The chief of the New South Wales Vice Squad told reporters that his officers had questioned booksellers stocking the novel and that all information would be passed on to the Chief Secretary's Department. The decision of whether to prosecute would be theirs. There was little doubt that there would be action, though: in a briefing for Willis, they wrote that *Portnoy* was 'flagrantly obscene in its detailed description of sex aberration'.[13]

Willis attempted to have the best of both worlds. On television on 31 August, he repeated his in-principle view that adults should be allowed to determine what they read, and admitted that standards were always in flux: 'Some of the books permitted today would not have been permitted twenty years ago.' He tried to argue that he was simply doing his duty as a minister — doing what the community wanted. But his abnegation of leadership was obvious: 'This [issue of obscenity] is left to the court to decide from time to time. On moral questions like gambling and obscene publications, I don't think it is the prerogative of the government to lead, but to reflect the attitudes of the time.'[14] Moreover, when asked for his opinion of the novel, Willis was scathing: 'I have read the book, and it is the greatest lot of filth and garbage I have ever read without even the redeeming feature of it being good literature.'[15]

In Victoria, police showed up at Penguin's offices at 10.45 on Monday morning.[16] In much the same way that Penguin in the UK had provided police with copies of *Lady Chatterley's Lover* to avoid incriminating booksellers while its legality was settled, the Victorian police believed the company would sell it copies of *Portnoy* and volunteer to withhold copies from sale until the courts had dealt with the matter. They claimed later that this was Penguin's idea, proffered by some intermediary as a conciliatory measure. John Hooker rubbished this: 'The intermediary certainly was not anyone from Penguin Books.'

By this point, however, Penguin's warehouse was nearly empty. The last of the shipments had long gone. Peter Froelich's changes had proved their worth. *Portnoy's Complaint* had left the building. The opportunity to handle the matter with Penguin alone had passed. Michie had known there would be action, and was aware that it would be 'quite a lively' week when the book came out: 'I think we will get 48 hours in Victoria before we are injuncted,' he had written to Greene.[17] Michie had made sure to have two copies of the book on his desk that morning — no more. When Detective Sergeant Kenneth Walters, head of the Vice Squad, arrived in his office, Michie pointed to them: 'There they are.'

Walters was dumbfounded. 'Any more stock?'

'No,' Michie replied, 'it's all gone.'

Walters purchased a copy for $1.35, made sure to receive a receipt, and left; then, sceptical that the books could have been distributed already, returned that afternoon with a search warrant. Police turned up three boxes that had been overlooked — containing 414 copies and intended for Cheshire's, on Little Collins Street — but otherwise went away empty-handed. They were shocked that the books had gone, and angered by Michie's refusal to direct booksellers to withhold *Portnoy* from sale. Critically, Michie had also refused to make any promises about refraining from another print run.

The excitement and action reached Western Australia. Arthur Williams, of the In Bookshop, in Perth, wrote to Greene to tell him that booksellers were resisting police attempts to restrict the book and were fully cooperating with Penguin.[18] Certainly that was the experience of the proprietors of the Terrace Arcade Bookshop, also in Perth. Claiming to be a friend of a regular customer, a detective visited the store, purchased a copy of *Portnoy*, thanked the bookseller, and returned three hours later with four members of the Vice Squad to seize all remaining stock. They were not thorough — they inexplicably left six copies behind — but they issued charges under section 2 of the state's *Indecent Publications Act*. Electing to pay the fine, the Terrace Arcade proprietors were not overly concerned. They were amused at how it was turning out, they told Greene:

> The whole situation has a delicious Gilbert & Sullivan flavour. One of our customers has ordered twenty copies and is going to have a treasure hunt with them. They are to be wrapped in plastic bags and hidden at an open-air theatre. This should provide some pleasant exercise for the Vice Squad.

'We will let you know how things progress,' they finished. 'Perhaps there will be such an outcry that the charges against us will be dropped before the hearing.'[19]

* * *

It quickly became clear that the state governments would each need to take responsibility themselves. Officials from the Department of Customs washed their hands of the matter. *Portnoy's Complaint* was a prohibited import, yes — but this was a locally published edition, they told enquiring reporters. They had no jurisdiction or grounds to prosecute anyone. There was only one possible way of using federal law to intervene, and that would require establishing where, when, and how *Portnoy's Complaint* had been smuggled into the country for use in the Penguin edition, and who had done so. A spokesperson promised that the department would investigate, but behind closed doors the department had already decided against it. Michie had told Customs officers that he had not imported the book, nor had it been imported through Penguin. 'He "acquired them from a friend",' recorded the sceptical but realistic Customs officer. 'I suggest NFA [no further action] on this aspect.'[20]

Nor could the state governments rely on one another to maintain a uniform resistance to *Portnoy's Complaint*. The Tasmanian government banned it immediately, and the Queensland government promised to do the same, but the South Australian government made the crucial and significant decision to break with its counterparts. Announcing on Monday 31 August that it believed adults were entitled to make their own decisions on what to read, Attorney-General Len King said that there would be no prosecutions, provided that booksellers sold the novel responsibly. 'If a bookseller keeps the book out of public view and confines sales to adults who make direct enquiry, and there are no other adverse features of the case,' he said, 'there will be no prosecution.'[21]

As well as being consistent with ALP policy, the decision had been spurred by Don Dunstan's aversion to censorship. As King later said, Dunstan was 'libertarian' about the issue: 'His view was that we shouldn't ever prosecute for indecency or any published material or theatrical productions and so on. People could make up their own minds. He was in favour of restricting any doubtful material to people over the age of eighteen, but beyond that he considered it was open slather.'[22] *Portnoy's Complaint* supposedly bored and 'nauseated' Dunstan, and its rapturous reception surprised him, but he pushed King to allow the book through.[23]

Although King's announcement would have been especially cutting for Griffin Press, its most important consequence was its effect on the agreement for uniform censorship. In one short press statement, the agreement had been broken. The consensus was gone. It was a vital victory for Penguin, instrumental in tearing through the otherwise blanket hostility toward *Portnoy*. Michie was elated. 'The complaint now endemic in Australia,' he telegrammed Greene, on 2 September. Hooker followed that with a letter: 'There's not a dry seat in the whole of Australia,' he crowed. Penguin had sold 68,000 copies already, and 'the whole place is in an uproar'.[24] 'That was a great moment,' Hilary McPhee recalled. 'A hole was punched in the system. It was a big victory, and it gave us a sense that it was very nearly won.'[25]

Officials from all of the state governments and the federal government were dismayed and critical. Though his own officials had noted in July that it might well happen, Don Chipp saw that the whole concept of uniform censorship in Australia would now require 'urgent re-appraisal'.[26] He said in the House of Representatives on 2 September that he was 'surprised and disappointed'.[27] A conference of state chief secretaries and federal ministers, at which they were going to discuss censorship, was only two weeks away. But now, the South Australian government had taken unilateral action. 'Whatever faults might have been discovered in the censorship laws in the last two years, at least there has been uniformity throughout Australia,' he said. 'I think it would be one of the great tragedies of our time so far as censorship is concerned if we returned to the insanity of having seven censorship systems, such as was the case prior to 1968.'[28]

Arthur Rylah, who had been on holiday, returned seething at

the 'unilateral' decision. 'That State seems to have given the green light for the printing and publishing of any obscene book whether prohibited in the past as an import or likely to be prohibited in the future,' he wrote to Don Chipp. 'I cannot imagine anything more calculated to destroy the edifice of Commonwealth and State uniformity in this area which we have so painstakingly built during the past two years ... I am not sure just what we can salvage from the wreck, but Victoria will be pleased to do everything it can to assist.'[29]

Matters were now escalating. Both sides were digging in. Boosted by the news from South Australia, Michie was in the newspapers, boasting that 70,000 copies of *Portnoy's Complaint* had been sold, dismissing Australia's censorship system as 'insidious, inconsistent, and ridiculous', and calling for wholesale reform.[30] Booksellers were emboldened: in Perth, Arthur Williams was making undisguised plans to circumvent police action in Western Australia by mailing copies of *Portnoy* from South Australia; in Sydney, James Thorburn was promising to continue selling copies, come what may; in Melbourne, with sales showing no signs of abating, Cheshire bookshop employee Bill Holl declared that *Portnoy* was 'the best thing that ever happened for bringing young people into the shop'.[31] The press was laughing. Journalists from *The Sydney Morning Herald* cracked open a phonebook and tracked down a Bankstown electrician who shared the surname of Roth's character. He had not read the novel. 'Who is this Portnoy in the book?' he asked.[32] *The Age* called the whole affair a 'Keystone Cop melodrama', and welcomed Penguin's demonstration of the 'absurdity' of the censorship system:

> In the present crisis, the State Government [of Victoria] has no option: it must immediately close the border with South Australia. Apart from the fact that South Australians who have read *Portnoy's Complaint* may decide to travel interstate, there is the clear and present danger that Victorians unwilling to do battle with

Melbourne's bookstores might cross the border and buy a copy without having to compete with plainclothes policemen. Anxious Victorians standing by their wireless sets can be comforted by the fact that the Minister for Customs (Mr Chipp) and the Acting Chief Secretary (Mr Smith) are keeping in touch.[33]

The embarrassment stung authorities into greater action. In New South Wales, with special warrants signed by Eric Willis, the Vice Squad raided three Sydney bookshops on 2 September: Angus & Robertson, on Castlereagh Street; the Pocket Bookshop, on King Street; and the Third World Bookshop, on Goulburn Street. Detectives had already visited all of these bookshops, but now they swooped to stop any further sales. They seized all unsold stock of *Portnoy*, netting nearly 800 copies from Angus & Robertson alone. Some bookshops, knowing that raids would come, had taken precautionary measures. Bob Gould had made an arrangement to store his copies of *Portnoy* offsite, in the basement of a nearby hotel. Copies, disguised in beer cartons, were brought to his shop only as they were needed. When officers arrived, Gould had sold three-quarters of his stock and had only twenty-three copies on the premises. Police seized those, and informed him that Willis had promised to prosecute anyone selling the book.

Gould affected innocence. 'I didn't know anything about it. How can I find out?'

'I suggest,' said one officer, drily, 'you read the papers, or listen to the radio.'

Police departed with the twenty-three copies — but without the hundreds more that sat untouched barely a block away.[34]

Reporters were present when police arrived to raid Thorburn's Pocket Bookshop. Quickly and quietly, they seized his stock — even plucking a copy from novelist Patrick White, just as he was about to purchase it.[35] Thorburn, aware that the publicity provided by press coverage was necessary for the fight, spoke freely about the raid: 'They were very nice about it.'

'Have you been depraved by it [the novel]?'

'I don't think so, whatever depraved might mean.'

'Do you think you're doing any harm by selling it?'

'I don't think so,' replied an amused Thorburn.[36]

Further raids in Sydney and elsewhere in New South Wales followed. Thorburn's shop was raided twice more. The pickings were not much bigger, but police managed to get their hands on just shy of 1,500 copies overall. In Victoria, police raided bookshops in Melbourne and seized copies. That Wednesday, they served Michie and Penguin with three summonses. The first was a charge for knowingly keeping obscene articles for gain; the second called on Penguin to show cause why the seized copies of *Portnoy* should not be destroyed; the third, to Michie personally, was a charge for selling obscene articles — that is, for having 'sold' the novel to police.

Penguin's staff knew that events were unfolding as they had foreseen. Writing to Greene on 8 September to inform him of the charges laid against Michie, Hooker admitted, 'This I suppose was inevitable.' But there was a hint of jangling nerves in his note that, for *Portnoy*'s release in South Australia, 'we must be thankful for small mercies'.[37] Peter Froelich recalled these days in similar terms. 'We knew they were going to have a go at us,' he said. 'We knew they would come for us.' But even that knowledge did not prevent him from feeling nervous. 'It was a scary time. We had stirred up a hornet's nest,' said Froelich, 'and we didn't think it'd be as big as it was. But, then again, we'd say, "Isn't that exactly what we set out to do?"'

Michie had reason to be nervous. He and Hilary McPhee had each recently left their marriages to be together, and both feared that muckraking journalists might seek to make hay of it.[38] But Michie remained calm. He did not waver. The personal summons that might have given others pause only reinforced Michie's determination to see the matter through. 'His thinking was that if this is the way that the establishment is going to treat him,' recalled Sessions, 'then he was going to fight back all the way.'

Publicly, Michie was defiant. Accusing police of trying to

use 'intimidation tactics' to dissuade booksellers from selling the novel, he announced that the entire print run had sold out and that Penguin was now planning a second print run. ('This will make the government really look up,' Hooker wrote to Greene.)[39] Michie said that Penguin had set aside $15,000 as a 'fighting fund' to defend itself, and repeated his promise to fight all the way to the High Court. Moreover, aware that the decision of the Menzies government to ban C.H. Rolph's *The Trial of Lady Chatterley* had drawn further attention to the issue of censorship, Michie announced Penguin's intention to publish an account of the court proceedings against them for *Portnoy's Complaint*. Penguin would do so, he said, irrespective of any verdict in the trials. 'I think the account of the court proceedings would be of world interest,' he told journalists. '… Censorship is an international issue.'[40]

This was no off-the-cuff promise. Hooker was already writing to Greene for records and information about his contacts with Chipp and other publishers; he was also making it clear that Penguin would do all it could to keep the issue, and the book, front and centre in the public consciousness: 'The writing of the trial book will, of course, take eighteen months or so because it looks as though we will have to appeal as far as the High Court of Australia.'[41]

Sydney-based writer and reporter Julie Rigg, then aged twenty-six, would be commissioned to write the book. A reporter since her teens, Rigg had worked on newspapers in Australia and the UK, and, since 1964, had written for *The Australian*, where she became a columnist. She had edited a collection of essays on women in Australia in 1969, and had a long interest in censorship. 'It was appalling and ridiculous,' she said later. After meeting with Hooker, she began amassing material — clippings, law reports, transcripts. From the beginning, C.H. Rolph's *The Trial of Lady Chatterley* was the model she intended to follow. The book would be the record of the public drama, contextualised and substantive, professional and fair.

There would be much to record. The efforts to suppress *Portnoy* were failing. Booksellers who had hesitated to sell it began to order copies; other sellers were daring the government to prosecute; consignments were still wending their way across the country; and police action to seize copies was inconsistent and at odds with the statements of various politicians. Internationally, the affair seemed farcical: advising Australia's authorities to 'relax a little', the *Guardian* said the fuss was not worth the bother and made Australia look 'ridiculous'.[44] On 4 September, *The Canberra Times* echoed this, editorialising that the ban had been mistaken, that attempts to enforce it were foolish, and that, if the novel could so easily deprave or corrupt, the problem was with the education system, not the book.[45]

Others poked fun at the absurdity of the whole affair. 'Does [Victorian acting chief secretary] Ian Smith seriously contemplate midnight raids on the quiet groves of suburbia wherein already lurk hundreds of smuggled copies of the dreaded *Complaint?*' asked Melbourne's scandal rag, *Truth*.[46] Journalist Maurice Dunlevy pointed out that the insistence of officials in New South Wales and Victoria to prosecute when South Australia had refrained meant that 'the right to be depraved and corrupted is not an equal right for all Australians'.[47] The next day, *The Sydney Morning Herald* carried a positive assessment of the novel by former editor John Douglas Pringle. Emphasising the book's humour, language, and subject, Pringle admitted that *Portnoy's Complaint* might be pornographic, but that it was also a 'cry from the heart of the human condition'. Eric Willis's scathing comments about the book, however, were ridiculous: the chief secretary was 'talking through his hat'.[48]

But the book's publication did not enjoy universal support among the public: there were those outraged by what Penguin had done. One correspondent wrote to Michie, accusing him of trying to make 'a fast buck by polluting minds impressionable and otherwise ... This kind of pornographic codswallop is socially decadent and for the cerebrally effete. I think that it is high time that

Australian booksellers like yourselves ceased serving pervs and set about trying to elevate our community above the level of the gutter.'[49] Penguin's staff were hurt neither by this nor by threats from the authorities. As Graham C. Greene wrote to John Hooker, 'If you get sent to prison, I will come out personally with the soup.'[50]

Officials at all levels of government continued to do whatever they could to halt *Portnoy*'s spread. On Monday 7 September, belying the Department of Customs' unwillingness to get involved, postmaster-general Alan Hulme announced that the Post Office would seize all copies of *Portnoy* that it found in the mail system. The Post Office had the right to intercept books and parcels, he said, and, if any parcel indicated that it contained a copy, it would be seized and burned. But, in the same breath, Hulme admitted that this would occur only by chance: the Post Office had no intention of opening every parcel, and it was unlikely to look hard for such parcels.

Only in places where the government exercised a close level of control could threats and intimidation be sustained. Canberra bookseller Teki Dalton sold thirty copies of *Portnoy* on 31 August before police visited and warned him of potential legal action. A worried Dalton pulled the book from sale and contacted officials at the Department of the Interior, which governed the ACT, with a simple question: was selling the book illegal? The answers were murky. There was no instrument for a ban on a book in the ACT, nor was any such ban in place regarding *Portnoy's Complaint*. But, Interior told Dalton, there was a risk of prosecution, with a potential penalty of up to $200 or imprisonment for six months. Who would decide whether to prosecute? The attorney-general, Tom Hughes, QC.[51] Dalton backed down. He undertook to not to sell any further copies in exchange for a promise that he would not be prosecuted for the sales already made.

This intimidation was roundly criticised. An Australian National University (ANU) criminal-law academic called it a 'mangling of the law', and the president of the Council for Civil

Liberties, Peter Stott, pointed out that by threatening Dalton the government had evaded settling whether the sale of *Portnoy* was illegal. 'If the book is to be stopped,' he said, 'it should be done in such a way that can be contested in the courts.'[52]

* * *

That contest now became the priority. In New South Wales, the government confronted the question of who, and in what order, it would prosecute. There were compelling reasons to aim first at the low-hanging fruit of booksellers such as Gould and Thorburn, rather than tackle Angus & Robertson employee Paul Grainger and Halstead Press managing director Aubrey Cousins. Gould and Thorburn would not have the resources to fight the charges properly; in the case of Gould, whose left-wing sympathies were overt, it would be easy to paint him as a disreputable seller of smut.

But there were equally compelling reasons to take an alternative course, as the Crown solicitor's office suggested. On grounds that evidence would be more straightforward, that cases could be resolved quickly, and that there was a fortuitous distinction to be made between obscenity and indecency, the Crown solicitor's office suggested that Eric Willis persuade the New South Wales attorney-general to institute an *ex officio* indictment against Thorburn and Grainger alone. Under this 'uncommon' plan, Grainger would be charged with selling an obscene publication, and Thorburn would be charged with publishing an indecent one.[53]

It was an egregious suggestion that would not survive the scrutiny of a week. It would have averted committal hearings at which Grainger or Thorburn would ordinarily have the opportunity to test the evidence against them; it plainly would have outraged the public; and it would certainly have provided fodder for Penguin and Michie to criticise the capriciousness of the censorship authorities. On 17 September, the Crown solicitor's office recanted. 'It was felt that, from both the practical point of view and a political point of view,' ran the judicious record of this conversation, 'there could be considerable criticism of any deprivation of rights of defendants in this important case. It is the view of the Crown, therefore, that the normal processes should be adopted.'

Now Angus & Robertson manoeuvred to position itself as the subject of the test case. Hugh Jamieson, an art-loving litigation solicitor at Allen Allen & Hemsley who was handling the case, wrote to the Crown solicitor's office to have Angus & Robertson substituted in Grainger's place.[54] Officials seized on the offer: the bookseller had offered to make 'certain formal admissions' about the circumstances of the sale of *Portnoy* in exchange for an assurance that no proceedings would be instituted against Grainger or any other employee.

What was there to lose in accepting this? It was unlikely that proceedings against Grainger would result in jail time, given that he had been carrying out his employer's instructions when he had sold *Portnoy*. What would be the good in pursuing him, then? There were only two reasons to pursue Grainger: to underscore the importance of the matter, and to provide a deterrent for publishers and sellers, to force them to think again about defying the kind of 'clear warning' that had been given by the government.

Neither reason proved compelling. The Crown solicitor decided that 'the companies are the principal offenders and it does seem desirable to have the "test" cases against them rather than their employees.' He recommended that once there was agreement with Allen Allen & Hemsley on a set of formal admissions, the government make the deal.[55] Willis approved the new course of action — and, in doing so, he ensured that Angus & Robertson, well-resourced, reputable, and wholly determined to fight, would be the test case for *Portnoy* in New South Wales.[56]

And what of the twenty other defendants? The Crown solicitor had a plan worked out: lay the charges, and then have them adjourned until resolution of the test case. After a fortnight of embarrassment and criticism, Willis was happy to approve a course of action that would allay suggestions of impropriety. 'Definitely,' he wrote of this plan. Do it, he added, 'as soon as possible'.[57]

His officials tried, but the proceedings were halting. On 13 October, the summonses against Angus & Robertson came up for hearing at the Court of Petty Sessions, on Liverpool Street, but were adjourned by agreement until a committal hearing on 14 December. That hearing would determine whether or not there was *prima facie* evidence to hold a full-scale trial against Angus & Robertson. Two weeks later, on 26 October, the police sought an order in the Court of Petty Sessions to have the seized copies of *Portnoy* destroyed, and Reginald Barrett had to rush, at the last minute, to have the matter adjourned until 14 December.[58] By now, the issue was boiling down to its essentials: by tacit agreement, the summonses against the other defendants would only be mentioned — nothing more. They would wait until the case against Angus & Robertson had been resolved.

* * *

The preparations in New South Wales were echoed in Victoria. Arthur Rylah was determined to make an example of Penguin. He had read *Portnoy* by now, and regarded it as 'a most obscene and objectionable book'.[59] His officials sought to have the Victorian Vice Squad allowed access to the reports written about the novel by National Literature Board of Review members, and Rylah, too, pressed for that access: the opinions cited therein could be of use in the trial, which they wanted before the end of the year.[60]

Penguin's lawyers stepped up their preparations. Strategies and tactics were honed, and prospective witnesses were approached and tested to see how they would stand up to questioning. Penguin's solicitor, David Walsh, partner at Melbourne establishment firm Mallesons, was already well into the work of preparing the case and working with the barristers who would lead the defence.

But there was no let-up in the public offensive that Michie

and Penguin were waging. Of the opinion that 'there is a lot of re-thinking going on by the various State authorities on censorship', Michie decided to write an article in the *Bulletin* to influence that thinking.[61]

It was a sustained and caustic attack on the censorship system. Writing that censorship was the product of a 'strong, wowser tradition' that relied on intimidation and confusion to maintain its sway, Michie argued that its foundations and mission were a farce. The concept of community standards, he wrote, was worthless.

The National Literature Board of Review was qualified to advise on literary merit, but the invitation of successive Customs ministers for it to act as a judge of community standards was 'completely inappropriate' in light of the board's composition. 'Any body that was set up to assess community standards should contain representatives from the younger section of the community,' Michie argued. What eventuated was a 'subjective and uninformed personal appreciation' of what might be community standards: 'No evidence is allowed to establish what are in fact the community's standards.'

The court system was similarly inadequate. Comparisons with books that were available were not permitted, and the use of a jury, which could go 'some way toward establishing a community standard', was precluded in all states but New South Wales. Nor were the supposed offences to community standards ever real: prosecutions were hypothetical only, based on feeling, and verdicts were based on the 'small, subjective reflection of the taste or moral outlook of individual judges'.

Michie admitted that there were legitimate grounds for censorship — in particular, to protect children from matter that was 'adverse to their own moral or physical wellbeing' — but argued that censorship laws needed to be overhauled: censorship should go no further than was absolutely necessary.

Michie did not mention *Portnoy*, but he made it clear that the impending trials were fundamentally wrong. Legislation on the exhibition of sex, violence, and cruelty was applied indiscriminately, irrespective of purpose, he pointed out. Someone who gave school-girls the 'most vile and nauseating writings imaginable' would be liable for a maximum $10 fine or three months' imprisonment, but someone who published a book of great literary merit that 'might tend to induce unchaste or immodest thoughts' could be imprisoned for up to two years or pay a $200 fine. New books that were of literary merit were discriminated against, as the recognition of that literary merit was impossible to establish if they were banned.

He did not hold back from criticising the motives of those in charge of the censorship system. 'It may in fact suit those opposed to censorship reform to maintain the present legislation,' he wrote, 'because of the scope its defects give for heading off "unacceptable" publications by threats rather than run the risk of possible political embarrassment by prosecution in the courts.' The overall effect of this system was 'to turn Australia into the Alabama of the literary world'.[62]

It was a bullish and blunt argument. Followed, a week later, by the order of a 50,000-copy reprint of *Portnoy*, it signalled the approach Penguin would take in a few weeks' time, as the first of the *Portnoy* trials began.[63]

CHAPTER 9

Literature and liberty

The first *Portnoy* trial began at 10.12 am on Monday 19 October 1970.[1] In the crowded, tizzy-pink courtroom of the Melbourne Magistrates' Court, on the corner of Russell Street and La Trobe, proceedings opened quietly, with the lawyers defining the contest at hand and setting the rules on what they would and would not discuss.

Then Leonard Flanagan began to rail against *Portnoy*: 'When taken as a whole, it is lewd; as to a large part of it, it is absolutely disgusting both in the sexual and other sense; and the content of the book as a whole offends against the ordinary standards of the average person in the community today — the ordinary, average person's standard of decency.' In tones that were strident and ringing, he declared *Portnoy's Complaint* to be obscene. It was obscene by its nature. It was obscene by its subject matter. It was obscene by its undue emphasis of sexual matters. 'This book is basically a book about sex, sexual matters,' Flanagan went on, 'and not restricted to just sexual behaviour between opposite sexes but to sexual behaviour between the same sexes, and to a very large extent the sexual behaviour of one person with himself in terms of his masturbation and matters of that nature.'[2]

A quick and intelligent man who had been educated by the De La Salle Brothers at Malvern and studied law at the University of Melbourne, Flanagan had been only thirty-one years old when he was appointed Crown prosecutor in 1965. At the time, his youth had prompted concern and amusement at the Bar. But his suitability for the role had only become more apparent in the years that had followed. Tough and shrewd, with an Irish-Catholic conservatism that could make him seem a little older than he was, 'Lennie the Lip' Flanagan was an apt prosecutor for *Portnoy's Complaint*: as one witness would recall, he seemed personally outraged by the book. 'His perversions of *that* practice,' he shuddered, when discussing Portnoy's masturbatory habits.

'The defence will be that this book is not obscene,' said Peter Brusey QC in turn. A tall, thin, English-born barrister best known for representing Ronald Ryan during his last-ditch appeals against the death sentence imposed in 1967 by the Bolte government, Brusey was Penguin's lead counsel. At the Bar he was regarded as articulate, charming, measured, and erudite: a man of integrity. While his chief expertise lay in equity law, Brusey had notable experience in obscenity cases: he had unsuccessfully defended actor Charles Little during the controversy over the play *The Boys in the Band*.

Brusey's junior, Stephen Charles, aged thirty-three, also possessed this interest in obscenity, though he had started on the opposing side. When the charges against Little and his fellow actors were initially dismissed on grounds of triviality, it had fallen to Charles to lead the Crown's appeal. His argument in that appeal was logically impeccable: if one agreed that the word *fuck* was obscene in any context, it could be no trivial offence when it was used over and over again, before audiences of hundreds of people, as repeat performances of the play demanded. Mr Justice Douglas Little, hearing this in the Supreme Court, leapt to agree, and convicted the *Boys in the Band* actors on that basis. Charles took satisfaction from the craft of his argument, but was distressed by its success. It was well-known that Little had walked to a newsvendor outside the Supreme Court building the evening after the trial and, within deliberate earshot of a group of barristers, invoked one of the contentious lines from the play: 'Who do I have to fuck to get a newspaper around here?' The hypocrisy had been widely noted, and confirmed Charles's existing interest in defending people charged with obscenity crimes.

'I didn't see any potential damage to people from the sorts of things that were then being held up as dangerous,' he recalled. 'I thought works like *Portnoy's Complaint* were good for people to read. I was honoured to be asked to take part in the trial.'[3]

So were the witnesses coming to appear on Penguin's behalf. They would come to reinforce the foundations of its defence: that the novel was possessed of literary merit, and that it would corrupt or deprave no one. John Michie had written to Graham C. Greene to emphasise that this would be the focus. 'Apart from literary merit,' Michie wrote, 'the Prosecution's main attack will be based on the effect of the book on adolescents, and [so] we will be producing a number of eminent psychiatrists to testify to this.'[4]

Both points appeared in Brusey's submissions that morning. After emphasising that *Portnoy's Complaint* was not obscene, Brusey declared that Penguin would demonstrate that it possessed recognised literary merit and that any argument about its potential to corrupt or deprave was mistaken.

After an hour and a half, the wrinkled and puzzled magistrate, Ewen Ross, adjourned the court so he could read the novel. When he resumed, at 2.15 the next afternoon, Tuesday 20 October, Flanagan opened his case proper by aiming to set literary merit aside. Nothing of the novel's artistic worth was relevant, he said. 'The law here is clear. You cannot, by skilfully dealing with some matter which is pure filth, [by] describing it pleasantly, change it from the very nature of what it is. It is still filth.' Roth's reputation and ability were immaterial. The literary merit was irrelevant. All of the witnesses that Penguin would summon were wasting their time. All that mattered was the book's obscenity — and that was plain.

Flanagan offered proof: a page on which he had tabulated, for the convenience of the court, every 'sex reference' and 'four-letter word' to appear in the novel. According to this list, there were such references and words on 125 of the book's 274 pages. Flanagan had even calculated the percentages: 28.1 per cent of the book's pages contained sex; 17.5 per cent contained four-letter words.

Next, the prosecutor sketched a connection between the novel's obscenity and Penguin's decision to publish it. An integral part of his case, Flanagan said, was Penguin's distribution of *Portnoy* without any care for the age of purchasers or their susceptibility to immoral influences. There had been no plan to restrict sales of the book, no guidelines on whether it should be displayed or hidden, no policy on selling it to people not yet eighteen. Even if the court were to find that the book was of literary merit, he went on, its indiscriminate distribution was not justified.

Flanagan called a single witness, Detective Sergeant Kenneth Walters, to testify that he had visited Michie at Penguin's offices on 31 August. Brusey's cross-examination played to the onlookers in the gallery. When had Walters first heard that *Portnoy* was to be published in Victoria?

'It would be the twenty-eighth,' said Walters.

'Of?'

'August.'

'Nineteen—?'

'Seventy.'

'Have you read the book?'

'Yes.'

'And do you feel alright?'

Flanagan objected immediately, and Ross ruled the question out of order. Brusey did not mind. Laughter achieved, he concentrated on drawing from Walters one admission: did he recognise that Penguin was a 'reputable publishing company'?

To the detective's grudging, one-word agreement, Brusey made sure to slip in an additional qualifier: 'About as distinguished a calibre as possible.'

Brusey opened the defence case on 21 October. Stating that the defence wished to fight on 'the real live issues' and not on any narrow, technical grounds, he argued that the prosecution should have to show a specific class or group that would be corrupted or depraved by *Portnoy* in order for its case to succeed. Citing a litany of precedents to support his argument, Brusey pointed to the lack of evidence that any such person, class, or age group had been harmed by the book. 'You have got no evidence at all in the present case about age groups,' he told Ross. Shouldn't that be in evidence?

Aware that the prevalence of sex in the novel had to be addressed, Brusey next told Ross that the coarse language and sex in *Portnoy* was akin to that in Shakespeare. Think back to your school days, he said. You would have read *Hamlet*. Remember the moments before the Mousetrap scene? 'Hamlet says to Ophelia something like this: "Shall I put my head in your lap?" And then a little later he says, "That's a fair thought — to lie between maids' legs. Do you think I meant country matters?" Now, the word *country*, there,' Brusey began to explain, 'is quite plainly a pun on a very ordinary four-letter word. You find that kind of example all over literature.' Disgust at this kind of language and subject matter, however, was not enough for a conviction. 'Supposing at the end of that you feel disgusted,' said Brusey. 'Is that sufficient for you to convict us under this act? The law has made a very clear and ringing answer to that question. The answer is no. That is not a relevant matter.'

Brusey argued that *Portnoy* was a sad book. Alexander Portnoy was bricked in by his duties to his family and his own desires. The story related was sexual, yes, but not pornographic. Ross would have come across pornography, he said. 'And my learned friend, Mr Flanagan, who deals largely, I believe, in such matters, no doubt has seen more than you or I, sir,' Brusey added, to laughter. Pornography displayed all sorts of activity — kinds where people hardly paused to draw breath as they engaged in a 'series of sexual acrobatics'.

But the sex in *Portnoy's Complaint* was not like that. The sex it portrayed would not prompt arousal or imitation. 'None of the sex is portrayed as being something which it might be advisable to copy.' Portnoy's sex was unhappy, furious, and angry. It was not pornographic. The book was a warning. It was a sad book.

Ross might not like reading it, but that was immaterial. 'What matters is: does this book constitute a threat to anybody's morals?' The answer was no. *Portnoy's Complaint* was not obscene. The evidence, Brusey said, would show that.

The defence had assembled 'as distinguished a body of testimony as it would be possible to call', a litany of witnesses of the 'greatest possible standing', said Brusey. Its case would be twofold: 'We will call evidence to show you that this work is of recognised literary merit in Victoria. Second, we shall call evidence from experts in the field to show that this work, so far from being damaging to the morals of the reader, is in fact a work likely to do good.'

* * *

The strategy for the literary merit defence was simple: weight of numbers. 'We wanted to get as many good people as we could to give evidence of literary merit,' Stephen Charles said later. 'We wanted to have as many witnesses as possible so that no one could deny that the book had literary merit.'[5]

They did not have trouble attracting witnesses. Graham C. Greene's telegram to Michie on the first day of the trial — 'ALL BEST WISHES FOR A RESOUNDING VICTORY FOR LITERATURE AND LIBERTY' — had been echoed in the large number of people willing to put themselves forward to speak for that exact cause.[6]

First to the stand was John McLaren, a critic and lecturer in English at the Secondary Teachers' College in Carlton. McLaren had experience devising syllabi for junior school students, and told the court that he had made a special study of the impact of literature on young minds. In testimony that occupied six hours of the hearing, over two days, McLaren said *Portnoy's Complaint* was 'very real, very serious, and very sensitive'. He ridiculed Flanagan's description of the novel as solely about sex: it was 'certainly not' the main topic. McLaren could be learned and witty: asked what Portnoy's complaint actually was, he deadpanned: 'A good subject for Empson's *Seven Types of Ambiguity*.'[7] At other times, his testimony was weighty, clear, and sharply put: 'The main theme of the book is Portnoy's inability to reconcile his sexuality with his idealism. It deals with his attempt to come to terms with his sexuality.'

McLaren did not believe that the novel could incite adolescents to similar behaviour. The only way that it would lead someone to masturbate was if they had not done so before, he said. 'However, amongst those who perhaps do masturbate and feel guilty about it — and they are by no means an insignificant group — the book could have a healthy consequence in making them realise that they are not alone.'

Flanagan's cross-examination was confrontational from the beginning. He wanted to tarnish McLaren's testimony and cut him down to size. He read aloud a line from the blurb: '*Portnoy's Complaint* must surely be the funniest book about sex ever written.' How did that square with McLaren's answer to Brusey that the novel was not just about sex? Flanagan asked about masturbation: 'You do not think that these detailed passages of sexual aberration, if I might use that expression, would influence an adolescent at all?' At another point, Flanagan thrust under McLaren's nose a lukewarm review of *Portnoy* from *Time* magazine and asked if he had read it. To McLaren's no, the prosecutor sneered: 'I see — you regard that as a bit beneath your field, do you?'

The disjuncture between Flanagan and McLaren was palpable. The prosecutor made no disguise of his view that Portnoy was a pervert who corrupted those around him; McLaren, however, insisted that Portnoy was much more than this, and that the depiction of his life created insight, understanding, and compassion. As all works of literary merit did, he said, the novel 'enlarges the reader's understanding of what human life is about'.

This view underscored McLaren's refusal to accept Flanagan's condemnation. The book was about a man's inability to reconcile his sexuality with his idealism, he said. 'The literary merit of the book is to be found in the extremes to which he is driven in his inadequacy and his disgust with himself.'

In turn, Flanagan was contemptuous of McLaren. To all the invocations of understanding and compassion, and the distinction between author and material, Flanagan saw only low standards. When McLaren said that he would regard Portnoy's 'perversions' as 'distasteful' only, not 'a form of depravation', Flanagan affected shock: 'That is all?'

Theirs was a duel, conducted at speed and with skill. Flanagan told McLaren off — for making speeches, for going 'a long way' from answering his questions, for interrupting, for failing to listen. McLaren continued to insist that there was disgust and shame evoked in the work, as well as sordidness. Flanagan, in turn, began to simply read passages of such sordidness and ask what they added, whether they were of literary merit, and what the point of them was. He read the passage of Portnoy's *ménage à trois* with the Monkey and an Italian prostitute and said, with considerable distaste, that it was descriptive, wasn't it?

'And so is the next sentence at the end of the paragraph,' said McLaren.

Flanagan paraphrased it: '"Then I got up and went into the bathroom and you will be happy to know regurgitated my dinner." Well, he could hardly be blamed for that, could he?'

'Exactly,' said McLaren, with the tone of one whose point has just been proved.

McLaren stood down so that *Age* editor Graham Perkin, the next witness, could be interposed. A solid, gruff, and brilliant newspaperman who had lately transformed the paper, Perkin had aimed at credibility and relevance by hiring young and ambitious journalists, overhauling the paper's layout, and broadening the scope of its coverage. A believer in the public importance of journalism and the role it could play, Perkin had given priority to the public interest. And, if wary of moves to publish *Portnoy* in 1969, he had no hesitation about engaging now on its behalf.

Perkin testified that *Portnoy's Complaint* was a serious literary work with an appeal that stemmed from 'its literary quality'. It did not outrage him in the slightest, he said, and although not all would find the book funny, a 'sensitive reader' would be highly amused by some of its passages.

Flanagan found Perkin to be hard going. When he put to him that the book was all about sex — citing the blurb again — Perkin was noncommittal: 'I am a compulsive non-reader of dust-jacket blurbs.' Pressed on the question, though, Perkin was firm. There was more to it: 'It is a quite rare combination of tragedy and high comedy. Roth uses illustrations of this man's sex to illustrate his whole personality.' Of the novel's merit, Perkin said, 'The book is well written, in a craftsman-like way, and the character of Portnoy is well sustained and treated with sympathy.' Roth had written the book 'with integrity'. Perkin's responses seemed to irritate Flanagan. When Perkin, answering whether sexual matters were foremost in Portnoy's mind, said that he would have thought they were 'in everyone's mind', the prosecutor was heard to mutter: 'Speak for yourself!'

After Perkin came another newspaperman. Scots-born journalist and editor John Douglas Pringle had proved himself an astute analyst of Australian culture and values. Progressive and wry, Pringle had trained his eye on the long history of censorship and puritanism in his adopted country when reviewing *Portnoy* in August. Now, on the stand, questioned by Charles, Pringle elaborated on his positive review. He told the court that *Portnoy* was well written: 'The writing is crisp and vigorous and fresh. The dialogue is vivid, the characters are real and alive, the picture of his family is extraordinarily human. You feel you live there.' The repeated use of four-letter words was justified by the course of the book, as were the detailed sexual passages that populated its pages. The novel's literary merit could not be denied. 'Nearly everywhere,' he declared, 'its literary merit has been recognised at once.'

Pringle, however, yielded considerable ground. When Flanagan put to him that passages in the book were ludicrous, Pringle agreed. When the prosecutor said that some were intended to startle and shock readers, Pringle agreed. He admitted that he did not think *Portnoy* was a great book, and then, during a discussion on whether Portnoy had fallen apart as an adult, Pringle himself seemed to fall apart under rapid-fire questioning. Was the book an uninhibited confession? Yes. Were Portnoy's problems self-inflicted? Yes. Were Portnoy's descriptions of masturbation detailed? Yes. But these perverted practices preceded his 'sexual repressions', didn't they? Yes. The book was not about repression, Flanagan said, rising to a peroration. It was about a man who had sunk as low as it was possible to sink, and it portrayed nothing of how to get out of that, didn't it?

There was sniping between Brusey and Flanagan throughout the hearing. Interrupted by objections, Flanagan would sigh: 'Mr Brusey, I will conduct the case, please.' Or: 'Mr Brusey, you know, an objection is not the occasion for a speech.' During a wrangle over whether the blurb should be in evidence, Flanagan laughed: 'Well, I understand my friend's submission at the moment, Your Worship, to be an admission to tender the book without the cover.' Brusey had a ready reply: 'My learned friend need not mutilate the book any more than he has done in his opening.' When Brusey asked Graham Perkin what would be left if the sexual episodes were culled from *Portnoy*, Flanagan heckled him: 'Ten pages!'

There were jokes, too. When Pringle suggested that Portnoy had fallen apart because he had visited a psychiatrist, Brusey could be heard murmuring to the prosecutor, *sotto voce*, 'You might be late for your own appointment tonight if you don't hurry up.'[8] When

Pringle stepped down at four o'clock, having discussed Portnoy's masturbation into the liver and its subsequent consumption at dinner, Brusey asked for an adjournment on grounds that he had 'not, as it were, got any witnesses left on the menu for today ...'

The evidence presented by McLaren, Perkin, and Pringle notwithstanding, the most notable point of the trial came in the morning, before Pringle took the stand, when Brusey and Charles made their arguments for the strategy that Michie had mentioned to Greene — to call psychiatric evidence.

'We could not call evidence of the tendency to deprave and corrupt at large — that is, to deprave and corrupt anyone and everyone,' Charles recalled. 'But once you narrowed it to a field such as the impact on children, and on boys, we believed we could justly argue that that was a narrow field on which there was recognised psychiatric knowledge.' Flanagan, during his opening remarks, had made reference to seventeen-year-old children. 'Because he had narrowed it in that way,' said Charles, 'we were entitled to say, "We can call evidence."' There was another element to this: the defence could argue that, far from corrupting or depraving young people, *Portnoy* would be a positive influence. 'It would remove the feeling of guilt about masturbation,' Charles recalled. 'It would be positively beneficial for them.'

They had prepared two witnesses for this point: La Trobe University professor Ronald Goldman, and Dr Allen Bartholemew, a psychiatrist with expertise in the relationship between psychiatry and the law. Bartholomew had extensive experience working in correctional institutions, and was the first psychiatrist superintendent at Coburg's notorious Pentridge Prison. The prospect of their testimony presented a dire threat to Flanagan's case.

'Flanagan leapt in immediately to say that the evidence could not be admitted,' Charles recalled. 'He realised that it would be damaging to his case. To say that there was nothing damaging about *Portnoy* was obviously ruinous for him.' In submissions that took up most of the morning, Flanagan argued that such evidence was inadmissible. The High Court, he argued, had made it clear that it was the content and the nature of the literature in question that required judgement. The scientific evidence that the defence hoped to present should be ruled inadmissible.

Brusey responded that the act under which Penguin had been charged made it clear that it was contemplating people who might be depraved or corrupted by the work in question. He argued that psychiatrists could therefore inform the court of the likelihood that *Portnoy* would do this.

After three hours of submissions, Ross ruled it out. No such evidence would be heard in his court. 'I keep coming back to the general core of the matter, which is that this court has to decide whether the matter [*Portnoy's Complaint*] is, or is not, obscene.' In that light, he said, there was no place for the evidence of psychiatrists, psychologists, or experts in similar fields.

Michie would call this ruling a 'disaster', but Brusey and Charles were far from devastated.[9] Why? Because it opened the prospect of an appeal. 'We felt, as soon as Ross ruled it out,' Charles recalled, 'that we had an appeal point. Right at that moment.' The knowledge that Ross's ruling had given Penguin an avenue to launch an appeal, in the event of a guilty verdict, made the defence increasingly confident — and willing to take further risks. 'We did not mind whether it was or wasn't [ruled out],' Charles said, 'so long as we got the opportunity to make the play; so long as we got to say that there was very considerable evidence, from an array of respected children's psychiatrists, saying that this was a book that was positively good for you. We were going to keep repeating that whenever the question of pornography and obscenity came up.'

Therefore, the next day, Friday 23 October, Brusey launched an attack on Ross himself. Noting that the magistrate had refused to hear scientific evidence, Brusey argued that the Crown had been allowed to put forward evidence that should have been inadmissible. Flanagan's recitation, during McLaren's testimony, of the negative views of *Portnoy* held by the National Literature Board of Review should not have been placed before the bench. That was 'totally improper', Brusey said. Flanagan's use of newspaper and magazine reviews that had not been entered into evidence had not been appropriate: 'There has been conveyed to you [Ross] a whole series of inadmissible evidence.' On these grounds, Brusey told Ross, he should recuse himself. 'If you feel that justice would be better done, I ask you to say that you think a fairer hearing of this case would be before another magistrate, [and therefore] you would discharge yourself as a judge would discharge a jury.'

It was an audacious move. While there was some benefit in drawing Ross's attention to the inadmissibility of what he had heard, and so pressuring him to bend the other way to maintain his impartiality, the request was also fraught with risks. It could offend Ross, personally and professionally, and endanger the rest of the defence case. 'I am not saying you are prejudiced,' Brusey said, to pre-empt any antipathy, 'but some matters should not have been admitted.'

Flanagan's response was heated and irate. He was offended. 'I feel that the submission he [Brusey] has made makes improper and outrageous remarks about my conduct of the case.' He disagreed with any suggestion that Ross should step aside: 'There is no legitimate reason that Your Worship should exclude yourself from hearing the rest of the case.'

Ross ruled against it. Conceding that some of the evidence he had heard should not have been admitted, he shrugged it off: it was a problem for magistrates everywhere. Restricting evidence to ensure it was admissible was never easy. 'I propose to continue this hearing,' he said. 'I would also like to say that I hope this will be the last of this matter and this sort of dissension which seems to have cropped up in this case.'

It was — but Brusey's challenge, and Ross's defiance of that challenge, was the headline for that day's press coverage. Within the court of public opinion, it was a win. For Penguin, this was almost worth whatever cost might eventuate. 'We thought that, by that point in the trial,' Charles explained, 'as we had lost the psychiatric evidence, there was nothing to lose in pushing for Ross to recuse himself. We did not expect to win it.' Was it a point for publicity, then? Said Charles: 'Yes, certainly in part.'

* * *

The case went on. The witnesses continued. Arthur Angell Phillips said that the book had a strong moral: 'There is an essential wholesomeness in this book, particularly in its sexual values. There are treatments of perverse sex and this book is partly concerned with perverse sex … [yet] you are always aware of an element of absurdity in the perverse incidents.'

Younger men followed: Brian Kiernan, of Swinburne Technical College; David Bradley, Noel McLachlan, and Dennis Douglas, all of Monash University. The treatment they received from Flanagan and the arguments they made were largely the same. The book had literary merit, they said. Its language was alive. Its characterisation was compelling. The incidents of sex were necessary and not salacious. The coarse words were part-and-parcel of Portnoy himself. 'The only question I was asked by the legal beagle on the other side was whether I cared about my children's education,' Douglas recalled. 'I said something to the effect that it was a major concern of mine.'[10] Kiernan, who had heard McLaren's testimony, made sure to deliver his evidence in a way that was 'low-key and respectable'.[11]

The manner and substance of the hearing seemed to change with each witness. It was a morality hearing, then a squabble over smut, then an English literature tutorial, then a comedy of embarrassment and prudery. Bradley was asked about his knowledge of the sex acts contained in the book. 'If I may make a confession to the court,' he answered, a little sheepishly, 'I must admit it educated me.' When he later remarked that he had found the book to be revealing about his Jewish friends, Flanagan started: 'And did you find it remarkably revealing in that sense …?'

'About their sexual habits?' Bradley said. 'No. I don't know what their sexual habits are.'

At this, laughter broke out and Flanagan fumed. 'I had not finished my question,' he said. 'I know the witness box is sometimes regarded as a stage, but at the moment I am putting serious questions on a serious topic.' At other times, though, Flanagan could laugh. 'We have a lot of fun in court,' he said, during Kiernan's testimony.

Some witnesses were better than others. Stephen Charles thought Douglas was 'a little too prepossessed by his own verbal skill'; during another witness's testimony, he scrawled two blunt sentences, added a large exclamation mark, and slid the page over to Brusey: 'An awful witness. As short as possible!'[12]

Dinny O'Hearn's evidence veered between a lecture, a performance, and a scolding. Barely allowing Charles room to ask his questions, the sub-dean of arts at the University of Melbourne spoke at length on the novel, reading passages to support his ideas, likening Portnoy's cloying family drama to that in an Irish-Catholic family's.

'I do not think I want great long tracts of this read out,' Ross interrupted, at one point.

But O'Hearn barely seemed to hear him. 'Well, could I go on about that?' he said, and continued just as he had before. To Ross's consternation, the galleries responded. Emphasising the comic aspects, O'Hearn read a long passage full of Jewish jokes that had spectators convulsing with laughter.[13] Then came the scolding: Flanagan asked about *Portnoy's* plot. Turning to the prosecutor haughtily, O'Hearn exclaimed, 'We don't use terms like *plot!*'

Court adjourned for the weekend and resumed on Monday 26 October. One after another, witnesses such as Vincent Buckley, David Martin, Jean Battersby, and Manning Clark lined up to scotch the prosecution's argument that *Portnoy's Complaint* was obscene and without literary merit. Martin spoke at considerable length, as though delivering a morning lecture; Battersby was firm and direct; Clark, with a glance at the tiny blue notebook in which he had scratched some notes, called the book a 'complaint against God', and said that Roth had held 'a mirror up to life'. Buckley, a poet and chair of English Literature at the University of Melbourne, gave serious evidence but later poked fun at the whole show. In 'Portnoy's Revenge', he described Ross snoozing, Flanagan humming *Dies Irae,* and a witness — 'the Famous Witness' — showboating on the stand:

> So you admit the book is disgusting,
> said Flanagan QC. It is your own word.
> Disgusting as life is disgusting, said the Famous Witness,
> and beautiful like life, full of despair and joy.
> Would you call it filthy? Pornographic? Sexually arousing?
> As Life is, said the Famous Witness. Radically
> filthy, pornographic, sexually ar …
> Aargh, said Flanagan QC, for God's sake.
> The Famous Witness sat down beside me
> and glanced at my averted eyes.
> How did I go? he whispered.
> I'll tell you later, I muttered, barely turning.
> After a minute, he got up and left.
> You should have finished the bloody book, I thought.[14]

Jennifer Strauss, of Monash University, also found the trial comical.[15] That morning, Flanagan stood and interrupted proceedings, saying, 'There is a child in this court, and it is not seemly that the ears of children should be polluted by the evidence that will be heard.' People looked around. Where was this child? Eventually, they realised that Flanagan was referring to a baby, cradled by its mother in the public gallery. Ross gave a serious pause as he decided how to respond.

'Well,' he said, 'it seems to me that the child is too young to be polluted by what it will not understand.'

This was a cheap move from Flanagan, thought Strauss, who also decided that he was 'exactly the kind of person to make you think that you are absolutely right to defend *Portnoy's Complaint.*' As she said later, 'He was running every *petit-bourgeois* objection to the novel. He was concentrating on the fact that it had sex in it, and bad language. He had no interest in the social dimensions, or the Freudian elements in it.' Strauss viewed this lack of interest dimly: 'They were so much of a piece with that ignorant, closed state of mind that made Australia at that time so insular.'

She also thought that the outcome was preordained. She felt that Ross's mood was somewhere between boredom and amusement, and it seemed to her that this was because he already knew the verdict. 'He had probably already decided that the book was obscene, but was just working out whether it had literary merit.'

Thirty-seven years old and a mother of three, Strauss was aware that she and the other women coming to the stand were living examples of the defence argument that *Portnoy's Complaint* was not a corrupting or depraving influence. She was also aware that they had been deliberately chosen. 'We thought that the magistrate, the press, and politicians,' Stephen Charles recalled, 'would be surprised and impressed by the fact that women — ordinary, decent women; the epitome of good women at the time — were prepared to stand up and talk about it.' They were also best placed, Hilary McPhee recalled, to rebut the argument that censorship was necessary for the protection of children.[16]

But Strauss was also determined that her voice and those of her fellow female witnesses be heeded in the matter — and not merely as mothers or wives or 'good women'. 'We were not to be passive recipients of what other people thought was proper for us to read or not read,' she said later. As teachers and scholars of expertise and credibility, they had informed views to offer: 'I suspect, in fact, that Flanagan was quite shocked at all of us.'

She knew that Brusey and Charles wanted their expertise and

credibility, but the emphasis that was placed on their respectability could be grating. 'They wanted us to wear dresses,' Strauss recalled. 'They did not want us to wear trousers.' They were also concerned about Strauss's determination to take an affirmation rather than an oath sworn on the Bible: 'They felt it dinted my respectability.'

Strauss persisted. She made an affirmation, and spoke on the nature of satire and exaggeration. 'One of the complaints about *Portnoy* was that it was negative and excessive,' she said, 'particularly about the mother. I argued that the point about complaint was that it was a form of satire, and by its very inherent nature it was excessive! That is the very definition of satire. It's about exaggerating flaws and foibles in order to make people see their absurdity.'

Joanne Lee Dow, aged thirty-two and an academic at both the University of Melbourne and Monash University, became involved in the trials via Strauss.[17] She did not need much convincing to appear. Lee Dow was scornful of censorship. It inhibited teaching, and it deprived readers of the fullness of life. The censors, she believed, did not understand literature, and their aims were inconsistent with their actions. 'The logic of it would have meant that they ban Shakespeare,' she said. 'It was just silly, and uptight.'

Ross looked tired and old, 'as though he needed oxygen', when she took the stand, and the courtroom was stuffy, even sleepy. The galleries remained full, but there was a clear sense that the important witnesses had come and gone. Attentiveness had waned. This left Lee Dow self-conscious. She was twice interrupted by objections from Flanagan, and became overwhelmed with embarrassment and nerves. She felt that her subsequent testimony was excruciating, and that Stephen Charles, who was leading her questioning, was no help to her. She was ashamed and infuriated when the lunchtime adjournment came and he indicated that he wished for her to return to the stand: 'I wanted to crawl into a hole.'

Lee Dow said this to Vincent Buckley over lunch. Buckley's reply surprised her. 'Charles is not as unhelpful as he seems, Joanne.

I was looking at the faces of the magistrate and the prosecutor — who cares about it more than any of us — and they were both actually listening to what you were saying.'

Buckley contrasted it with his own testimony. 'I was too formal, too impersonal,' he said, 'and Dinny [O'Hearn] was, at best, ineffectual.' He smiled at Lee Dow. 'Stephen Charles has got you in there and he's called you back because they are all listening to you and you are talking in ways that they can understand.'

This was a consistent theme for the women who appeared for the defence. Experienced in reaching students who were uninterested in or baffled by literature, witnesses like Lee Dow could situate *Portnoy's Complaint* in a place where it was interesting, relevant, and accessible. Brusey and Charles knew it, and were happy to do all they could to make it so. It helped, too, that Lee Dow was 'hopelessly candid' about the book. When she returned to the stand, she remarked that for a book about an adolescent boy there was less masturbation in it than might be expected; when Flanagan sought to discomfort her by asking her to read aloud the passage where Portnoy masturbates into the liver, she did so unperturbed. Then he sought to embarrass her by asking if she would read it to her children as a bedtime story. She gave this short shrift: 'Don't be stupid.'

Lucy Frost, aged twenty-nine and a lecturer at La Trobe University, came next.[18] An American who had moved to Australia with her husband after finishing her PhD on contemporary American fiction, Frost had been infuriated when the Australian censors 'relieved' her of a good portion of her books. 'Everything by William Burroughs, including *Naked Lunch*, was taken away. All of my copies of Henry Miller's books were taken,' she recalled. 'I was just beside myself with fury.' In addition to galvanising her willingness to participate in the *Portnoy* trial, Frost's involvement in the civil rights and anti-war movements in the US had given her an awareness of the theatre involved in court proceedings. A mother already, and with another baby on the way, Frost knew that she appeared wholesome, virtuous, demure. She played it up, particularly as Ross offered her water, offered a chair, and took her gently through the particulars of her oath.

But then she began to answer questions, developing her argument that *Portnoy* was drawing on a theme interrogated in literature as old as classical Greece. 'At the centre of the book is a struggle, a problem of the mind and the body being split,' she said later. 'That was my line. I talked about how important it was to have the frame story, of Portnoy talking to a psychiatrist, because he's so completely obsessed with that body part of himself and with masturbation that he can't overcome that split. I was trying to set his masturbating into the liver in a context of literary tradition.'

Frost knew that understanding this might be difficult for a magistrate more familiar with grubby questions of assault, murder, and petty crime. She was careful to speak plainly and to make connections obvious, using examples that Ross was likely to have encountered. She had the feeling she was successful: he asked questions with a degree of seriousness that indicated he was engaged. 'I felt that he was listening to me very carefully. But,' she added, 'that he was also uncomfortable.'

* * *

Witnesses continued to testify that day: Stephen Murray-Smith, the editor of *Overland* and a lecturer in education at the University of Melbourne, and Josephine Barnes, a West Australian academic. The next day, Tuesday 27 October, it was the turn of ANU academic Bob Brissenden, La Trobe University lecturer Jennifer Gribble, and Patrick White, the future Nobel Prize–winning author of *The Tree of Man*, *Voss*, *Riders in the Chariot*, and *The Solid Mandala*.[19] All testified that *Portnoy's Complaint* was a work of literary merit and not obscene. The overlap of their evidence and repetition of their arguments was such that Barnes questioned its value. 'This has been stated over and over again,' she said to Brusey, when he asked her to detail the book's themes. 'I can only repeat it.'

'I am afraid each witness, as it were, starts again,' Brusey replied, gently. 'And so without you necessarily repeating everything else said, we do want to hear what your expert testimony is.'

White was aware of the humour and the theatre of the proceedings.[20] He arrived at court in an austere black coat and homburg, looking for all the world like a British banker.[21] Onlookers were astonished, not least by the hat. 'He must have had it stashed away from the days when, after leaving Cambridge, he was cutting a dash in London,' remarked Geoffrey Dutton later.[22]

The respectability that this costume lent, when added to his stature, made White an imposing, if modest, witness. Asked if he had made a special study of English literature, he affected nonchalance: 'Well, I have been reading it all my life.' He agreed that he was the author of eight books, and dismissed his poetry: 'Oh, that's something we forget about.' He testified that *Portnoy's Complaint* was 'in the tradition of great comic novels', that it was 'written with great style', possessed convincing characterisation, and was 'terribly funny'. He had no problems with the use of *cunt*, *prick*, or *fuck*: 'Bad language is used all around one. I use it myself, daily. It prevents me blowing up.'

White knew he might be undermining the defence case by emphasising the book's humour. 'The whole thing has to be conducted with great solemnity, I realise,' he wrote to Tom Maschler afterwards, 'but I couldn't resist saying what a funny book I think *Portnoy* is: I hope I didn't put my foot in it.'[23]

Nobody but White believed that he might have. Hilary McPhee recalled his appearance as the most impressive moment of the trial. 'He knew exactly what he was saying. He spoke slowly, and he didn't mock the questions. He answered them with great deliberation, and spoke of the quality of the writing and the appropriateness of the writing.' Brian Kiernan recalled White's appearance in similar terms. 'Very confident, assertive, with nothing histrionic,' he said later. 'Everything was quietly, firmly, decisively spoken.'[24]

The defence team felt good about the trial. The support that Penguin enjoyed was always palpable. 'We had everyone in the courtroom with us except the coppers who were in there, Walters — who was the head of the Vice Squad — Len Flanagan, and the magistrate,' recalled Stephen Charles. 'Everyone else who was there was with us, enthusiastically supporting *Portnoy's Complaint* and the right for that book to be published.' More importantly, there had not been a moment in the trial where Flanagan had surprised them. 'We knew the sort of evidence they were going to give. We knew the law. We knew the problems we were going to have to overcome. We thought that we were likely to get a good result, one way or the other.' And they could not help but be amused at Flanagan's hackneyed attempts to provoke outrage: 'Flanagan was reading parts of the book out — really scaly bits — and expecting people to cringe and react with disgust. But they were hooting with laughter.'

Brusey gave his closing address, requesting that Ross find Penguin not guilty on grounds that *Portnoy* was not obscene, that *Portnoy* was possessed of literary merit, and that the publication, distribution, and keeping of the novel was justified. 'Looking at this case on the evidence, Your Worship,' Brusey said, 'you must feel uncomfortable about convicting. I ask for an acquittal on each of the charges, including the show-cause summons.'

Flanagan's address was consistent with what he had said all along. 'We say the book is obscene. It is obscene by contemporary standards of decency of the people in the street. It suggests that young people's minds are likely to be affected by reading the book.' All but ceding the ground of literary merit — leaving that for Ross to determine — Flanagan pointed to the circumstances of the book's publication as reason to find Penguin guilty. 'Even if you were to find that the book did have literary merit, we say: whatever its literary merit, the publication in the circumstances was not justified.' A guilty verdict was the only correct verdict.

When Flanagan finished, Ross nodded. He would consider the evidence, and reserve his decision until 9 November. Court was adjourned.

CHAPTER 10

Peppercorns and pyrrhic victories

Ross was as good as his word: he handed down his verdict at ten o'clock on Monday 9 November.[1] The whole affair was 'quite extraordinary', thought Hilary McPhee: television crews were massed outside, and the courtroom was crowded with people. Both sides played nice for the observing press. Flanagan, sporting a fresh haircut and a black-and-white checked shirt — 'a concession to fashion', McPhee called it — joked and chatted with Brusey as they waited for matters to get underway. Eventually, an elegant clerk whom no one had ever seen before appeared in the courtroom, boomed for them to stand for Ross's entry, and then mangled the name of the case, confusing it with another. 'Is it possible it's *not* the most important case going through the City Court?' McPhee laughed, at this.

Ross walked to his seat without looking at anyone, sat, and read his judgement in its entirety. From a first reading, he said, it was obvious that a considerable portion of *Portnoy's Complaint* was devoted to sexual matters: 'Adjectives such as disgusting, indecent, filthy, sordid, [and] shocking apply to this book.' Section 154 of the Victorian *Obscenity Act* defined an obscene work as one that unduly emphasised matters of sex. 'This book,' Ross said, 'by its bulk comes under this category.' Was this undue? Standards do change from time to time, and there was a 'new frankness' in the community regarding matters of sex. But, he went on, 'I find it does offend against the ordinary man.' The book was obscene.

Penguin had expected little else. The next question that Ross considered was crucial: whether the book possessed the literary merit that the defence had claimed. Ross noted the strengths of the defence case, in particular the gallery of witnesses it had assembled. 'One could not fail to be impressed by [the] witnesses.' With 'no evidence to support a contrary view', Ross said he was 'satisfied that the book had literary merit before Penguin published it'. The qualifier was important. *Portnoy's Complaint* was still relatively new when it was published in Australia, and some might well have argued that the defence of literary merit had been a convenient, after-the-fact justification for defying the law. Had the literary merit been recognised before this, then? Yes, Ross judged. It had been. The defence had discharged its onus.

But even as the defence celebrated this, Ross made clear his judgement that the book had been distributed and sold in a manner intended for the 'widest possible distribution'. The cheap price implied no restriction of availability: 'All classes and age groups could have it.' The blurb described *Portnoy's Complaint* as a dirty book. Penguin, he went on gravely, had promoted it as such. That dirtiness might even have had the effect of putting off serious readers. Therefore, Ross ruled, the book was obscene, and the plans for its distribution were indiscriminate.

'I find that the publication, distribution, and keeping were not justified in the circumstances,' he said. 'I find the charge proved.'

Almost immediately, Brusey broke in with a question. Ross had mentioned *Portnoy's* availability to various age groups. Would Ross expand on that, Brusey asked, perhaps to clarify what age groups he was referring to?

The magistrate went red. No doubt he had realised that in referring to age groups he might have given Penguin further grounds for an appeal. After a long pause, he told Brusey in halting, careful terms that he was not bound to answer the question, and that he would not expand or clarify his answer.

'This is odd and is much discussed by Brusey and co. as to the actual sense of Ross's *no*,' Hilary McPhee wrote afterwards. 'Brusey seems to feel this is the moment on which we might have a chance to appeal for [the] admission of psychiatric evidence.' Certainly it was peculiar for Ross to have so erred; nonetheless, Brusey began lobbying for leniency.

He told Ross that he should take into account the difficulties in Victoria for a publisher about to publish a work of recognised literary merit. There were uncertainties with which Penguin had struggled before its decision to publish. Victoria was the first place in the world where *Portnoy's Complaint* had been prosecuted under an obscenity law. That should count for something. This was not a deliberate offence, Brusey argued, with considerable chutzpah. It had been committed by a company of international standing and reputation — a company 'to which we are all indebted', he argued. Ross should therefore impose a nominal penalty only.

Ross, who had looked puzzled and gazed heavenward while Brusey spoke, turned to Flanagan. The Crown prosecutor put his motion: the 414 copies of *Portnoy's Complaint* that police had seized should be destroyed. In light of Ross's decision, he sought an order for that destruction.

In that case, Brusey said immediately, he sought a stay on any destruction order in case of an appeal.

Ross dealt with this quickly. He wanted the matter over. He stayed the destruction, subject to the date by which an appeal had to be filed, and handed down his sentence before vanishing into his chambers: a $50 fine for publishing an obscene article, a $25 fine for distributing an obscene article, another $25 fine for keeping an obscene article for gain, and $4.50 for court costs.

'We're obscene but with some literary merit and our crime against society has been measured at $100 plus $4.50 costs,' McPhee wrote. 'It's all rather heartening and at this stage we seem fairly certain to appeal upwards.' The penalty, certainly, was lenient. 'It was token,' Peter Froelich recalled. 'It was a peppercorn.'[2] There was widespread agreement that public opinion had influenced the court on this front. How else to account for it? 'Certainly weird when you consider the 100,000-odd copies sold and the rumours of righteous anger against this publication for gain,' McPhee thought. It boded well for Michie's yet-to-be-tried case: even if found guilty, he could surely not be dealt with any more harshly than Penguin.

Stephen Charles thought the verdict was positive. Although he lamented that Ross had bowed to political pressure to find Penguin guilty, he saw that the verdict left the state government in an impossible position: there was nothing more that they were able to do. 'All the steam went out of the prosecution,' he said later. '… As soon as [Ross] announced it, we knew that Bolte and Rylah would be furious. This decision effectively stuffed them.'[3]

The verdict did not dent Penguin's resolve. Though he had been less certain that Ross would accept *Portnoy*'s possession of literary merit, Michie had predicted that the magistrate would not, ultimately, rule in Penguin's favour.[4] But that would not be the final word. 'He was always going to appeal,' said McPhee, later. 'Penguin were not going to just take it.'[5] Michie had ensured that Penguin remained resolved. Three days before the verdict, the board of Penguin Australia determined that an unfavourable verdict would be met with an immediate appeal.[6] The attitude among staff, recalled Bob Sessions, was 'a sense of, "This is just part of the fight. We'll win this, and we'll win the next one, too." We felt we were doing the right thing.'

Outside the court, in front of the press, Michie sounded defiant.

The battle was not over. Yes, Penguin had been found guilty. And yes, for now, Penguin could not distribute *Portnoy's Complaint* in Victoria. But it should be recalled that almost 100,000 copies had already been sold in Australia. The book was legally available in South Australia, and Ross had found that *Portnoy's Complaint* was a work of recognised literary merit. That finding vindicated Penguin's decision to publish the book. This was to his liking, Michie said, but he was 'very disappointed with the overall finding'. And so Michie told the press that Penguin would appeal: 'We will take it to the High Court if our solicitors advise us there are grounds to do so.' And if that were not enough, Michie intimated that Penguin could make further challenges to Australia's censorship and obscenity laws. It had other books that it could seek to do so with, he said.[7]

Privately, he remained combative. 'Again, the press reaction has been very favourable and we have, at this stage at least, won a moral victory,' he wrote to Graham C. Greene. 'The situation is becoming increasingly ludicrous, especially when you consider that we have sold 100,000 copies and have been fined a total of $100 for doing so.'[8] Hooker would echo this point when he wrote to Greene: the verdict was 'basically ludicrous', though it was also a 'slight advance' on decisions made in the past in similar cases. Moreover, Hooker went on, 'There is something almost apologetic in the magistrate's tone.'[9]

Press reaction to Ross's verdict was caustic. *The Age* scorned the 'exquisite ambiguity' in his declaration that it was notorious that community standards had changed. 'Did he mean *notorious* in the simple sense of being well-known, or did he intend to impart a connotation of disapproval? ... It is of course notorious that citizens of this virtuous State are more easily offended and disgusted than those of any part of the English-speaking world.' It rubbished his exclusion of the scientific evidence: 'If medical specialists in mental conditions and professional analysts of human behaviour are not qualified to submit evidence on this point, then who is?' Finally, the paper derided the failure of Ross and the censors that had banned *Portnoy's Complaint* to understand that it was a funny book: 'So lacking are they in insight and humour that they cannot perceive laughter is one of the best safeguards against depravity and corruption.'[10] Elsewhere, *The Canberra Times* lamented that the 'uninformative' decision failed to clarify the nature of obscenity, and argued that it caught in sharp focus the failing agreement between the Commonwealth and the states for uniform censorship. 'Whatever the merits or demerits of the Victorian decision,' the paper editorialised, '… the puzzling assumption remains that different community standards apply in different parts of Australia.'[11]

* * *

Meanwhile, preparations for the trial in New South Wales were continuing. Government solicitors keeping an eye on Victoria were reckoning with how they would handle the litany of expert witnesses testifying to *Portnoy's* literary merit. How would they rebut those arguments? Approaches — for guidance, advice, and even a few damning comments — to members of the National Literature Board of Review were rebuffed. Those members wanted nothing to do with the court action, and any opinions they offered would likely have been equally of help to the defence.[12]

Eric Willis looked for help among contacts of his own, and came away disillusioned. 'I feel it would be difficult to get any recognised expert to say the book [*Portnoy's Complaint*] has little literary merit and impossible to find one to say it has none,' he wrote to the Crown solicitor's office.[13]

The government was still grappling with this when the committal hearing began on Monday 14 December in the Sydney Court of Petty Sessions.[14] Appearing before Magistrate Harold Berman, for Angus & Robertson, was George Masterman, who had been retained for his links with Allens and his experience with obscenity law in the Dennis Altman case.

Opposing Masterman was Robert Vine-Hall. An experienced

prosecutor who had edited Bignold's famous guide to the *Police Offences* and *Vagrancy Acts* in 1967, and prosecuted Wendy Bacon in the Sydney Magistrates' Court earlier that year, Vine-Hall knew exactly what was required of him. He called Detective Constable Terrence Mitchell to the stand, and took him through his testimony. In the company of Detective Sergeant Edward Quill, Mitchell said, he had gone to Angus & Robertson at around noon on 31 August. They had gone to the paperback section, queued, and purchased a copy of *Portnoy's Complaint*.

'Did you notice anybody in particular in the queue?'

'Yes,' said the detective, 'directly in front of me in the queue was a schoolgirl, in school uniform.'

This was surprising to the defence — and potentially ruinous. A schoolgirl had been able to purchase the book? A *schoolgirl*?

Masterman, however, initially ignored this. His cross-examination of Mitchell was focused on the manner of the sale of *Portnoy*: he wanted to demonstrate that Angus & Robertson had sold the book responsibly, without sensationalising its contents or playing on its notoriety. He had the detective confirm, grudgingly, that the book was not on display in the shop window ('I didn't see it on display'), that it was sold from the back of the store, that there were no signs advertising the book ('Well, there could have been but I didn't see any'), and that even at the counter where the book was being purchased, there still were no copies to be seen ('I didn't see them on display').

Then, aware that the only real threat to that strategy was this schoolgirl that Mitchell had mentioned, Masterman sought more information. How had Mitchell determined that she was a schoolgirl? Did he speak to her at all?

'No, I never spoke to her.'

'So, all the help that you give us in attempting to identify this girl is that you say she's about sixteen, was wearing a navy uniform, had long dark hair, [and] possibly was wearing a navy hat?'

'Yes, I can give you more,' Mitchell said, agreeably. 'She was carrying a school case. I noticed that she had white socks on with black shoes and I couldn't see the name of the school on her blazer or anywhere and I didn't take particular notice if she was wearing a tie. I couldn't identify the school.'

'You mean there was no name on the blazer?' Masterman asked. 'Did you look for it?'

'No, I didn't look for it.'

'Anyway, she was about sixteen? I suppose she could have been seventeen or eighteen?'

'I wouldn't put her age at any more than sixteen,' said Mitchell. 'She had no make-up on and she looked very young in the face.'

'Well, your best estimate is about sixteen?'

'About sixteen.'

Detective Sergeant Edward Quill came next. His evidence with Vine-Hall was brief, confirming what his colleague had said, but with Masterman it was extended and contentious. They started with Masterman's request to see what Quill had written in his notebook about the Angus & Robertson visit. Quill handed the notebook over, but added as he did that it contained nothing of his visit to Angus & Robertson. Those notes were on two pieces of foolscap paper that he had typed, 'shortly after, on the day', at the Vice Squad office.

Masterman zeroed in on this. 'Why did you think it appropriate to put some observations and conversations in your ordinary police notebook, and some in —?'

'Well, the purchase of the book at Angus & Robertson was a matter that had been considered should be done unostentatiously,' Quill interrupted. 'Consequently I did not think it was prudent for me or anyone else to be making notes in the shop whilst this was going on.'

'This gives you the advantage that you are the only one who can give evidence about this purchase. You and Mitchell.'

'I don't think so. There was — any other person there that could have seen what we saw.'

'And they would be expected, I suppose,' said Masterman, 'to remember this visit by Constable Mitchell and the schoolgirl in front of him?'

To Quill's feigned ignorance, Masterman was blunt: 'What I suggest to you is that this schoolgirl is an invention of yours and Mr Mitchell's.'

Quill denied it, but he was on the back foot. He did not alter that when Masterman asked for a copy of his notes about the visit. Quill had not tendered them to Vine-Hall, nor had he brought them to court. He did not think, he explained, that they would be required.

They were, Berman interrupted. The magistrate adjourned the court for ten minutes, and ordered Quill to retrieve the notes.

The subsequent examination of those notes was brutal. Masterman established that they had been typed on 1 September, not 31 August, as Quill had just testified; that Quill had barely opened *Portnoy's Complaint* — 'I commenced to read it, and I gave up,' Quill said — and that his testimony about seeing people younger than twenty queueing to buy the book on 1 September was profoundly flawed. 'You can't tell us whether in fact they actually purchased the book or not?'

'No, that's correct.'

Immediately after Quill stepped down, Masterman put it to Berman that the case should be dismissed on the grounds that there was no case to answer. It is likely that the weakness of the police testimony about the schoolgirl, and the grudging admissions of the lack of signage in the Angus & Robertson store, were what spurred the request. Berman, however, refused it. 'I find there's a *prima facie* case, Mr Masterman, and now it's a matter for you whether you wish to call any witnesses on behalf of the defendant company.'

Masterman had lined up three witnesses to testify that *Portnoy's Complaint* was a work of literary merit. The first was H.W. Piper, head of the School of English at Macquarie University. Aged

ABOVE: John Michie, *c.*1969.
COURTESY OF HILARY MCPHEE

RIGHT: Peter Froelich, *c.*1970.
COURTESY OF PETER FROELICH

BELOW: John Hooker, *c.*1970.
MICHAEL CURTAIN, COURTESY OF
JAKE HOOKER

Arthur Rylah, deputy premier of Victoria and chief secretary. *VICTORIAN PARLIAMENTARY LIBRARY & INFORMATION SERVICES*

LEFT: Eric Willis, chief secretary in New South Wales. *NSW PARLIAMENTARY LIBRARY & INFORMATION SERVICES*

BELOW: Don Chipp, minister for customs 1969–72. *AUSTRALIAN INFORMATION SERVICES, STATE LIBRARY OF VICTORIA*

ABOVE: Philip Roth, on the cusp of publication of *Portnoy's Complaint*. *BOB PETERSON, LIFE IMAGES COLLECTION, GETTY*

LEFT: The 24 June 1969 telegram announcing a ban on *Portnoy's Complaint*. *NAA: A425, 72/4378*

BELOW: John Michie's telegram to Don Chipp, July 1970. *NAA: A425, 72/4378*

TELEPRINT

CUSTOMS CBA 320   24.6.69
FROM GORDON
TO LITERATURE - ALL STATES
MF 69/2702
    ''PORTNOY'S COMPLAINT'' BY PHILIP ROTH PROHIBITED
REG. 4A

ENDS

AUSTRALIAN POST OFFICE
TELEGRAM

MELBOURNE   VIC   58   11–30A

MR D L CHIPP
PHONE 994264
MELBOURNE VIC

WE HOLD AUSTRALIAN RIGHTS PHILLIP ROTH NOVEL PORTMOYS COMPLAINTS STOP
PROPOSE PUBLISHING THIS WORK IN AUSTRALIA IN THE NEAR FUTURE STOP
IN VIEW OF YOUR OFFER OF PRIOR CONSULATIONS ON MATTERS OF CENSORSHIP
HAVE BEEN ANXIOUS TO DISCUSS THIS MATTER WITH YOU BEFORE PROCEEDING
                    --JOHN MICHIE PENGIUN BOOKS AUST LTD

CPDKM11-53A

MINISTER'S MEETING WITH MR. J. MICHIE -
PENGUIN BOOKS AUST. LTD.
_____

Points for Discussion

1. Department of Customs & Excise responsible for
   importation of goods.

2. Publication and distribution of literature in Australia
   is the responsibility of State Governments and Federal
   Territories.

3. Spirit of Commonwealth/State Agreement on censorship
   of works of literary merit is that Commonwealth and
   State Ministers will act uniformly on imported and
   locally produced publications submitted to the
   National Literature Board of Review - although
   the States are legally free to take any action
   for or against a book under their own respective
   laws (Clause 18 of Agreement).

4. The matter of publishing "Portnoy's Complaint" in
   Australia is one which you should discuss with the
   State Governments.

5. Unless my specific permission has been obtained,
   any copy of "Portnoy's Complaint" in Australia is
   a prohibited import - should it come to my notice
   that there are such prohibited copies in Australia
   I will have to consider what action I shall take
   (seizure and/or prosecution for possession).

6. There is provision for you to contest the prohibition
   in Court.

LEFT: The points provided to Don Chipp for his meeting with John Michie, July 1970. *NAA: A425, 72/4378*

BELOW: NSW Vice Squad officers raid the Angus & Robertson store on Castlereagh Street, Sydney, 3 September 1970. *FAIRFAX MEDIA*

ABOVE: Pocket Bookshop proprietor James Thorburn goes to the Chief Secretary's Department to present a copy of *Portnoy's Complaint*. *GRANT PETERSON, FAIRFAX MEDIA*

RIGHT: Police raid the Pioneer Bookshop, September 1970. *ROD LOCKE, WEST AUSTRALIAN NEWSPAPERS LTD*

Joan Broomhall sells a copy of *Portnoy's Complaint* to Laurence Wishart, September 1970. *WEST AUSTRALIAN NEWSPAPERS LTD*

William Deane, QC (right) with NSW premier Sir Robin Askin, *c.*1973. *JOHN MANOLATO, FAIRFAX MEDIA*

'Portnoy' jury fails to agree

After a 10-day trial a Sydney Quarter Sessions jury was unable to agree last night if the American novel "Portnoy's Complaint" was obscene. Judge Goran remanded Angus and Rob-... the Sud-...

sold in Angus and Robertsons store to a 16-year-old girl in school uniform Seve... by the book w... literary In h... terda...

Banned novel: Vic will prosecute publis...

The Victori... ernment will ... Penguin Bool... tralia Ltd over ing of the novel "Portno... plaint".

Publishers to defy ban on U.S. novel

"Potnoy's Complaint," an American novel banned by Customs, will be published in Australia by Penguin Books next week.

The company will go ahead with publication despite warnings yesterday that the publishers, distributors and sellers would be prosecuted. "Portnoy's Com... by Philip ...

given by the Queensland Minister of Justice, Dr P. Delamothe, and Victoria's acting Chief Secretary, Mr I. W. Smith.

'Portnoy' ban battle is not yet ended

MELBOURNE, Monday. — "We will take it to the High Court if our solicitors advise us there are grounds to do so."

The managing director of Penguin Books in Australia, Mr John Michie, said this today after Mr E. Ross, SM, had ruled that the novel, "Portnoy's Complaint," was obscene. Mr Ross fined the company $100 with costs on th... latt...

quired nominal penalties only. Mr Ross agreed to make an order that 414 copies of the novel seized by the Vice Squad...

Mr Ross said he was impressed by evidence from professors, lecturers, teachers and author...

A selection of headlines from *The Sydney Morning Herald*, August 1970 to February 1971. *SYDNEY MORNING HERALD ARCHIVE*

```
CUSTOMS CBA  262      17.6.71

FROM GORDON

TO LITERATURE  -  ALL STATES

     IN ACCORDANCE WITH MINISTER'S PRESS STATEMENT IMPORTATION

OF ''PORTNOY'S COMPLAINT'' MAY BE ALLOWED.


ENDS
```

The telegram that went out on 17 June 1971, rescinding the ban on *Portnoy's Complaint*.
NAA: A425, 72/4378

On the corner of Hunter and Castlereagh Streets, Sydney, the P. & O. Shippi
has completed its contribution to the Australian Ugliness—the P. & O. Building, o
opened by the Prime Minister in January. To alleviate the severe drabness of its sa
facade, sculptor Tom Bass has set an attractive bronze urinal in the wall for the conv
of passers-by. This is no ordinary urinal. It has a continual flushing system and
handily set at different standing heights. There is a nominal charge, of course, bu
worry, there is no need to pay immediately. Just P. & O. Pictured is a trio of
natives P. & O'ing in the Bass urinal.

Sunday Review

OCTOBER 25, 1970   No. 3   Fifteen cents

J. K. GALBRAITH ON RICHARD NIXON

THE COLLECTED WISDOM OF R. G. MENZIES

Harris versus Humphries (round 2)

ONANISM ON TRIAL

TOP: The cover of the infamous February 1964 issue of *Oz*.
UNIVERSITY OF WOLLONGONG LIBRARY, COURTESY OF RICHARD WALSH

ABOVE: An extract from the March 1970 issue of *Tharunka*.
ARC

LEFT: Michael Leunig's cartoon of the Melbourne trial, printed in the *Sunday Review*, 25 October 1970. *COURTESY OF MICHAEL LEUNIG*

fifty-five, Piper brought considerable credibility to the defence case. He agreed that *Portnoy's Complaint* was possessed of literary merit, and confidently discussed its literary heritage. The book contained tragedy and comedy. It was a savage comedy, of exaggeration and grotesquerie, that was commonplace in literature. 'If you want literary ancestry for it, go back to Aristophanes,' he said. 'It's been through literature, always.'

Under Vine-Hall's cross-examination, however, Piper became nervous and anxious. His hands began to tremble, noticeably, and his answers became hesitant, vague, and then uncertain. Vine-Hall asked Piper whether he had heard of Jacqueline Susann's famous quip — that while she would like to meet Philip Roth, she would not like to shake his hand. 'Do you agree with that?'

'No, I'm not even quite sure what it means.'

'Aren't you, Professor?'

'If this could mean that they think the book is well-written, but is something that no decent man should have written ...' Piper tried. 'Is that what they mean?'

'You are the critic, not I,' Vine-Hall said breezily. Quizzing Piper about literary merit and what it was, he became sarcastic and cutting. When Piper suggested that works of literary merit made 'a comment on our experience', Vine-Hall directed him to the passage where Portnoy, masturbating in the bathroom, ejaculates with such vigour that he splatters a light bulb and calls himself the Raskolnikov of jerking off. 'Who on earth, Professor, is Raskolnikov?'

'Raskolnikov is a character who, in Dostoevsky's *Crime and Punishment*, commits a murder and gets away with it until eventually his conscience betrays him.'

'And what has that to do with —? I mean,' said Vine-Hall, stopping, 'does he ever damage any light bulbs?'

'No, of course he doesn't damage any light bulbs,' said Piper. 'He commits a particularly bloody axe murder. And this is the point of using Raskolnikov there — to indicate wild guilt, absurd guilt.'

'Absurdity?'

'Yes.'

'Extremely humourous,' said Vine-Hall, drily. Then he began asking about the connection between realism and literary merit. Pressed, at length, on this line of questioning, Piper's nerves now got the better of him. He flailed. He babbled, backtracked, apologised. He agreed, then added caveats; admitted possibilities, then asked for clarification. He was all over the place.

Vine-Hall did not let up. 'Don't you follow at all?' he demanded. Smelling blood, he pressed Piper on the book's accuracy and Piper's ability to evaluate it. 'You would agree that it is to a large extent a novel about class?'

'Yes. It's to a large extent a novel about a class, yes.'

'It does not truly present that class. Does that detract from its literary merit?'

'It could, it could, yes.'

'It could, considerably, depending on how far its accuracy was?'

'Yes, and the nature of the inaccuracy.'

'Have you met many North American Jewish mothers lately?'

'I haven't met any for ten years, and only one then. I have known Jewish families.'

'In North America?'

'No, some North American, others in Australia, others in England.'

'Have you known lately a large number of young Jewish men who were products of North American Jewish families?'

'Not a great number, no,' Piper admitted. 'Getting down to cases, probably I've known about three or four. That's all.'

'You are, in fact, in no position to judge the accuracy of the picture with which we are presented here, are you?' said Vine-Hall.

'Of those aspects of it, no.'

'So, you are in no position to know to what extent inaccuracies may deprive this book of literary merit?'

All Piper could do was agree.

* * *

Peter Bennie — known as 'the Toad' to his students at St Paul's College, where he was warden — followed Piper to the stand. A tutor of English and an ordained priest in the Church of England, Bennie was a witty, liberal man with experience in appearing at obscenity trials, having testified during Richard Neville's trials. He was clear and absolute about *Portnoy*. Merit could be found in the words and form of an artwork: 'So that if the words and the form are a perfect expression of the subject matter, then you have literary merit, and the more serious the subject matter, the greater the literary merit.'

Bennie was definitive about reality and exaggerration. A work of art did not need to mimic reality: 'A work of literature is not necessarily dealing with reality at all. It's a work of imagination,' he argued. 'For example, I have no acquaintance with the royal family of Denmark, but I still read *Hamlet* entranced. A literal realism is not necessary in a work of art.' Nor was it inappropriate that masturbation be discussed in *Portnoy*: 'I understand from the Kinsey Report that the practice is almost universal at some stage or another in the career of males, and therefore I think that this subject is quite a normal one in discussing the career of an adolescent.' Nor was the derivative necessarily derivative. Invoking Polonius's advice to Claudius in *Hamlet*, Bennie pointed out that it contained all sorts of popular witticisms and stories. 'Nothing in any book can be completely original, in the sense that even unconsciously the author himself may have repeated something he's heard somebody tell him months or years ago, without knowing that he hasn't made it up in his imagination.'

Vine-Hall tried, but his cross-examination was toothless. Attempting to trip up Bennie on the relationship between reality and literary merit, he was shrugged off, chided, respectfully reproached ('With respect, sir, the question is too general'), or simply rejected.

'Has reality much or little relation to literary merit?' he asked.

'I can go no further than to say *some*,' said Bennie. 'For example, take *A Midsummer Night's Dream*. How much reality is there in that play of Shakespeare's? And yet none of us would come forward and say that it wasn't an exquisite work of art with some literary merit.'

'And of course,' Vine-Hall said, 'that rather depends on the purpose of the work, doesn't it?'

'No,' said Bennie.

Nothing much seemed to work. Bennie spoke again about realism and credibility, invoked Russian winters to make his point. 'I'm quite unacquainted with Russian neologist intellectuals,' he said, 'but after reading Dostoevsky one can look out the window and expect to see a wolf peering into the door, so credible is the whole thing that you feel that you've moved out of this world and into the world that the artist is describing. I don't have to be a Russian historian of the nineteenth century to understand this.'

Masterman's final witness was Maureen Colman.[15] Thirty-nine years old and a lecturer in English in the adult education department at the University of Sydney, Colman was well travelled, of an independent mind, and unabashed about her opinions. Like her husband, Adrian Colman, who had testified on behalf of Martin Sharp for the cartoon 'The Gas Lash' in 1964, she had no truck with censorship. 'I just thought it was stupid, and had no place,' she said later. 'It was pointless. If you say a book is forbidden, a lot of people will want to read it — they will think it must be an exciting read.' And though she did find *Portnoy* rather frank, Colman believed that prosecution of it was ridiculous. 'You don't have to read a book,' she said later. 'You can't complain about it that way. If you think it's dreadful, you can just stop reading it. No one is making you read it.'

On the stand, Colman argued that *Portnoy* did what George Eliot had prescribed art should do: enlarge our sympathies. 'I think that this is one of the things that *Portnoy's Complaint* does pre-eminently. It enlarges our sympathies for another human being.'

People felt sorry for Portnoy, by the end, and the techniques used to present him and evoke that sympathy were highly developed and suitable.

Vine-Hall's cross-examination was not difficult for Colman. He tried to take her on over George Eliot: what about works that did not enlarge the reader's sympathy? Would they be disqualified from this realm of literary merit? What about a novel about, say, Himmler, that presented him sympathetically? Would that be a work of literary merit?

Colman had no trouble again. Citing Bulstrode, from *Middlemarch*, she argued that even an unsavoury character could be shown to be human. Vine-Hall disliked this response immensely: 'As long as you can get some sympathy for the postman, it doesn't matter about the rest, is that right?'

Well, Colman said, yes.

What about Portnoy? Isn't he a scoundrel? Why should you have sympathy for him? Isn't he having a whale of a time?

To this, Colman pointed out that the book ends with Portnoy screaming in agony. But Vine-Hall scoffed: 'You're a charitable soul, Mrs Colman.'

* * *

Masterman's closing address was to the point. He told Berman that no jury would find *Portnoy's Complaint* obscene or indecent. Citing Justice Windeyer, Masterman argued that for a work to be obscene or indecent it needed to do more than offend or surprise. It needed to shock, he said. *Portnoy's Complaint* could not do that; therefore, Berman should dismiss the case.

Even if he did not do so, Masterman argued, works of literary merit were exempt from prosecution. The Crown's failure to call rebutting witnesses on this point, Masterman said, meant that it had implicitly conceded the point. 'And the position where the Crown takes the course of not calling any evidence in the proceedings at this stage is, in my submission, that that issue is determined in favour of the defence and must be so determined.'

Finally, Masterman argued that once the possession of literary merit was decided, the onus was on the prosecution to demonstrate that the manner of sale was 'not justified in the circumstances'. Masterman reminded Berman that there were no signs in Angus & Robertson advertising *Portnoy*; copies were not on display; and those who sought a copy had to ask for it. And although Masterman did not push back hard on the police testimony, he emphasised that the prosecution had failed to show any reason why the book should not have been sold to people who wanted it, who asked for it, who were all of such an age to read a book of 'undoubted literary merit'. That included, he added, that girl of sixteen.

Vine-Hall's argument was much easier to make. He shrugged off Masterman's suggestion that no jury could find the book obscene or indecent in light of new community standards: 'It is pointless and exceedingly tedious to talk about changing community standards, and one hears about it in the newspapers, one hears about it on the television, one hears about it even from erudite people like Masterman — and no one ever tells us what the standards are changing from or to or where they are. Now, there's one very good cross-section of community standards, and that is a jury.'

He did not agree that the Crown had conceded anything about *Portnoy*'s literary merit. That matter, he said, was not suitable for the Crown to argue in a committal hearing. But even if it were, and the Crown had to deal with the manner of sale — well, look at the book! Vine-Hall pointed to the dust jacket: 'The funniest book about sex ever written,' he repeated. '... It's as clear an indication as Your Worship could want that it [the novel] was intended to fall into the hands of anyone with $1.35, and it would have done — and, in fact, until the sale of it was stopped, it did.'

'Your Worship's only duty at the moment,' Vine-Hall finished, 'since Your Worship has found a *prima facie* case, is to consider whether in the light of the evidence already given a jury, properly instructed, would find this book either indecent or obscene.'

Berman wasted no time. 'The matters are ones which should go to trial before a jury, and I therefore make an order in each case authorising an indictment to be filed for the offences to be named in the information.'

It was not unexpected. Angus & Robertson knew that the committal hearing was a formality. Trying to have the case dismissed had been a long shot. For several months now, Angus & Robertson and their lawyers had turned their attention to finding a top-notch Queen's Counsel to appear at the full trial that Berman had just ordered.[16] The company was defiant. It wanted victory. And Masterman made sure to put this on the record straightaway: 'We welcome a trial before a jury.'

CHAPTER 11

A kick in the ribs

Now the *Portnoy* trials shifted to Western Australia, where, in the final days of 1970, Joan Broomhall appeared in the Perth Court of Petty Sessions before Magistrate N.J. Malley, charged with selling an obscene publication.

A fifty-eight-year-old English-born woman with wavy grey hair, plump cheeks, and glasses, Broomhall was the manager of the Pioneer Bookshop, in Perth. Owned by the Communist Party of Australia, of which Broomhall was a member, the Pioneer was housed in an ageing cottage on the corner of Bulwer and Stirling streets. Its shabby front room was packed with books: the requisite communist material — magazines and newspapers from the Soviet Union, China, and Soviet-bloc countries; novels and plays by favoured writers; and, of course, the works of the 'saints', Marx, Engels, Lenin, and Stalin — but also, unusually, mainstream works from local publishers, including Penguin.[1]

Broomhall had been determined to stock *Portnoy's Complaint*.[2] She and the party were anti-censorship: 'I think censorship of books for adults is an insult.'[3] Prompted by the quick sale of an

162

initial fifteen copies in September, she ordered more: 200 copies, then 300, then more again. Aware that the police would soon swoop, Broomhall hid the stock in her home and in those of fellow party members, which they retrieved and brought to the store as needed.[4] With a 47 cent profit on each sold copy, Broomhall and the party were intent on maximising sales; thus the party allowed members to sell the book individually and take a 20c cut. Soon enough, party members were appearing in hotel gardens, on the streets, in Forrest Place, and at the University of Western Australia with copies in arm, ready for sale.[5] This operation, which was stepped up as the controversy spread in the east, was unabashed, even brazen. On 11 September — the day police raided the Pioneer, seized twenty-three copies of *Portnoy*, and informed Broomhall that she would be charged — party secretary John Rivo Gandini came to the shop, on foot, laden with copies of *Portnoy* for Broomhall to put on sale. He did so within full sight of the press, which splashed photographs of his arrival in the newspapers.

Police retaliated by serving a summons on Gandini and by raiding the store again, on 15 September.[6] This time, they made sure to make hay of the raid. With the press in tow, they turned the shop over, to the point of climbing into the ceiling to ensure they had seized everything illicit. They managed to find 267 copies, and photographs of the raid — police officers in trilbies and suits, clambering up bookshelves and diving through boxes — were splashed about. But it was to limited effect. Party members continued to sell the book, pushing sales to about 2,000 copies, and providing a welcome influx of funds to the party coffers. There was also the benefit of considerable publicity: at a meeting in October, party members crowed that the advertising they had gained from all the fuss had been 'fabulous'.[7]

But the potential penalties for the fuss — a $200 fine, or six months' imprisonment — were not so fabulous. Moreover, Broomhall's was to be the test case in Western Australia: by agreement between police and eight other booksellers, her prosecution would determine whether *Portnoy* would be banned in the state and whether the other booksellers would be prosecuted.

Prosecutor Ian Viner was aware of the government's desire for success. Aged thirty-seven, he was a rangy and experienced barrister of six years' standing.[8] Though he had heard of *Portnoy* before the trial, Viner had not read it before it landed on his desk in his brief. What he found was both underwhelming and grotesque. 'I was very bored by it,' he said later. 'I found it tedious to read.' He was in no doubt whatsoever, though, about the book's obscenity: 'I was disgusted by it … I didn't have any problems saying it was obscene.'

Influences on that view, he acknowledged later, included his upbringing and the social climate of his state. 'In Western Australia, we were a socially conservative society,' he said. 'I did not have strong views one way or the other about censorship at the time. I grew up in a family where there was no discussion of sex, and swear words were not used.' People were hostile to obscenity and the use of profanities, Viner believed; censorship, which helped to stamp that out, was therefore uncontroversial. It was regarded as an immutable fact of life, 'an accepted part of social regulation'. For Viner, the case was not one that aroused great passions or conflicts of principle. He accepted the case as a cab off the rank, and he prosecuted it in that vein.[9]

The cause meant more for his counterpart at Broomhall's trial. A friend of Broomhall and a fellow traveller in the Communist Party, Lloyd Davies was a forty-eight-year-old barrister with dark, stringy hair, bright eyes, brow-line glasses, and a beard that ringed his face like a lion's mane. He was gentle, if slightly eccentric, and he was delighted to have received the brief. He regarded the trial as an opportunity to show that Western Australia was not a conservative state.

After a preliminary hearing on 27 November, which was adjourned so that magistrate Malley could read *Portnoy* — explaining to the press as he left that he had not done so until then because it would have been illegal — the trial resumed on

30 November with Viner calling Lawrence Wishart to the stand.[10]
A thin-faced truck driver who had purchased a copy of *Portnoy*
from Broomhall on 8 September, Wishart testified that he had
heard via his radio that the Pioneer was selling *Portnoy*. Interested,
because it had been mentioned in the newspapers, he went to the
shop, where television journalists were interviewing Broomhall
about the book. 'I saw them buy a copy of *Portnoy's Complaint* from
Mrs Broomhall,' Wishart testified. 'They asked how many she had
left, and she said four or five. I said I'd better have one, too. She
produced a book from under the counter. I paid $1.35 for it.'

Viner had called Wishart to complete his evidence that
Broomhall had sold *Portnoy's Complaint*. But his doing so offered
an opportunity for Davies to prove his own point. Under cross-
examination, Wishart denied that he had been depraved or
corrupted as a result of reading *Portnoy*. The response delighted
Davies: it was a 'point duly scored'.[11]

Wishart's answer was the main grounds upon which Davies
then asked Malley to dismiss the case. It was a short-lived request,
not least because Wishart's answer, as Viner pointed out, did not
foreclose the possibility that the court could find *Portnoy* obscene.

Davies was not disheartened. He was confident that his overall
strategy was sound: namely, to establish the merit of *Portnoy's
Complaint* through expert testimony. Much as Penguin had done
in Victoria, Davies intended to call writers, critics, and academics to rebut the charge of obscenity and to testify to the novel's
possession of merit. Given the result in Victoria, this might not
appear a sure path to victory. But Davies had an advantage that
Penguin did not — a stronger exemption in the West Australian
Indecent Publications Act. Section 5 declared that 'nothing in this
Act relates to any work of recognised literary, artistic, or scientific
merit'. Although there was the possibility Malley could decide that
exemption was restricted to 'classic' works that were obscene, it was
the best option that Davies had — and he intended to make the
most of it.

* * *

During his preparations, Davies had been doubtful that there would be many witnesses willing to testify on behalf of *Portnoy*. 'It was an unworthy doubt,' he remarked later. 'Almost every West Australian with literary or academic qualifications who was approached readily consented to do so, even though many of them were heavily engaged in marking public and university exam papers, writing books, or producing plays.' According to Davies, it was only the timing of the trial — near the end of the academic year — that prevented *more* experts from testifying. But he had some reason to be nervous. There had been little opportunity for Davies to confer with his witnesses. But for a fleeting telephone call, he had not been able to speak with them at length about their views. 'Their testimony therefore had a unique spontaneity about it. There was much ad-libbing and a great deal of wit which enlivened the proceedings, even if it did not always further the defence.'[12]

This was the case with T.A.G. 'Tom' Hungerford, who came to the stand after Broomhall. A veteran who had served in Papua New Guinea during World War II, a novelist and critic with a long involvement in Australia's literary community, Hungerford had also been press secretary for West Australian premiers John Tonkin and Charles Court. He testified that *Portnoy's Complaint* was a 'turning point in literature'. It was a 'very fine, well written, superlative human document'. Hungerford was matter-of-fact about the use of four-letter words, noting that it was both appropriate for Portnoy's character and the context of his speaking on the psychologist's couch. The book was not a 'cauldron of filth', he said. It was a 'stew of ingredients out of which something remarkable has been achieved'.

Peppered throughout Hungerford's testimony were caustic comments about the censorship regime. 'From personal experience,' he said, 'I know how truncating it is to have to tailor dialogue to fit censorship.' Citing his novel *The Ridge and the River*, Hungerford pointed out how frustrating it was to make characters — soldiers in the jungles of Papua New Guinea — feel real, while depriving them of the expletives common to their speech.[13] He wanted reform of the censorship laws to ensure that books like *Portnoy* were available and hardcore pornography restricted. He did not think that the present censorship reflected community standards, nor did he think *Portnoy's Complaint* was an 'attack on the censor and the sensibilities of the public'.

Viner's cross-examination of Hungerford was of a piece with his challenge to all the defence witnesses to come. He had surmised that the defence would aim at the exemption that section 5 afforded, and that he would need to rebut the claims to literary merit in order to win the trial. Viner knew he was at something of a disadvantage. 'The witnesses appearing for the defence were lecturers and academics of writing and literature, largely from the University of Western Australia,' he said later. 'They were out to sustain the book. I wasn't going to get too far by challenging them with a definition of literary merit. Not with those kind of witnesses.'

So what should his strategy be? 'I decided that my best option was to challenge the objectivity of what the experts were saying.' Suspecting that it was an in-principle opposition to censorship that motivated those witnesses, Viner decided to challenge the veracity of their opinions, especially their claims to the excellence of the humour in *Portnoy*. 'My line was to read aloud slabs of the book — such as the passage where he masturbates into a liver, or masturbates while on the bus — and ask, "What's funny about that?" I was asking this question sincerely. For myself, I could not see that it was funny. I thought that asking if it really was as funny as the witnesses were claiming was the best way to refute that argument.'[14]

It was, at times, an effective strategy. To such questions, the explanations of jokes, puns, and exaggerations could seem laboured and underwhelming; the claims for excellence could sound insincere and exaggerated. But the gross nature of the material could also seem unexceptional if the witnesses were laconic or willing to temper their praise of it. Hungerford, for example, shrugged off questions about the necessity of chapter titles such as 'Cunt crazy' ('If Roth felt it was necessary, it was necessary'), downplayed the use of terms like *cocksucker* ('Very common in the United States'), and laughed off the suggestion that the liver episode was revolting ('I belly laughed').

Writer Peter Cowan, of *Angry Penguins* notoriety, similarly withstood Viner's questions about passages that provoked a feeling of revulsion. Having stated under Davies' questioning that *Portnoy* had a 'high degree of literary merit' and had contributed to a 'new freedom in writing', Cowan pointed out that *Portnoy*'s ability to prompt revulsion was not accidental: doing so required the exercise of considerable skill from the writer. Moreover, any sexual revulsion prompted was not as bad, nor as easily achieved, as revulsion to violence or destruction. Roth was exploring why people could be revolted. It was his job: 'The writer's job is often to revolt.'

Allan Edwards, professor of English at the University of Western Australia, provided what Davies later called a 'highlight' of the trial with his answers to Viner's questions.[15] A devotee of literature with a lilting voice and a guru's manner, Edwards was highly regarded in the West Australian literary community, and was well connected — even Davies was a former student. Edwards said that there was 'no doubt' that *Portnoy's Complaint* had literary merit, and was effusive about the realism of Portnoy's psychology. 'Normally one only finds such an account in history books,' he said. '... There is a great difference in understanding something in one's head and in feeling inside yourself that you are this particular victim. It is here that I find the book very powerful. It deals with a peculiarly Jewish problem, but enables one to understand this problem from the inside. It is at once pathetic and moving, and it is so because, not in spite of, the jokes.'

Viner's cross-examination focused on those jokes. 'I would ask,

"How can you say it has literary merit?'" he said later. "'Is it really funny to read that someone is masturbating into a piece of liver, and then goes home and eats it? Is that really so funny?'"[16] He read aloud, at length, passages that appeared to be disgusting; he read aloud passages containing an abundance of four-letter words; he even asked about the epigraph that prefaced the book and provided the explanation of the title.

This question backfired conspicuously. Edwards shrugged. 'Very funny,' he said, of the epigraph. 'It is a take-off of solemn scholarly journals.'

Was the title of the fictional scholarly journal in which the complaint was published — *The Puzzled Penis* — relevant, Viner asked. Was the joke there really necessary?

'The expression is very succinct,' replied Edwards. 'That was Portnoy's problem. He didn't know whether to put it in or pull it out.'

Guffaws of laughter filled the court. Even Malley covered his mouth to hide his snicker.[17] It was the best laugh of the case, Davies thought, and it all but terminated Viner's cross-examination.

* * *

Viner's strategy did not alter with subsequent witnesses. Again and again, he would read a licentious passage and ask for opinions. Sometimes he could get witnesses to hesitate. 'Not beautiful,' said John Deakin, a retired superintendent in the education system and book reviewer for Perth's *Sunday Times*, who appeared the next day, 2 December, and was asked about Portnoy's adolescent sexual experiences. But passages that were grotesque could also provoke defence and explanation. 'Without this writing there is no book,' Deakin said, at another instance. 'The novel must be accepted as a whole.'

The librarian at the University of Western Australia, Leonard Jolley, echoed Deakin's views. There were objectionable passages, but the book had to be taken as a whole, he said. He had read of the novel in newspapers and magazines — and had read the extract of *Portnoy* that had appeared in *Partisan Review*, which had come to Australia unimpeded by censorship. On the basis of the reviews and the extract, Jolley had ordered the novel for the university library. 'When I got the book,' he said, 'I thought I was justified in ordering it.'

James Lumsden, a psychologist with a PhD and expertise in literature, sang from the same songsheet, though he added another tune — one about the book's psychological acuity. 'The book has the truth of a tone poem or landscape,' Lumsden said. 'No case-history can be quite like this, but it looks like case-history.' In a claim that would make headlines across Australia, Lumsden argued that *Portnoy's Complaint* had a utility beyond entertainment: 'The book would be of use to a student of psychology. The understanding of the origins of Portnoy's problems would be of assistance to society generally.'

Viner avoided probing this claim, and instead continued his attempts to puncture claims of literary merit. 'What is funny about this?' he asked, after reading out a colourful passage. 'What is poetic about that?'

Eventually, he read out the passage about Portnoy and the liver. Lumsden agreed that it was shocking, but added that it was intended to shock. The tension was then punctured, deliberately, he said, by Portnoy's subsequent comment that the worst thing he had done was to fuck his own family's dinner.

'And what's funny about that?'

Lumsden smiled. 'If you don't think that's funny, I can't help you.'[18]

Subsequent witnesses continued to build the case. Journalist and writer Hal G.P. Colebatch had been convinced to appear at the trial by Dorothy Hewett; despite his subsequent regret at appearing, Colebatch testified that *Portnoy's Complaint* had merit, that it was well written, and that — as a study of one human — it had an 'essential educational function'.[19] The poet Fay Zwicky, who followed Colebatch, argued similarly: she had read the book three times, and thought it a 'work of considerable literary merit, particularly on re-reading'. A psychology lecturer at the University of Western Australia, Arthur 'Jock' Bownes, testified that Roth's psychological mapping of Portnoy's character was valid. 'Extreme behaviour of Portnoy is characteristic of an upbringing such as he had,' he said. 'Going from woman to woman, in a desperate attempt to find his manhood and finding little satisfaction, is a common problem to clinical psychologists.' Bownes echoed Lumsden's claim for the book's utility. He recommended it for students of abnormal psychology; during his cross-examination, he went even further: the novel was 'scientifically valid'.

Ronald Downie, who testified the next day, Thursday 3 December, continued this claim. A clinical psychologist and part-time tutor of English at the Adult Education Board, Downie said that the novel followed 'the line of American literature' that ran from Mark Twain to Hemingway. *Portnoy's Complaint* was about alienation. 'This is today's problem,' he said. 'I find this so as a clinical psychologist.' Downie was emphatic that the profanities were appropriate. 'In clinical practice, one endeavours to allow the client complete freedom of expression. After all, this is the setting of the book … In this book, Portnoy's outpourings seem highly probable. Clients tend to speak without self-censorship, from depths of feelings. It is the only way in which a person can grow therapeutically.' Viewed as a clinical case, he said, *Portnoy's Complaint* had a 'tremendous amount of fidelity'; moreover, for it to have the kind of impact and the truth that he had described, it had to have 'complete literary merit'.

Next came G.M. Glaskin. The author of *No End to the Way* described how he had heard of the novel and had ordered a copy from New Zealand. At the time, he said, it was not on the official list of banned books, and he had been outraged that he had not been permitted to read it. It was only after negotiations with Customs that he was allowed to: he had to read it within one month and, in the company of a customs officer, post it back *out* of Australia.

Viner's cross-examination sought to damage Glaskin's objectivity. Glaskin admitted that he had made his difficulties with Customs public, and that he had spoken about his disagreements with censorship policy. But, Glaskin added, lest the court think otherwise, he did not believe that censorship should be wholly abolished. He believed that people aged sixteen and over should be able to judge for themselves whether to read a book. This view was not out of line with the community, he said. It was a common view.

More and more witnesses followed: Ronald Unger, a reviewer for the *Weekend News*; Kenneth Munro and John MacLaurin, both English schoolteachers; Merv Lilley, a poet and short-story writer; David Ambrose, a classics tutor at the University of Western Australia; and Donald Stuart, a novelist and short-story writer. All testified to much the same point: *Portnoy's Complaint* was a work of literary merit. Roth had bought considerable skill to bear upon it. He had approached his material with serious intent. The language was necessary, and the subject matter was worthy of writing about. It was a convincing book. 'I've felt compassion for many people, in many books,' Stuart testified. 'Portnoy is one for whom I feel utmost compassion.'

The final witness was Dorothy Hewett. A former communist, former wife to Lloyd Davies, and now married to Merv Lilley, Hewett was already the author of a novel — the acclaimed *Bobbin Up* — three plays, and two collections of poetry. She was writing and teaching at the University of Western Australia, and on the stand she lauded *Portnoy* for reasons that were different from those of witnesses who had preceded her, adding another reason to read the novel:

> It is a comment on modern society. It tells more of what it is like to be a Jew and comment on man in his society. Not man the hero or centre of the universe, but man the anti-hero, unable to

cope with the environment he made himself ... [The] value of the novel seems to be, in fact, that it can teach Australians, notorious for their prudery, how to be honest about and with themselves. It should be prescribed reading for all mothers and sons. It is invaluable in a puritan, male-oriented society. It is a novel which helps women to understand men and all of us who live with the disease of sex-hatred.

Viner had no questions for Hewett. And with that, the defence case was closed.

* * *

Malley reserved his decision until the new year. In his judgement, handed down on 18 January 1971, he was forthright about the novel's obscenity. 'Having read the work in question and applying the principles laid down [from a survey of Justice Windeyer's opinion, in *Crowe v Graham*],' he said, 'I have no hesitation in reaching the conclusion that *Portnoy's Complaint* is patently and often nauseatingly obscene.'

Malley brusquely disposed of the facts of the sale of *Portnoy's Complaint*. Broomhall had not contested testimony about the novel being on sale, and her testimony about the limits she had applied on its sale — that is, not selling it to children — was immaterial, given that he had found the novel to be obscene. He moved on to the exemption provided by section 5 of the *Indecent Publications Act*, and its likely definition: 'What constitutes a work of recognised literary merit?'

He had heard the evidence of a large number of witnesses, all of whom were qualified. Although there was considerable variation in their interpretation of *Portnoy's Complaint*, all of them were unanimous that it had literary merit. 'From the positions and qualifications, or by virtue of their own writing skills,' Malley said, 'many of these persons are in a position to pass a considered judgement on the work in question and all have been prepared to put their professional reputation to the test in asserting and therefore recognising the literary merit of this book. No contrary evidence has been tendered, and I therefore conclude that *Portnoy's Complaint* has recognised literary merit within the meaning of section 5 of the Act.'

Malley now paused to interrogate what 'recognised literary merit' meant. Was it the case that the legislature, while enacting section 5, only intended to provide protection for 'old and recognised standard works in which there may be some obscene or mischievous manner'?

If this was the case, the defence might well have failed. No new work, if Malley agreed that this intention was reflected in the law, could ever fall within the purview of section 5, no matter how acclaimed or well received.

But he did not. 'The relevant words of the section appear to me to have a plain and unambiguous meaning,' he said. '… I consider that even though there be a finding that a book is obscene, once it is accepted as having recognised literary merit, then it is exempted from the penal provisions of the Act …

'The complaint therefore fails,' finished Malley, 'and the charge will be dismissed.'[20]

Broomhall and Davies had won. *Portnoy's Complaint* could be sold, legally, in Western Australia.

Broomhall was ecstatic. People were queueing at the doors of the Pioneer Bookshop the next day to purchase copies; within days, the police had trooped in to return the copies they had seized, muttering as they did that there were no hard feelings.[21] Bookshops that had held off from further sales while Broomhall's case was heard had put copies back on sale: 'I've sold about 9,000 in all,' an elated Arthur Williams, of the In Bookshop, told the press, 'and they're still going!'[22] The matter had turned out almost entirely in favour of Broomhall and the Communist Party. At meetings in March, Broomhall and Gandini would be commended for sticking 'their necks out', and the party resolved to use the *Portnoy* profits to renovate the Pioneer 'with wall to wall carpet' to stop it looking like 'a second-hand junk shop'.[23]

Davies, for his part, was especially pleased. He saw the verdict as a decisive rejection of the prosecution's arguments that Western Australia was unwilling to accept the language and frankness of *Portnoy's Complaint*. The isolationism and provincialism implicit in those arguments, he wrote later, had been rejected. There was a 'regional significance' in the verdict, and a national significance, too, he claimed. The outcome in Western Australia had dealt the censorship system 'a heavy kick in the ribs'.[24]

That was certainly true. Though banned in Victoria, and with court action pending elsewhere, *Portnoy's Complaint* was now freely available in two states. Was it possible that this state of affairs could be maintained? What would happen if more states allowed the book's distribution and sale? Prodded by his departmental officials, Don Chipp wrote to the West Australian police minister, James Craig, to find out what the government would do. Would the verdict be appealed? Would it be overturned? 'The recent decision handed down in Perth,' wrote Chipp, 'gives cause for doubts about the practical application of such an agreement [of uniform action on obscene publications] in Western Australia. I would be interested to learn what problems you consider may now arise in attempts by your government to support the scheme of uniform censorship, and whether you can overcome these problems.'[25]

But the West Australians seemed paralysed. Craig was unwilling to appeal the decision, and, although he ordered his department to have the exemption in the act closed off, the impending state election meant that work could not proceed much further.[26] Attention to it would not resume until late in February, when Jerry Dolan was appointed to succeed Craig as police minister after David Brand's Liberal–Country Party government lost office to the Labor Party, led by John Tonkin. It took until May for Dolan to take to cabinet proposals to amend the *Indecent Publications Act*. Changes would include the repeal of section 5 and its replacement with a new section that would, in effect, give protection only to works of 'dated origin' — which would have rendered defenceless any new work found to be obscene. There were also proposed changes to include the possession of obscene material as an offence under section 2, in order to prosecute offenders who would otherwise escape prosecution, and to move jurisdiction of the act to the chief secretary, who otherwise held responsibility for censorship matters in the state.[27] On 1 June, the West Australian cabinet agreed to transfer the jurisdiction of the act to the chief secretary, but otherwise held off on further changes.[28]

The signs of strain in the censorship system were clear. On 9 January, nine days before the verdict had been handed down in Western Australia, Don Chipp had announced that the Literary Review Board had decided to revoke its ban on seven novels by the American writer Henry Miller, including his 1934 novel, *Tropic of Cancer*. Booksellers who had furtively sold copies now moved them from under the counter to above it, and were forthright when asked for their reactions to the news. Bob Gould pointed out that he had already been selling *Cancer* for a long time. Angus & Robertson store manager Ronald Dingley contrasted the treatment of Miller with *Portnoy's Complaint*: 'Miller has been around so long most people have read something of his, despite the ban. He's not contemporary like *Portnoy* is. And Miller is legal now, while *Portnoy* isn't. Once people can buy a book legitimately they lose interest.' That was a point that James Thorburn agreed with: people would buy *Tropic of Cancer* because they could, now — 'But they won't finish it.'[29]

This change, the result of the West Australian trial, and the subsequent scramble to prevent any repetition of that result caused eyes to turn to New South Wales, where plans were still in place to try Angus & Robertson for selling *Portnoy*. Would the trials still go ahead?

Eric Willis was not about to give up the fight. 'I don't know whether the law in Western Australia is the same as in New South Wales,' he said. 'Proceedings here are already before a court and it is no longer a matter for me to decide their future.'[30]

CHAPTER 12

The beginning of the game

The Darlinghurst Courthouse in Sydney was scrupulous, dull, ponderous, and grand. Built in the 1830s, this sandstone block of Doric pillars — Greece revived in the Antipodes — crowned Darlinghurst Hill and lent order to the streets that stemmed from it. Its sweeping driveway, bound on each end by a black wrought-iron fence, flowed into Oxford Street and Taylor Square, seeming to invite Sydney's citizens in; beneath its shallow portico on any given weekday was a democratic mingle of court officials, barristers, witnesses, and half-interested spectators.

What aesthetic appeal it had — and there were those who thought the Doric columns especially fine — lay largely in the exterior. The inside of the courthouse was worn and shabby. The aged, cedar-lined courtrooms had a functional elegance, but dust motes gleamed in the white light from the windows overhead, and the bench was a grim shadow looming at the front of the court, as though to project the state's power. And despite the presence of standing fans to supplement the overtaxed ventilation system, the courthouse in the summer months was near unbearable for its robed, gowned, and bewigged actors.

When the next *Portnoy* trial began, on 2 February 1971, against Angus & Robertson, the summer was at its most severe, a litany of sultry 30-degree days accompanied by afternoon storms. Everyone was hot. The judge looked hot. The prosecutor looked hot. The defence looked hot. The all-male Anglo-Saxon jury looked especially hot. And, as though it might burst into flame and add to that heat, a paperback copy of *Portnoy* was propped on a shelf set across the dock and guarded by an armed police officer.[1]

There was something dangerous about the book. This trial was going to be pivotal. With victories evenly split between the censors and the anti-censorship campaigners; with a jury, for the first time, assembled to hear and decide the matter; and with the most populous state in the country to finally weigh in, the third trial was crucial. For the anti-censorship campaigners, victory would render the schism over *Portnoy* unworkable.[2] It would all but end the matter. 'If you couldn't ban a book in New South Wales,' one of those involved said later, 'it couldn't be banned effectively anywhere.'[3] For the prosecution, victory in New South Wales would represent a major triumph. The tide would be turned; they could go after all of the booksellers who had stocked and sold *Portnoy*; they could ensure that no such stunt ever happened again. The stakes, for both sides, were high.

P.J. 'Jack' Kenny QC, counsel for the Crown, was well aware of this. A short Irish-Australian with a gaunt face, wet, blue eyes, and rimless glasses, Kenny was fifty-eight years old and an antiquity of the New South Wales Bar. He had a standing brief with the Commissioner of Railways, notorious at the Bar, to prosecute for trespass people who had fallen beneath oncoming trains.[4] Indomitable, even brutal, with a theatrical courtroom manner, he was a prosecutor from central casting — a living incarnation of the maxim that common law barristers do not cross-examine but, rather, examine crossly. Canny, cunning, audacious, and blunt, Kenny was dismissive of *Portnoy's Complaint* and the claims that it was a serious literary work. As he and his junior, Robert Vine-Hall, would later write, the book was 'more offensive to generally accepted standards than most pornographic novels'.[5]

But Kenny's objections to *Portnoy* did not blind him to the difficulties that he would encounter in trying to secure a conviction. The first problem he saw was the jury itself. Kenny believed there were two types of people in the community-at-large: first, those who 'confuse[d] freedom of expression' and believed that authors could write about whatever they wanted, in whatever manner they wanted; second, those who believed that banning a pornographic book only fuelled its notoriety and gave it attention, undermining the efforts to minimise harm. 'Both categories tend to regard opposition to censorship in any form as a moral principle to be rigidly adhered to,' Kenny would write, 'and it is extremely probable that in any jury there will be one or more persons falling into one or other of those categories.'[6]

Nonetheless, he set to work undaunted. After the jury selection was over and Angus & Robertson had entered its plea, Kenny opened his case with a sharp, simple address. The case was straightforward. It should take only a week. *Portnoy's Complaint* was an American novel that had been reprinted in Australia as a paperback. It described a young man narrating his sexual experiences to a psychiatrist, and it had been called one of the funniest books ever written about sex. But, Kenny said sharply, this was mere badinage. It was not accurate. 'There are one or two passages dealing with normal sexual relations between men and women, but they don't receive a great deal of attention,' he said. What was important to this trial were the repeated and detailed descriptions of sex that was not normal: 'There are also acts of perversion which, as far as I know, there are no Anglo-Saxon words to describe. The whole of it is described in [the] most coarse and vulgar language which may be regarded in this community as unprintable.'

This was the key point, one that Kenny sought to home in on: a book was obscene if it offended any age group or any other group in the community. The contents of *Portnoy's Complaint* 'deal with sex and go beyond anything accepted in our community. The Crown submits [that] the book transgresses the accepted bounds of decency accepted in this country.'[7] The book was obscene. Its sale, he said, was against the law.

From there, Kenny called the first of his two witnesses: Detective Constable Terrence Mitchell, of the Vice Squad, Criminal Investigation Branch, New South Wales Police.[8]

Kenny's strategy with Mitchell and with Quill, who would follow Mitchell to the stand, was geared toward defeating Angus & Robertson before it had even opened its case. Kenny knew that the defence case would be premised on two points: first, that *Portnoy* was not an obscene publication and that its sale did not, therefore, violate the law; second, that even if the book were obscene, it had literary merit. If this was accepted, Angus & Robertson could avail itself of provisions in the *Obscene and Indecent Publications Act* that allowed vendors to sell an obscene work that was possessed of literary merit. But there was a rider on this: the sale had to be justified. The method of sale had to be responsible. Foreshadowed in the December committal hearings, Kenny knew he had to tackle this point, to pre-empt it. Thus, after having Mitchell detail how he had purchased a copy of *Portnoy*, Kenny asked about the people in the queue ahead of him. Was there anyone inappropriate in the queue? Anyone who managed to purchase a copy who should not have? A schoolgirl, perhaps?

'Directly in front of me there was a girl,' Mitchell testified. 'I would say she would have been about sixteen years of age and she was dressed in a school uniform.'

'Do you remember the details of the uniform?'

'Yes, from memory it was a navy-blue uniform, she had on a blazer and black shoes with white socks, and she was carrying a Globite case in her right hand.'

'She was immediately in front of you?'

'She was directly in front,' Mitchell said.

There it was: Angus & Robertson had irresponsibly and unjustifiably allowed an obscene publication to come into the hands of a minor. This was the point to which Kenny guided Mitchell's testimony, and the fact that he sought to fix in the minds of the jury members.

The only hiccups came when humour intruded on proceedings. When Mitchell, at Kenny's prompting, began to describe other people in the queue, he became snagged on the details of a young man standing in front of the girl. 'He looked to be about twenty years of age,' Mitchell said. 'He was of a hippie appearance. He was dressed in a blue —'

The defence interrupted, objecting to the pejorative of *hippie*. Justice Alfred Goran QC — a wry, quizzical, and owlish judge who had studied law at night while working as a teacher, and then become one of the top criminal law barristers in the state before being raised to the bench in 1965 — sought clarification.[9] 'It depends what he means,' he said drily. 'I suppose a hippie person is a person with large hips.'

'Is that what you mean?' asked Kenny, as laughter bubbled in the galleries.

'No,' Mitchell replied, 'he was of an untidy appearance, sir.'

Now William Deane QC rose to begin the cross-examination. Notwithstanding that he was then forty years old, Deane was still in the early days of a glittering career. A graduate of the University of Sydney and the Hague Academy of International Law, Deane had been called to the Bar in 1957, when he was twenty-six, and been appointed Queen's Counsel only nine years later.[10] The perception, intellect, and legal skills he showed were considerable: the president of the New South Wales Bar Association would later say that Deane 'absolutely dominated' the Bar during this period.[11] Later to become a High Court judge and then governor-general, Deane was a heavyweight lawyer, 'the barrister of choice', said one colleague.[12]

But he was also a somewhat unusual choice for the defence. Given that he was a Catholic and former, if very short-lived, member of the socially conservative Democratic Labor Party (DLP), there might well have been bemusement at the thought of Deane defending a novel about a sex-crazed American Jew. Deane was aware of this, as a joking remark to Reginald Barrett in the months before the trial suggested: 'Don't forget to tell them that your leading counsel is a conservative Irish Catholic.'[13] There were also questions over whether his practice — generally as an equity lawyer — was broad enough to succeed in a criminal law matter. But there were good reasons for his selection: in addition to his intellect and skills, Deane's manner would make for a marked contrast to Kenny. Eloquent and gentlemanly, he was ideally suited to mount arguments about artistic merit, civility, and obscenity.[14]

His skill was on show with his cross-examination of Mitchell. Reasonably, but in great detail, Deane took the detective through the visit to Angus & Robertson. He had Mitchell admit the responsible and unobtrusive way in which Angus & Robertson had sold the book. There was no sign announcing that one could buy *Portnoy's Complaint*, no notice in the window, no copy on display. The premises were large, the counter at which Mitchell had purchased *Portnoy* was at the very back, and the people purchasing *Portnoy* did so without even seeing it.

Then Deane moved to the schoolgirl. For the benefit of the jury, he asked whether Mitchell made any record in his notebook of this visit.

'No, I didn't.'

'Did you make any record yourself at all of this visit?'

'Not in my notebook; in my official diary there would be a record of having attended the store.'

'Were there any details of what happened?'

'No.'

The facts were catalogued: Mitchell made his statement about what had happened in the shop the day after, and he and Quill had collaborated on these notes. Deane drew a link between Mitchell's and Quill's reconstruction of the purchase and their evidence about the girl. Did they think her presence was significant? Did they think her relevant to the purpose of their visit? Did they think her age important? Did they take a particular note of her age? Did they ask the girl her age?

'No, I had no conversation with her,' Mitchell said.

Deane asked if the detectives were familiar with the practice of leaving a note on someone's car to alert them that they were to be charged with a parking offence. 'The purpose of that,' he explained, 'is as a matter of ordinary fairness when somebody is going to be charged with an offence, it is customary in this community, it is possible, to give them an opportunity of knowing the circumstances surrounding the event with which they are going to be charged?'

'Yes, that is correct.'

So, Deane went on, it was true that Angus & Robertson was unaware of the detectives' visit — indeed, that was the point of the visit, wasn't it? Moreover, once Angus & Robertson had sold the book to Mitchell, was it not the case that Mitchell and Quill left it until the next day to inform the store that it had, potentially, committed a criminal offence, thereby depriving it of the opportunity to check, follow up, or even defend itself?

The suggestion that the detectives had been underhanded was allowed to hang in the air, a wispy possibility.

Deane moved on. Was Mitchell aware that it was the school holidays at the time of his visit to Angus & Robertson? Did he have an answer to why a girl would wear her school uniform during the school holidays? 'Didn't it surprise you that a schoolgirl of about this age would be, in school holidays, actually wearing the school uniform and carrying a Globite bag?'

Mitchell, a tad unconvincingly, sought to be stoic: 'No, it didn't.'

Deane suggested that the detectives had been mistaken. Did Mitchell know that the uniforms worn by female employees of the Commonwealth Bank, the NRMA, and the Bank of New

South Wales were similar to his description? Was he certain that it was a school uniform? Was he certain it was a *particular* school's uniform?

'No, I had no idea what school it belonged to.'

Now Deane ceased his overly credulous questions. 'See, Detective, so there can be no mistake about it,' he said, 'I suggest to you that this sixteen-year-old schoolgirl is a figment of your imagination.'

* * *

When Quill took the stand he was far more definitive about the existence of the girl. Under Kenny's questioning, he described her clothing in detail — a navy tunic dress, a blazer, black shoes, white socks, and a brown bag. With apparent certainty, he identified her school: Fort Street Girls' High School.

Deane probed this evidence closely. How did Quill know that it was the uniform of Fort Street Girls' High School, he asked. Quill had testified in the committal hearing that he had no idea what school the girl was from. That was correct, wasn't it? How could he now be so certain? 'As I understand it, what you now tell the gentlemen of the jury is that you purport to identify the school by saying that you subsequently had a closer look at some other uniform?'

'That is true,' Quill said.

'A closer look than the look you had had on the original occasion at Angus & Robertson?'

'That is right.'

'And you found out from the wearer of that uniform at which you had a closer look what school it was, is that so?'

'A closer look showed me that the name of the school was written on the crest of the badge.'

'But of course you could not see the name of the school on the blazer of the girl you saw in Angus & Robertson?'

'Not where I was standing, no.'

'You did not see it?'

'I saw the badge, yes,' said Quill. 'I could not read the writing.'

Deane noted again that Quill and Mitchell had not informed Angus & Robertson of their visit until the next day, that they had done nothing to inform Angus & Robertson that they had sold *Portnoy* to a minor, and that both men had failed to record information about the visit in their notebooks — even about the girl. And, again, Deane pointed out that they had visited the store during the school holidays. 'Would you agree with me that the first thing the average sixteen-year-old schoolgirl does when holidays come round is to put the uniform away until school goes back in?' Turning Quill's certainty and use of detail against him, Deane also pointed out that the uniform Quill had described was the summer uniform for Fort Street Girls' High School — not the winter uniform, which would have been in use in August.

At this, like a cockroach flipped onto its back, Quill was helpless. Then Deane had him describe how he had decided that the girl was from Fort Street Girls' High School. It had happened on a bus, a few days later, Quill explained. He had noticed a girl who had the same badge on her blazer as the girl in Angus & Robertson. 'The wording on the second girl's blazer was merely *Fort Street*.'

Eventually, Deane stopped. 'So that there can be no doubt about this, what I am suggesting to you is that this Fort Street High School girl is an absolute invention.'

'That is entirely wrong,' said Quill.

'And I am suggesting to you that at no stage did you see any girl in school uniform on 31 August or on any other day being sold a copy of the book *Portnoy's Complaint*.'

Quill sought to be stoic: 'What I have said is true.'

But he was blowing in the wind. How — if the detectives did not speak to the girl — did they establish that she was sixteen? Who suggested that she was? How did they agree? How did they reconstruct all this? Would it be true to say that the supposed age of the girl was 'the result of an agreed state of affairs' between Quill and Mitchell?

'Yes.'

'Is that the way that you and members of the police force working with you normally prepare accounts as to —?'

'Yes, men working together, naturally.'

'What — agree together as to what the situation was?'

'Well, if there is any dispute it would be ironed out.'

But then another, plainly disconcerted voice broke in. 'How do you do that?' asked Judge Goran.

'Well,' said Quill, turning, 'if I said the chap looked twenty and Mitchell said he looked thirty, he would have to stick with that.'

'But that is not ironing it out,' Goran said. 'That is an agreement to differ. Do you agree to differ?'

'No.'

'You do not?'

'No,' said Quill.

To this, Deane noted that 'ironing things out' and refusing to agree to differ removed the possibility that conflicting evidence could be given in the witness box; moreover, the clandestine nature of the detectives' visit to Angus & Robertson, as well as their failure to alert staff at the store to the alleged sale of *Portnoy's Complaint* to a minor, meant that there was no possible way to check their evidence. What reason was there for this? What, after all, had there been to stop the detectives from identifying themselves? What reason could they have had for not speaking with the girl, and establishing the vital details about her?

Quill stonewalled, but Goran was so unimpressed that he continued to interrupt and press for answers. 'Why could you not have asked her when she went out of the shop, "Would you mind telling me how old you are?"' he asked Quill. 'How would that have affected your whole case?'

'I can only say if we had done that we would have been trying to get the name and address of every person we saw buying the book.'

'What was to stop you asking her name?' Deane asked.

Finally, Quill gave up: 'Nothing.'

* * *

At the time of the *Portnoy* trial in New South Wales, David Marr was a twenty-three-year-old articled clerk employed by Allen Allen & Hemsley. Though soon to leave the law for a career in journalism, Marr had been plucked out of the clerks' room by instructing solicitor Hugh Jamieson to serve as the dogsbody for the defence team. His job was to herd and brief witnesses, relay messages, and cart files and documents about. Though potentially dreary, he found instead that the work was absorbing, exciting. *Portnoy's Complaint*, he thought, was 'fabulous — just completely wonderful', and his involvement in the defence of it was cause for considerable pride. 'I had read all the stuff about the *Lady Chatterley* case,' he said later, 'and I had no doubt that with *Portnoy* we were doing something important. The firm knew it. So did Penguin. So did Angus & Robertson. This case mattered. It was the best thing I did in my — admittedly, short — legal career.'[15]

It would also offer instruction in litigation tactics. When he arrived at the courthouse that morning, Marr had noticed that parked in the driveway was a hire car in which a woman sat in the back, waiting.

Evelyn McEwan, the principal of Fort Street Girls' High School, had been subpoenaed by Allen Allen & Hemsley to testify. Under questioning, the defence believed, McEwan would blow apart the police claims that one of her students had purchased the book. She would point out that it was during the school holidays; that students would hardly wear a uniform that they did not need to; and that it was completely the wrong uniform in use at the time. 'I was all for calling her to the stand,' Marr said later. He thought McEwan would be a lethal witness, exposing the police claims about a schoolgirl for what they were: brazen inventions and lies. 'So I was saying, "Call her! Call her! When are we going to call her?"'

But Deane, Masterman, and Jamieson had begun to rethink the idea of calling McEwan to the stand. Yes, McEwan would undoubtedly do them much good under questioning. Yes, she would easily be able to scotch the police claims. But what about the cross-examination? What might happen then? What would Kenny ask her? And what might she say in response?

'She would be invited to condemn *Portnoy's Complaint*,' said Marr. 'And, as the headmistress of a girls' school, she would almost certainly accept the invitation to put the boot into it.'

The danger was obvious; the question was stark. Was the damage that McEwan might do to the prosecution's case worth the damage she would do to the defence's?

Wiser heads prevailed. 'It was an early lesson for me,' said Marr. 'There are dangers you don't run, questions you don't allow the other side to ask.' Deane, Masterman, and Jamieson opted to be satisfied with the cross-examinations of Mitchell and Quill. They had punched crucial holes in the police testimony; those would suffice.

Word was sent out to McEwan. She would not be called to testify. The hire car and its silent passenger were sent away.

* * *

The time had come for the jury to read the book. Deane, doubtless with an eye to the effects of reading the novel among the realities of family life, lobbied for jurors to take the book home. 'We would submit that that jury would be in a much better situation to form a view of this book if they were permitted to take it to their homes and read it in the ordinary comforts of their home where a book like this is read, rather than to read it in the uncomfortable and barren atmosphere of the jury room.'

Justice Goran was sympathetic, but refused. 'I think I am going to be unpopular, but I must do this,' he said. 'I am going to ask the jury to read it in what you call the *uncomfortable and particularly barren* atmosphere of the jury room.'

There would be a two-day adjournment in proceedings. Jurors would attend court the next day, Wednesday 3 February, and read *Portnoy's Complaint* in the jury room. They could have all the time that they might require. 'Take your time about it,' said Goran. However, he went on, jurors needed to remember that they had not yet heard all the evidence. The defence would make its case next, and there might yet be further evidence from the Crown. Then there would be closing addresses, and he too would sum up. Do not make conclusions before all the evidence has been heard, he instructed. Suspend your judgement, he said. 'You have only seen the beginning of the game.'

CHAPTER 13

The subject of expert evidence

Deane had opened his defence before the jury had begun reading the book. He dismissed the schoolgirl from consideration: she was only relevant if the jury decided that literature should be of a standard suitable for a sixteen-year-old — and 'God forbid for the sake of English literature *that* situation could arise'.[1] The bigger point was that *Portnoy's Complaint* was not an obscene work. The passages of sex and immorality were neither pornographic, depraving, nor corrupting. 'You might find some of the sexual references a trifle disgusting, and not in the best of taste,' Deane said, 'but they do not titillate and could never encourage perversion or anything else.' Far from obscene, the novel was a work of literature, with considerable merit. The defence would prove this, Deane said, 'through the mouths of witnesses who would carry weight; witnesses whose names were bywords in the literary world'.[2] Thus, on the afternoon of Thursday 4 February, Deane called Harry Heseltine to the stand.

Heseltine was almost tailor-made for the case. An associate

professor at the University of New South Wales, a Fulbright and Carnegie scholar, he had pronounced expertise on American literature, and opposed censorship. He had testified in defence of the *Oz* editors — Richard Neville had been a student of his — in 1964, and he had much sympathy for what Penguin was doing with *Portnoy*.[3] 'Well, it just seemed to me the thing one had to do,' he said later, of his decision to appear. 'If you were supposed to know something about literature, particularly American literature, and you believe that the book had merit, you should be prepared to get up publicly and say so.'[4]

Kenny was aware that Heseltine was a dangerous witness: he could define the discussion of literary merit for the trial, and offer a clear and credible argument for its existence in *Portnoy*. So, when Deane invited Heseltine to detail the literary merits of *Portnoy's Complaint*, the prosecutor objected, arguing that this had to be determined by the jury, and that evidence on this matter by experts was opinion — and therefore not admissible as evidence.

'Your basic objection to this evidence is that expert evidence — as to the opinion of the expert on the literary merit — cannot be given at all?' asked an incredulous Justice Goran. 'It is not just the question that has been asked, but the fact that the evidence cannot be given at all?'

'Yes,' Kenny replied, 'it is not the subject of expert evidence.'

It was the first indication of Kenny's perspicacity — and it succeeded.[5] After a long exchange with Kenny, Goran sustained the objection, ruling that witnesses first had to affirm and describe objective standards of literary merit before applying them to *Portnoy*. It created an immediate obstacle for the jury: they would have to understand those standards first to make any sense of how they applied in *Portnoy*. The effect was instantaneous. When Deane asked Heseltine to identify the recognised criteria for determining whether a book had literary merit, Heseltine split the question: first, into a test of establishing whether a work was literary; second, whether it had merit.

He was prepared to state that literature could not be defined by its subject matter; it depended on 'the use of the language [that] is brought to bear by the authors choosing the subject'. As for merit, Heseltine argued that it was demonstrable if the 'verbal model' of human behaviour used in response to the subject matter — that is, the language the author brought to bear upon the subject — was shown to have 'consistency and coherence'.

'In light of what you have said,' Deane asked, 'is this work in your view a work of literature?'

Yes, said Heseltine.

And did the use of vulgar language, four-letter words, and crude situations detract from the work's literariness, or its merit?

No, said Heseltine. They were essential. To remove them from the book would be akin to 'cutting the lines of the Prince of Denmark from the play *Hamlet*'.

Deane referred him to a passage describing the sexual fantasy of the Monkey's first husband: a black woman would shit on a glass table beneath which he masturbated, all in view of the Monkey, who was to drink cognac and watch from the remove of a red damask sofa. Did this detract from the novel's literary merit?

Heseltine was unambiguous: no, it did not.

* * *

Kenny was aware that success for his side required his discrediting of the defence claims about the literary merit of *Portnoy's Complaint*. How should he do so? The previous tactics adopted by Flanagan and Viner — emphasising the four-letter words, reading aloud the licentious passages to evince a cringe from the witness — had hardly been shown to be a sure-fire way to secure a conviction. What should he do?

Kenny answered that with an eye to the jury. Resourcefully and shrewdly, he formulated tactics predicated on playing to the twelve silent men assembled in the jury box. First, he aimed to make Heseltine look grubby by suggesting that his diagnosis of Portnoy and the Monkey — as 'two mutually inadequate people' — stemmed from a skewered view of sexual deviancy. Citing the passage Deane had referred to, Kenny asked Heseltine if he regarded it as a 'moral offence'.

'I regard it as morally and physically unpleasant,' said Heseltine.

'Do you regard it as a matter of moral guilt?'

'I regard all the sexual deviances in this book as objects of pity.'

'If you take a man who squats on a table and behaves in this manner in front of his wife, do you find him incurring any moral guilt?'

'Moral disapprobation, perhaps.'

'Disapprobation means disapproval?'

Heseltine rephrased it: 'What do you mean by guilt?'

To these deflections, Kenny began to strain: has he done anything wrong? Is this unnatural? Would you agree that what Portnoy has done is against the natural law?

But Heseltine calmly quoted the Roman playwright Terence: 'Nihil humani mihi alienum puto.' *I find nothing that is human is alien to me.* 'It is possible,' he continued, 'to disapprove and react in moral shame and horror but still feel compassion, and I think this is what Philip Roth is doing in the book.' He felt compassion for all those involved, he said — the Monkey, her husband, and the black woman fantasised about.

To this, Kenny moved to a different line: he suggested that Heseltine was too intellectual a reader to be representative of the public. Heseltine had a ready response: 'We would have to compare IQ.'

Kenny moved on again, engaging Heseltine on what literary merit meant, and suggesting that at crucial points *Portnoy* did not live up to the standards of literature. Roth had not written *everything* of the character of Portnoy, and the book was therefore deficient, he suggested. Citing a fleeting reference to a quiz-show scandal in the 1950s, Kenny said it had been dealt with far too quickly, and that Portnoy's failure to speak more about it was a flaw in the work.

'If I go to a doctor to treat a big toe,' Heseltine replied, 'I don't necessarily tell him that I teach English.'

Finally, Kenny took up Heseltine's description of the purpose of literature: 'the enrichment of human understanding'. He set up a question he could be sure would linger in the minds of the jury. 'So, if any work of writing, any piece of writing, is to be literature, it will have enlightened our understanding of some problem?'

'It if has literary merit, yes,' Heseltine said.

Did *Portnoy's Complaint* enlighten or enrich understanding of human nature? Or was it an exercise in filth and depravity that offered nothing to anyone? Those questions hung over the court, until Deane, moving to re-examine, asked Heseltine what he would say of *Portnoy's Complaint*.

'I would say that it has literary merit and it has enriched my understanding of certain aspects of human behaviour and would therefore, I hope,' said Heseltine, 'contribute to the moral quality of my own life.'

* * *

Testimony from the literary witnesses was interspersed with evidence from Angus & Robertson's employees to rebut the evidence about the sixteen-year-old schoolgirl. Ronald Dingley, the manager of the Castlereagh Street store, testified about the circumstances in which *Portnoy* had been sold.

Deane was careful to emphasise the schoolgirl. 'When was the first occasion that you heard the suggestion that this book had been sold to a sixteen-year-old schoolgirl?' he asked.

'I think I read it in the paper first, sir.'

And when was that?

'Long after the sale of the book.'

Kenny focused on attempting to demonstrate that Angus &

Robertson's sale of *Portnoy* had been irresponsible. He cited the restrictions that the bookseller had taken while selling the book, and turned them back on the defence. All of those measures, he pointed out, were exceptional: no other book had been kept from the shelves, kept under a counter, or placed directly in a bag when it was purchased. Didn't that suggest what Angus & Robertson thought of the book?

It was an effective line, and one that Kenny underscored — testing the licence of the court as he did — by asking Dingley to confirm that *Portnoy* had been banned by Customs. It was a way of sneaking in the information; unsurprisingly, Deane objected.

Goran scolded Kenny: 'The question should never have been asked.' But Kenny's combativeness and lack of deference to the bench led him to protest. Goran cut across him immediately: 'You are very experienced in these matters. You occupy a particular position in this court, and I am saying you should never have asked that question.'

Kenny bowed his head and moved on. He put to Dingley that *Portnoy* could be loaned, resold, or circulated in libraries after it had been purchased from Angus & Robertson. Once unleashed, he seemed to suggest, *Portnoy* could spread like a virus, infectious and uncontrolled.

It seemed a good point. But Dingley dismissed it. It would be a waste of time for people to buy *Portnoy* and resell it, he said. The book cost only $1.35. 'They would not make much money if they bought them from us and resold them.'

* * *

The following week saw Kenny stepping up his attacks, and Goran stepping in to push for clarity and specificity. This became acute during the testimony given by Barbara Jefferis, a novelist and book reviewer. She had testified that *Portnoy* had literary merit for its possession of emotional truth. It added to 'our knowledge and understanding of human nature', she said, and was a 'beautifully written' book with profanities that were realistic and fitting.

Goran pushed Jefferis on this. Why did this constitute literary merit?

'I didn't intend to imply that the things you mentioned make it so,' Jefferis replied. 'The thing that makes it a work of literary merit is this deep understanding of the central character and his very real plight.'

So, Goran went on, what is presented is a convincing human being? And it is that which makes *Portnoy* a work of literary merit?

'Yes,' said Jefferis.

Goran's questioning gave Kenny his most audacious line of attack: discrediting literary merit as a concept altogether, portraying it as subjective and arbitrary, even negligible. As he would later argue, the phrase as inserted in the act had no commonly accepted meaning. There were 'as many views [on its meaning] amongst persons purporting to be experts [on literary merit] as there are persons'.[6] Discrediting those views would require him to lock horns with the defence witnesses on the territory of their expertise — but where Ian Viner had shied away, Kenny was bold.

He bombarded Jefferis with questions about the distinctions between literature and merit, boxing her in and always reducing her caveated answers to absolutes. When she said that the distinctions were difficult, and that his definitions were unclear, he barked that he was talking about her definition: 'I said according to your definition, not mine. Don't worry about mine. According to your definition of *literature* there is no literature which is not meritorious literature, using your definition of the word.'

Eventually, Goran intervened to impose order. Take the books generally called 'pot-boilers', he said to Jefferis. Using your definition, would you regard them as having literary merit? Would you put a James Bond or a Mickey Spillane novel into the same category as *Portnoy's Complaint?* What was the difference?

Jefferis obliged. Those were formulaic novels. They had been put together to sell. 'It is usually a more commercial operation, and has very little to do with what a serious novelist is trying to do in making a book.'

Was *Portnoy's Complaint* written to a formula, Kenny asked. Was it not the case that the pornographic elements had been included to aid commercial success?

Jefferis took exception to this. *Portnoy's Complaint* was not pornographic: the depiction of sex had a deliberate artistic purpose. A serious writer, she argued, begins a book with a theme, with 'some pressing thing that he feels he has to say'. The writer devises a framework — essentially, a plot — to deliver that theme.

In offering this, Jefferis had opened a door for Kenny. He could use Jefferis — and did — to suggest that Roth had made a deliberate decision to write an obscene work, thinly guised as literature, in order to generate controversy and drive sales. 'So you think, then,' he said, drippingly, 'we may look forward to other novels in which this device will be freely used?'

Kenny continued this sarcasm and scorn when Cyril Pearl came to the stand. A longtime activist and agitator, Pearl had been a founding member of the Book Censorship Abolition League, and had campaigned during World War II against the federal government's attempts to enforce censorship of the press.[7] Now a grand old man of letters, he sprinkled his evidence with literary references and humour. His view of literary merit, he testified, stemmed from James Joyce: 'The supreme question about a work of art is out of how deep a life has it sprung.' One could read Joyce or Spillane, and sense Joyce's 'greater feeling for life' and 'deeper appreciation'. *Portnoy's Complaint* had that sense, and bore evidence of extraordinary technical skill, particularly in its form and content. As for its profanities, Pearl was not concerned: 'A number of great writers have used them, from Chaucer to Shakespeare.'

Kenny's cross-examination quickly diverged from *Portnoy* into how Pearl had come to participate in the trial. Who had approached him, Kenny asked. Had he discussed the book beforehand? Kenny was sceptical of Pearl's calm answers. 'Suddenly,' he scoffed, 'out of the blue last week, you got a letter asking you to give evidence?'

'Not out of the blue — out of the postbox,' Pearl replied, to chuckles.

Kenny was indomitable. He submitted to Goran that Pearl was so biased that his testimony was compromised. But Pearl evaded this. To questions on whether he would allow novels to be sold indiscriminately, whether he would allow books containing sex to be available to adolescents, and whether there should be restrictions on the sale of novels with sexual elements, Pearl repeatedly sought more information. Finally, Kenny simply barked, 'Where do you draw the line?'

'I do not draw the line,' said Pearl. 'That is for Mr Chipp [the Customs minister] to do.'

Kenny had to move on. He demanded to know whether Pearl's opinion of *Portnoy* derived from whether or not he liked it. Pearl's answer — that this was the ultimate position, but that it was buttressed by reasoned criticism — delighted Kenny, but flummoxed Goran. He took over the cross-examination to ask whether, when people reported favourable opinions of *Hamlet*, they were ultimately saying simply that they liked it.

Yes, said Pearl.

What about students at school and university, Goran asked. Is the ultimate aim of all that education, the expertise of all those tutors and lecturers, just to have students say whether or not they like a play like *Hamlet*?

'Unfortunately,' Pearl replied, 'they do not like it at school.'

'Some people come to the conclusion it is great literature,' Goran huffed, perhaps thinking of his time as a schoolteacher. His final question was plaintive: 'Is ultimately what they say, "I like it?"'

Pearl shrugged. 'As you like it, Your Honour.'

Nancy Keesing was next. A poet and longtime reviewer for the *Bulletin*, Keesing was no stranger to *Portnoy's Complaint*. Thanks to her husband, a friend from England, and Allen Allen & Hemsley, she possessed three copies of the novel.[8] Much like Barbara Jefferis, Keesing appeared a respectable housewife, a point that Deane emphasised with his first question: 'Your main occupation these days would probably be described as domestic duties?'

Yes, Keesing said — but went on to argue with force and clarity that *Portnoy* made the reader see the world in a 'fresh and new way', and, on the basis of its characterisation, form, style, content, and language, had considerable literary merit.

Kenny continued his assault on the concept of literary merit. He put to Keesing a hypothetical: we stand in a stream with literature on one bank, and non-literature on the other bank. 'How do you go about determining what you put on the left-hand bank as literature? What is it you apply? What is the test?' Could he take it, Kenny went on, that there was no universally accepted test determining on which side of the stream a work should belong?

Keesing admitted that there was not. She was certain that *Portnoy's Complaint* was literature and possessed literary merit, but there were works that she would puzzle over when faced with this question.

Then came Paul Grainger, manager of the Angus & Robertson paperback section, and the man who had sold *Portnoy's Complaint* to police. He answered questions quickly and clearly. Yes, he had been selling *Portnoy* on 31 August 1970. No, he did not sell a copy to any schoolgirl. No, he did not sell a copy to any girl in any school uniform. He did not sell it to *anyone* who he or the staff thought might have been under eighteen years of age. 'I had explicit instructions from the manager of the store,' Grainger said, and he had stuck to those instructions. Like Dingley, Grainger testified that he had heard about the supposed existence of this girl a month after the detectives visited.

Kenny used his cross-examination to remind the jury how quickly Angus & Robertson had sold the book, and to suggest the impossibility of its strict control of who had bought a copy. Selling

100 copies in forty-five minutes — 'Yes,' said Grainger — was something over two a minute, wasn't it? And 500 copies in 150 minutes — 'Yes,' said Grainger — was something over three per minute, wasn't it?

Yes, Grainger said.

There was no point changing what had happened, Grainger said later. *Portnoy* had sold well. Why lie about that? It might not sound good, but that was what had happened. 'I thought the most fatal thing to do would be to make changes to the story,' he said later. 'So I told them what happened.' But he was not worried. What Grainger had seen of the defence left him confident. They were in control.[9]

* * *

Deane, Masterman, and Jamieson had been conscious of the need to call a variety of witnesses. Like the defence in Victoria, they wanted a mix of youthful experts and grey eminences. They especially wanted women. Calling Jefferis and Keesing was but a start. They had convinced Maureen Colman to reappear, and had approached Margaret Harris, a lecturer in English at the University of Sydney, who also agreed. Harris in turn suggested they also approach Maria Szewcow, a tutor in English at Sancta Sophia College at the University of Sydney. The defence team were delighted with this prospect: a witness from the Catholic women's residential college would be living proof that *Portnoy* did not corrupt or deprave. 'In this quest for youth and virtue,' Harris asked, wryly, 'what could be more virtuous than a tutor from Sancta Sophia?'[10]

Szewcow came to court on Tuesday 9 February, and argued that *Portnoy* was 'an important document about contemporary literature, perhaps about contemporary experience'. It was morally and psychologically acute — a study of a 'nervous, insecure, self-conscious, self-aware individual, very critical of himself, tremendously worried, an anxious kind of character'. The novel was part of a contemporary American tradition, she said, similar to works by Saul Bellow, Norman Mailer, and even Samuel Beckett.

'In case one or two members of the jury do not know the names of the authors you have mentioned, are all those authors of a high standing?'

'Yes,' said Szewcow.

Kenny was rough with Szewcow. Privately, he was to be scornful of her and the other young women witnesses. While there were some with 'high literary qualifications', he wrote later, there were also some with nothing more than a degree in Arts. 'But in these latter cases they were mainly of the female sex,' he added, 'and had allied to their degrees good looks or charm, and an association with young people as teachers or tutors.'[11]

David Marr, who watched witnesses in between shepherding them into and out of the courtroom, recalled how this dim regard manifested itself. 'Kenny's voice — this great Australian nasal artillery — was designed to cut witnesses down to size. It was a blast of scorn that he directed across the court.' Kenny barraged them with questions, jabbing his index finger at them accusatorily, to impugn their reputability as though they had done all that Portnoy had done. That finger — so vivid and so prominent, at times, that it seemed to Marr to have another joint — was relentless. 'He would point it at the witnesses as he berated them,' Marr said. It was a form of indictment, intimidating and unsubtle. 'It wasn't subtle at all.'[12]

In the trial, Kenny railed at Szewcow, seeking to embarrass her and then to find moral fault with her. He read at length a passage that described Portnoy having sex with the Monkey and an Italian prostitute:

Into whose hole, into what *sort* of hole, I deposited my final load is entirely a matter for conjecture. It could be that in the end I wound up fucking some dank, odoriferous combination of sopping Italian pubic hair, greasy American buttock, and absolutely rank bedsheet.

He demanded: 'Do you regard that as coarse or not coarse?'

He did not let up when Maureen Colman came to the stand. Kenny seemed 'very primitive' and 'outraged' by the book, she said later, and he dripped contempt for both it and her. He seemed to want to 'terrify' her for testifying.[13] To her statement that there must be some evidence of 'moral concern' in a work of literary merit, Kenny snorted and asked what the moral concern of *Portnoy* was. To her answer that it was the relationship between parents and children, he scoffed: '*That* is the matter of serious moral concern? What does it tell us about this situation?' In response to her explanation, he simplified it: 'He tells us people brought up in this way have difficulties?'

On and on it went. When Colman suggested that a reader might understand and even forgive Portnoy for his promiscuity, Kenny lampooned her: 'The understanding which is enlarged then is the understanding about why a man in America somewhere goes on from one woman to another and is not satisfied with the individual relationship?'

The reduction and sarcasm annoyed Colman, and prompted her to push back. She described Portnoy's relationship with the Monkey, and pointed out that the story of the West Point officers that Kenny was dismissing went to the heart of their relationship. Against her detail and command, Kenny's scorn became smoke and bluster. When Colman finished, Marr congratulated her: 'That was terrific!' he said. 'You were good!'

'He was very pleased with me,' Colman explained later, 'because I had stood up to that bloke.'[14]

But Kenny was dogged. After a short appearance from novelist and short-story writer Dal Stivens, Margaret Harris came to the stand and delivered what she later called 'standard lit-crit' arguments about *Portnoy*.[15] Aged twenty-nine and an expert on

Victorian novels, Harris's answers were clear and comprehensible, and prompted Goran to ask his own searching questions. It was a mark of Harris's credibility and the gravity of her evidence that, when it came time to cross-examine, Kenny treated her much as he had Heseltine. He first implied that Harris was too fine a reader to be representative: would the public understand the puns and humour that she described? Then he suggested that she might be grubby for finding the instances of humour funny: 'Do you think the account of the incident involving the black woman on the table funny?'

He next sought to take a hatchet to literary merit. Wasn't this merely the way that an author uses words?

Goran, too, pressed for answers on this. What about scenes? What about characters? What about events and conflict? 'Are those part of what you look for in literary merit?' To Harris's cautious yes, with caveats, Goran had to extrapolate: 'It is a matter of taking the bricks and building certain buildings?'

'Yes.'

'It is a matter of the skill with which he uses words for various purposes?' asked Kenny, seizing the moment.

'Yes.'

'Literary merit has nothing to do with anything other than skill with words?'

'Basically —'

But Kenny cut her off: 'Yes.'

'No,' Harris said, but the prosecutor was moving on.

'Of course, the ultimate test,' Kenny said, 'is it not, is whether the reader appreciates that the work has merit?' He steadily built his argument that Harris was too scrupulous a reader. Some readers might see the merit and some might not, he said. Those who did would need to have read with 'close care'. But this was not the only way to read, was it?

Harris's fine distinctions were repeatedly brushed over, made general, but finally she stopped Kenny dead: 'This is a sort of process that I referred to earlier in saying that the literary critic, in chipping down the wall and looking at the different bricks and way the mortar is being used, is perhaps doing only in slow motion, with a greater intensity, the kind of thing — and perhaps greater capacity — the kind of thing any reader is doing in making sense of the words on the page before him.'

* * *

Harris was still being cross-examined when Patrick White arrived at the courthouse the next day, on a 'deadly steaming' Sydney morning, to repeat his defence of *Portnoy*. Thinking that White needed to be entertained, Hugh Jamieson called Marr over: 'Would you go outside and keep Patrick calm?'

But White needed no nursing. Aware of Marr's own nervousness, the novelist was sweetness and light. He passed the time in the corridors by telling his future biographer stories about the kids at Centennial Park, where White lived. He had spied them biting the heads of day-old chicks, he said. It was a fiction, as Marr would discover, but it filled in the time.[16]

White was not enthusiastic about repeating his appearance. He had become tired of *Portnoy*. 'I find the whole business rather boring by now,' he wrote to Geoffrey Dutton, 'but thought I'd better agree to do it as I've been so consistent in refusing A[ngus] and R[obertson] everything they want.'[17] However true his reluctance, White again brought immense prestige to the stand. Of all the witnesses to appear at the Sydney trial, his was the most anticipated and the most dramatic. Standing aloof in his heavy Prince of Wales check suit and drawling in his patrician's voice, White repeated the best of his Victorian performance.

Yes, he was a novelist. Yes, he had written *Voss* and *The Vivisector*, and yes, he had written some plays. No, he did not like his poetry to be mentioned in the same breath as his novels: 'I try to forget about that.'

Asked to describe the criteria that would establish whether a novel had literary merit, White replied that he could define what he looked for in a novel: for his sense of reality to be heightened, for there to be style — anything from 'limpid simplicity to elaborate ornamentation' — and for a work to be durable and to withstand multiple readings. Characterisation was another important point.

'In *Portnoy's Complaint*,' said Deane, 'the words *fuck, cunt, prick* and that type of word are frequently used.'

'Yes.'

Did they detract from the literary merit? Were they relevant to literary merit?

'Well, they are the kind of words that that man would use.'

Deane brought up the passage describing the sexual fantasy of the Monkey's ex-husband: her watching as a black woman shits upon a glass table beneath which her husband lies, masturbating. 'What in your view is the effect of such passages as that on the literary merit?'

'Well, if you take a passage out like that, it does seem very crude, but I think you have got to take the picture as a whole, not certain passages.'

The thrust of Kenny's cross-examination, when it came, was potentially mistaken. Marr, observing, thought that Kenny wished for White to blush, to reach for euphemisms, to avoid the four-letter words, to maintain a Victorian-like decorum. It was a misreading of White. He responded to the questions forthrightly, succinctly, without artifice — 'with patrician nonchalance', Marr recalled. 'He was just so aloof, so untouched by Kenny's efforts to make him look grubby for liking the book.'[18]

Asked whether he would like to forget about certain incidents in the book, such as that of the Monkey and the negress, White shrugged. 'I had just forgotten about it,' he said. 'I had heard of worse in Sydney, actually. It is a part of life which the book reflects.'

Kenny scowled and continued to press him. Was it relevant to the book? How did it show Portnoy's development and character?

'You, as I understand it, say that any incident that takes place in real life can be reproduced in detail in a book?'

'It depends,' said White.

'It depends on what?'

'I think it was quite relevant to introduce it there.'

'Introduce what?'

'That incident.'

'Which one?'

'Of the negress shitting on the table.'

White took no enjoyment from the trial, but the questioning left him with special scorn for Kenny. Writing to Dutton that night, White was unequivocal: 'The prosecutor I can only describe as a cunt.'[19]

* * *

Alec Chisholm came last. A slight man with an imperious manner that belied a querulous voice, Chisholm was, like so many of those who had preceded him to the stand, a veritable man of letters.[20] But his evidence was short. Kenny's cross-examination was near lethal. He dismantled Chisholm's reputation: 'It is a reputation as a naturalist, isn't it?' What works of 'imaginative literature' have you written, he asked. What novels? What, *no* novels? And your work as literary editor for *The Daily Telegraph* — that is the same paper that went out of existence in the 1920s, correct?

It was a small mercy when Chisholm retired and the defence case was closed. Kenny offered no case-in-reply. In spite of considerable efforts by him and officials from the Crown solicitor's office, no expert had been prepared to give evidence for the prosecution on *Portnoy*'s possession of literary merit. Kenny later suggested that this was due to ideological conformity:

To qualify as an expert in the relevant field a witness must be either an academic, a writer, or a critic. Such persons either espouse the point of view that an author should be free to write as he wills without any legal restriction whatsoever, or alternatively, because of the fear of professional ostracism or of loss of opportunities of preferment which they think likely to follow any apparent opposition to that point of view, purport to adopt it, and will not give evidence of lack of merit of a book.[21]

He was aware of the weakness that this exposed. The bulk of the evidence had been adverse to the prosecution, and had relegated the detail of the sale of *Portnoy's Complaint* to a sideshow. Moreover, the impression created in the minds of the jury was that there was no dispute among literary experts as to whether or not *Portnoy* possessed literary merit.

But there was nothing he could do about that now. Thus the trial moved to the next stage: Deane's closing address. Here, Deane's manner — his calmness, reasonableness, and articulateness — shone. He deftly set aside the jurors' feelings for *Portnoy*. You might dislike it, he said, and that was fine: 'Not everyone enjoys Shakespeare.' It was okay to dislike the book. But one had to recognise that it was a work of literary merit. Yes, *Portnoy* contained depictions of sex that were off-putting. 'But there is nothing wrong, and there is nothing evil, about sex as such,' Deane said. 'Sex is also the touch of a hand and the exchange of the eye and the feeling of unity and the feeling that two people have become physically one. That is true sex, and in a way that is what this book is about.' The scenes that depicted masturbation had to be included because they established Portnoy's underlying problems. 'That is his introduction to sex: on his own, no love, no other party. On his own.' Deane counselled compassion and understanding, and recalled Heseltine's testimony: 'Nothing in human nature or nothing in humanity should be condemned simply out of hand. Professor Heseltine said the purpose of literature, certainly one of the purposes of life, is understanding and compassion.'

Portnoy's Complaint was a moral book. It did not encourage perverted sex; it discouraged it. Treating sex as a taboo was simply replicating the conditions that Roth had illustrated in the novel: 'Little Portnoy, the little boy, no one to talk to about his sex problems,' Deane said. The message of the book was to explain how Portnoy got to the psychiatrist's couch, to say: *Look what happened to him.* It did not encourage copying.

Deane pointed to the witnesses and their evidence on literary merit. He mocked the evidence from detectives Mitchell and Quill. Their schoolgirl was a 'patent invention'. He reminded the jury how Quill had determined the girl was from Fort Street Girls' High School: 'Gentlemen, the coincidence!' It was school holidays at the time, too: 'Well, I ask you!'

'There is only one thing involved, ultimately, in this trial,' Deane said, 'and that is whether an Australian bookseller and publishing company going back into the nineteenth century, taking the care it has taken, treating this book — which, of course, is an unusual book — in the light of the evidence you have heard, treating it as something that it handles with every consideration as to way of sale and everything else, the question is ultimately whether that company should be convicted of a crime, of a serious crime.'

The answer, he finished, should be no. The verdict should be not guilty.

* * *

Kenny's closing address reinforced the contrast between the two counsel. Where Deane had talked of compassion and understanding, Kenny talked only of *Portnoy*'s tendency to deprave and corrupt. Everything came back to this: the obscenity, the literary merit, the manner of the sale. 'The thing that is material is what in fact the book tends to do,' Kenny declared. 'The material question is what is its tendency, what is its effect likely to be.' This was the only question for the jury to decide: 'What is the likely tendency of this book?'

He scorned Deane's suggestion that *Portnoy* was moral, and dismissed Deane's talk about the beauty of sex. The book was simply obscene. 'Obscene means filthy or lewd or lascivious, leading to carnal desires, leading to carnal thoughts, leading to dirty-mindedness.' Kenny pressed that upon the jury and asked them to predict what might happen should people read *Portnoy*. He cited passages: was this likely to corrupt? Was this likely to injure? What about this? What about this? 'Test it for yourself,' Kenny said. 'Would you take it home and leave it lying around the house?'

At this question there was an immediate, and visibly adverse, reaction from the jury. Kenny saw it at once; so did Vine-Hall. It was 'so strong' a reaction that Kenny abandoned the rhetorical questions and returned to railing against the novel.[22] 'It is about sex, written in a dirty way, in an explicit way,' he said. Roth could have written about any number of issues, but had deliberately chosen to deal with sex, and via a technique 'which enables him to speak of it in the most vivid and fulsome details'.

The book promoted an unacceptable view of sex, and offered prurient descriptions of sexual acts. And with a few exceptions, it would not be read as the 'so-called experts' did. The great majority of people, Kenny said, 'do not study the book, they study the story, and the only thing they are concerned with is what the book says'. What would such readers remember of the book? Only the events. Only the depravity.

The prosecutor's arguments were at times extraordinarily bold. He lauded Roth's prose for its accessibility, and then indicted it for that same quality: 'It makes it all the worse.' He admitted to perceiving the humour, but declared it reprehensible since it brought matters of sex and dirtiness 'more vividly' to hand. He read passages aloud, made apologies for the language, and made as though to shy away, saying as he did so that the jury probably remembered this notorious event anyway in shock. It was a performance, and Kenny sought to milk it for all it was worth.

He urged the jury to disregard the view of the defence witnesses:

nothing they could say would justify the publication of *Portnoy's Complaint*, let alone its sale. He spoke of the degradation of the public that would follow should a not-guilty verdict be returned. Teenagers would be the most affected, he said. They would rebel against proper moral authority. In *Portnoy's Complaint*, they would not see a role model for resolving their problems — only an example of how to rebel, how to act out. They would wonder, Kenny said, 'Why should not I behave in the same way as the character in this book?'

'Having applied your own mind and your own interpretation,' Kenny finished, '… you will have no hesitation in finding that there should be a conviction.'

* * *

Justice Goran's summing-up was judicious. He did not know what Deane was speaking of when he talked of 'beautiful sex', and he did not think much of Kenny's suggestion that some aspects of sex were not worth portraying. 'I can recall some teacher at school telling me when I wanted to know on what to write a composition that any peg was good enough to hang your coat on. And so it is with a novel.' He urged the jury not to go through *Portnoy* 'on a witch hunt', nor to quantify how often sex appeared in its pages. They should consider the book's effects on readers, yes, but be realistic. 'Obviously, toddlers of five are not going to read it,' he said. 'You may look at the possibility of whether this is going to come into the hands of children of ten or twelve, some age like that, but you may well think that this is a book which will come into the hands of people of about, say, eighteen years, and some adolescents of a few years below that. Will it tend to corrupt or deprave, or injure their morals?' He told them, notably, not to impose higher standards than they themselves would live by, but to draw from experience: 'What is your experience of young people today? Would they be depraved by reading a book?'

He said that they did not need to accept the evidence from the literary experts, but he stressed the gravity of that evidence. Citing Patrick White's appearance, he asked, 'Do you discard those things lightly?' He reminded the jury of the evidence from detectives Mitchell and Quill that *Portnoy* was on 'unrestricted sale'. The defence had contested this, he said, but it could not be brushed aside.

And what of the sixteen-year-old schoolgirl? Goran brushed her aside: 'I am not going to deal with the evidence of the sixteen-year-old schoolgirl in uniform with Globite schoolcase in hand during school vacation, that is, in one hand, and her money in the other hand seeking to buy *Portnoy's Complaint*. You have heard that evidence,' he said, 'and it is entirely a matter for you as to whether you accept that version or not or whether in fact you are left in doubt about it.'

Finally, Goran asked the jury to retire. He sounded for all the world like the convenor of an afternoon debating society when he added, 'I have a feeling, gentlemen, that you will have an interesting if not a profitable time in discussing these matters.'

CHAPTER 14

Figures in dusty light

The defence team was satisfied as it settled in to await the verdict. They had done well. The witnesses had done well. Deane had done especially well, David Marr believed: 'Deane was wonderful. He was unflinching in his praise for the book.'[1] His closing address, in particular, had been pitched at exactly the right level: 'He made poor, sick Portnoy sound like St Augustine — with a dash of Jerry Seinfeld.' Kenny's tactics had been predictable. Rubbishing the book, dismissing Angus & Robertson, wildly predicting what teenagers might do when they read it — none of this was surprising. 'He personified the moralisers in Australia that wanted this book banned,' said Marr. Perhaps most important of all to the defence's mood was Goran's summing-up. It had been generous in its direction, expansive on the claims and arguments: 'We felt that he was summing up for a not-guilty verdict.'

The defence team thought that victory was likely. 'We were pretty confident that the jury would not convict,' said Marr.

And yet Marr, at least, could not help but lament the necessity of the trial. As he had arrived for each day's hearings, Marr had thought there was something fitting about the architecture of the courthouse, with its Doric columns, portico, and triangular pediment: 'It just seemed to me that what we needed was a spirit of Greek-style easy morals and freedom.' The cause had been worthy, but also surreal. Fighting it out in the elegant but shabby courtroom, where its figures had stood in the dusty light talking about masturbation and arguing about perversion was, truly, bizarre.

But Kenny was unhappy with the summing-up. Immediately after the jury left, he pressed Goran to call them back and amend his directions. He wanted a definition of *depraved, corrupt,* and *injure morals*, and he wanted an especially restrictive definition of *literary merit*. The definition Kenny wanted was, in effect, to make the hurdle higher and higher. '*Merit* means more than mere skill in the use of words,' he said, by way of suggestion. After forty minutes of argument, Goran reluctantly agreed. He amended his directions and told the jury to retire again.

It was not helpful. The number of witnesses and the complicated directions had so unsettled the jury that it came back at 3.30 pm, asking for clarification; retired again; and was then recalled an hour later and asked if they needed further help. 'Sometimes in a case like this,' Goran said, 'one is reminded of Omar Khayyam, who said amongst other matters that he frequented places of great argument, and evermore came out by that same door where he went.'

The jury retired once more. By now, they could have been forgiven for tossing in the towel. Their arguments would have gone back and forth: what did literary merit mean? How could *Portnoy*'s possession of literary merit possibly overcome its obscenity? What would be the effect of a not-guilty verdict — more books like this? Another three hours passed. They had taken the job seriously, aware of the responsibility entrusted to them, but by 7.40 pm the jury was at an impasse. Goran recalled them to the court. He understood from the foreman that they were unable to agree. If he offered more time — the jury could have all the time it needed

— was it possible that they would come to a verdict?

'We have discussed this point, Your Honour,' said the foreman, 'and we do not feel that we could reach a decision.'

That was it. That was the result of the trial: no verdict.

Goran was philosophical: 'It is better that you disagree than you arrive at a situation which is an injustice to somebody, merely for the sake of agreement.' He thanked the jury, urged them not to feel disappointed, and excused them from further jury service for five years.

'As to the accused company,' he said, 'I suppose the only order that I can make is that I remand the matter for retrial to such court as the attorney-general may appoint.'

* * *

The New South Wales government was lucky. Word of the lack of verdict came too late in the evening to make a proper splash: the news was crowded out by Australia's loss of the seventh Ashes test and the re-election of the Askin Liberal government on 13 February.

But there was no getting away from the damage that was being done to the censorship system, which was left battered and reeling from the forces of change. This seemed to manifest itself physically. In Victoria, embattled and exhausted by controversy and party infighting, Arthur Rylah had at last given way. Announcing his retirement on 3 February, he suffered a brain haemorrhage a fortnight later and collapsed at his desk, forcing his immediate resignation from parliament. The Customs department, meanwhile, had felt forced to release forty-eight books from the banned list, including *Peyton Place* by Grace Metalious, *The Carpetbaggers* by Harold Robbins, and *The Other Victorians* by Steven Marcus, on 12 February. These concessions begged the inevitable question: what would be next? Would Customs now remove the ban on *Portnoy?*[2]

The failure to secure a conviction over *Portnoy* compounded the embarrassment and the sense that change was in the air. The lack of verdict had come only days after Wendy Bacon had been tried in the courtroom next door for wearing her embroidered nun's habit. She had made a farce of those proceedings by refusing to enter a plea, by conducting her own defence, by citing Socrates' dialogue with Euthyphro, and then by refusing to give any information about her family to police and the court when found guilty by the jury. Was the whole system falling down? Why could it not resolve these matters? Most importantly, would another trial against Angus & Robertson end any differently?

The state government could not even take solace from the deadlock in the jury. John Michie wrote to Graham C. Greene to relay the apparent voting in the juryroom: 10–2 that the book was obscene, 9–3 that it had literary merit, and 9–3 again that its publication was justified. 'Meanwhile,' Michie went on, 'with South Australia and Western Australia going strong and with some underground sales in other States, we have notched up sales of over 120,000 so far.'[3]

In federal parliament, the opponents of censorship leapt on the lack of verdict and *Portnoy*'s continued sales. On 16 February, after presenting a petition calling for adults to be allowed to decide what they watched, read, and heard, Labor MP Richard Klugman pointed out that *Portnoy* could legally be sold in South Australia and Western Australia, and that the New South Wales jury had 'refused to declare' the book was obscene. Then, addressing Don Chipp, Klugman asked: 'In view of the fact that there has been no obvious increase in rape cases, either among those who have read the Australian edition, or the minister, his staff and parliamentarians who have read the imported edition, will he remove this book from the list of prohibited imports?'

Chipp would not budge an inch. The government would not relax the ban on importing *Portnoy*. His hands, he told the House, were tied by the *Customs Act* and by regulations. By law, he had to prohibit the import of any obscene or indecent publication. But this aside, there were clear grounds to accept that *Portnoy's Complaint* was obscene. 'We now have one court in the nation — in Victoria — which has pronounced unequivocally this novel to be obscene,' he said. 'We have another court in Western Australia which also has pronounced unequivocally this publication to be obscene.' Setting aside the peculiarities of the West Australian legislation that saw the charges there dismissed, Chipp reiterated that he could not allow the import of a novel that had already been declared obscene in two separate courts.[4]

But his dismissal of the question could not end the matter. On 22 February, debate resumed in the House on Chipp's ministerial statement on censorship from the year before.[5] MPs on both sides criticised the arbitrary nature of the censorship system, pointing to the works that had managed to slip through the cracks, and offered varying rationales for maintaining some degree of censorship. And although all commended Chipp for his willingness to draw scrutiny and to debate the issue, there were clear schisms in views about the worth and value of censorship.

Liberal MP Robert Solomon said that he disagreed with Chipp's abhorrence of censorship. He was in favour of moderation, he said; in favour of judgement in context, of appreciation of real sensitivity, of social responsibility, for the uplifting over the hurtful, and 'for restricting the portrayal of ultimate degrees of explicit experience in favour of some appeal to the imagination'.

Labor's Moss Cass argued that censorship itself caused harm by disconnecting repugnant actions from their consequences: in excising the repugnant action from a work, the censor also excised the feeling of repugnance itself that was necessary to the maintenance of a just society. 'We should be exposed, through good literature, to all these problems of human relationships — the good and the bad — because we have to be able to cope with the lot if we are to live a reasonably happy life.'

Liberal MP Neil Brown affirmed his belief in the merits of a censorship system administered in light of community standards and values. It was on this basis that he bemoaned the South Australian government's decision to break with other state governments and allow the sale of *Portnoy's Complaint*: 'The action of the South Australian government is a breach of the spirit of the legislation, if not the letter.'

Labor's Ray Sherry doubted that censorship improved or maintained the morals of a society, but pleaded for the debate to move from 'the Dickensian attitude' to an 'enlightened and contemporary' one.

Liberal MP Bob Katter (Sr.) set himself against the tide by arguing that the abandonment of the moral standards that girded censorship was a tragedy and would lead to greater moral degradation. Liberalisation had gone far enough: 'We should not go any further in this matter of censorship'. Klugman mocked this, noting that Katter did not appear to have been degraded or corrupted by seeing obscene material: 'I have not noticed any difference in his behaviour now from that before he left here.' Liberal MP Don Cameron, meanwhile, caused uproar when, demonstrating the existence of dirty material in magazines, he read out advertisements for sex toys, one-off liaisons, and swingers' parties. Cried one MP: 'You are corrupting the *Hansard* writer!'

Portnoy got a run during the debate. Labor MP Clyde Cameron said that he had read most of the books subject to censorship; although he hesitated to say it should be censored, he thought *Portnoy* was 'thoroughly disgusting', with one or two pages that made it 'thoroughly unacceptable'. Liberal MP Alan Jarman was less damning — claiming only to be 'not particularly impressed' — but was ambivalent about banning it. Cameron and Jarman, along with Labor MP Gil Duthie, were, however, in no doubt that there should be age-based restrictions on films that were unsuitable for young people.

Debate went on.[6] Liberal MP John McLeay suggested that the liberalisation of censorship could be connected with a higher abortion rate and the spread of sexually transmitted diseases, ridiculed literary and artistic merit defences, and dismissed the adverse international reputation that Australia had attracted for the censorship regime: 'To heck with overseas critics!' McLeay was no fan of *Portnoy*. Calling it a 'collection of pure rubbish', he argued that nothing would change even if all the four-letter words were eliminated from it. 'It would still be garbage,' he said. Liberal MP Michael MacKellar shied from such arguments, and instead called for more critical discussion of censorship. Labor's Norm Foster turned the debate towards censorship of Australia's military, intelligence, and foreign policy, arguing that there should be debate about activities at Pine Gap, at the North West Cape, and at Innisfail.

Nobody was willing to engage on these matters. When Liberal MP David Hamer — whose brother, Dick, was soon to become premier of Victoria — spoke, he talked of a British government report that argued laws on obscenity 'provide[d] no serious benefit to the public' and should be repealed. But, citing Disraeli, he added that the overwhelming majority of people in Australia supported the retention of censorship, and 'in a democracy, it is occasionally necessary for a government to bow to the will of the people'.

* * *

What was the will of the people? To look at one sector suggested that the position was clear: censorship should be abolished. That month, students at the Australian National University opened the Orientation Week issue of their campus newspaper, *Woroni*, to find advice on abortion and contraceptives, and excerpts from *Portnoy*. 'As the sale of *Portnoy's Complaint* is quite legal and above board in two states — South Australia and Western Australia,' the paper explained, 'there is no sane reason why the residents of the ACT should not have the same chance to become depraved and corrupt.' If readers 'groove[d] on the depraving effects' of those excerpts, they should buy a copy — perhaps from the *Woroni* offices.[7] Yet not even

Woroni was sure it should be selling the book: it defended its 65 cent mark-up as a prudent necessity should there be legal action.[8]

The provocation worked. Three days later, amid a debate in the Senate over adding student representation to the ANU's University Council, senators of the socially conservative Democratic Labor Party successfully moved an amendment calling on ANU council members to 'show a sense of responsibility and regard for the good name of the university' by rejecting the inclusion of 'crude pornography' in student publications. Those senators specifically cited the *Woroni* issue and its excerpts from *Portnoy*. As one government senator who supported the amendment commented, *Woroni*'s actions were 'an offence against any conceivable standards of decency, the ultimate in human degradation'.[9] This ruckus had consequences: at a subsequent meeting of the student association, the director of student publications was censured and then removed from office, by 95 votes to 85. *Woroni* editor Ken O'Neill refused to be cowed by any of this: 'Student newspapers are today the only papers in Australia free of pressure-group censorship.'

The trials over *Portnoy* continued. Police in the Northern Territory had raided two bookshops owned by Darwin city alderman Christopher Nathanael in September and October 1970; now, late in March 1971, they brought Nathanael to court on charges of 'exposing an obscene book' and offering it for sale. The first exhibit was one of the forty-seven copies of *Portnoy* that police had seized in those raids. With a potential sentence of six months' jail and no exemptions in Northern Territory law for works of literary merit, Nathanael's best hope was for a sympathetic magistrate. But Donald Miles SM was scathing about the novel. He compared it to writing found on lavatory walls, described it as 'dirty, dirty', and found Nathanael guilty on 1 April.[10] But Miles was also persuaded that Nathanael was a man of good standing, and so discharged the matter with a lecture and a nominal penalty of a six-month good-behaviour bond.[11]

Meanwhile, in Tasmania, *Portnoy* was causing problems. The

Tasmanian government's decision to ban the novel even before Penguin had published it had prompted Charles Wooley, an editor of the University of Tasmania's student newspaper, *Togatus*, to run a review in March 1970. It was not a particularly favourable article — 'Not really worth all that fuss,' ran the opening line — and the anonymous reviewer commented that finding passages to quote for the 'illegal delight' of the paper's readers had been difficult. The best the reviewer could do was quote the scene where Portnoy and the Monkey have sex with an Italian prostitute: 'Could this sort of passage justify the banning of the book?'[12]

After the issue was published, Wooley received a summons for a meeting with the state attorney-general, Max Bingham QC. A Rhodes scholar and Oxford graduate, Bingham was a recent entrant to politics, swept into government in the May 1969 election that had brought the Liberal Party to power after twenty-three years in opposition. Why the meeting? Bingham was well known to be a progressive force within the Liberal Party, Wooley recalled, and was — ostensibly — opposed to censorship. He couldn't possibly be angry about the review, could he?

The meeting was about the review, but Wooley had been correct in thinking that Bingham was not angry about it. Wooley came in, was offered a cup of tea and a slice of cake, and he and Bingham talked the matter over in entirely civil terms. 'Although the book is banned,' Bingham said to him, 'I don't think that should preclude a measured appraisal of the work — even though you have, technically, broken the law.'

Wooley caught the subtext. 'He didn't say it directly,' he recalled, 'but it was clear that Bingham thought the review was fine. He all but said we should not do it again, though, as it would make things difficult for him.'[13]

Wooley was correct. Bingham was not about to raise a storm over the matter. The meeting had been arranged for him to pass on a friendly warning, in case Wooley and his colleagues had plans to run extracts of the novel in future issues of the newspaper. 'One expects a bit of entertainment from university students,' Bingham explained later, 'but one needs to have regard to what the law of the land is.'[14]

Both men said their piece. And, with their respective positions made clear, they finished their tea and cake, and went their respective ways.

But there was more entertainment to come from students when John Reid, a scruffy, young PhD candidate in physics at the University of Tasmania and a part-time mathematics teacher at Fahan School, was charged with selling and distributing *Portnoy*.[15] Reid had been concerned with the restrictions that censorship imposed on freedom of speech, and though he had no particular liking for *Portnoy* as a novel, he believed that its publication in Australia was a pivotal moment in the fight against censorship: 'I believed Penguin deserved some support for publishing it.'[16]

When the book came out, he and like-minded students purchased 250 copies directly from Penguin and sold them in the university cafeteria as a protest against the ban. Making a profit was not their aim: 'We were just selling the book to point toward freedom-of-speech issues.' To ensure that their motivation was clear, they promised to donate all profits to ABSCHOL, the scholarship program for Aboriginal university students. But the protest had little impact. Said Reid: 'Of course, nobody took any notice of us.'

Reid realised that he could make his point more cogently by selling copies of the book at Tasmania's Parliament House. He therefore went to Salamanca Place in the evening of 15 September with half-a-dozen copies of *Portnoy*, and began to sell them in the foyer outside. The politicians hurrying out to dinner mostly ignored him. Only two stopped and bought copies; otherwise, there seemed to be an almost complete lack of interest. A Liberal MP whom Reid knew socially stopped and, idly, asked what he was doing there. At Reid's explanation, the MP laughed that he would not buy a copy, but that he would take one. Reid felt again that his point had not been made. No one was offended. No one was indignant. Where there was a reaction, it was only amusement.

Then the police showed up. Inspector Leslie Southern, who — according to Reid — already seemed outraged, seized the remaining copies of *Portnoy* and flipped through a few pages. What he read scandalised him. He passed the book to Reid and told him to read it aloud. Did he think it was indecent, he asked. What about this? What about that? 'Would you want your daughter to read this?' he demanded.

Reid was nonplussed. 'As a young and single man,' he recalled, 'that question seemed a *bit* irrelevant.'

Told he might be charged, Reid sheepishly agreed to leave. 'Yes, it looks as though I will be the bunny,' he said, according to the police.

Max Bingham regarded the matter coolly when it was brought to him. Aware that the censorship debate had widened to include the role of community standards, he believed it was appropriate to gauge whether *Portnoy* was tolerable by the community standards of his state. 'You had to bear in mind,' he explained later, 'that standards in Tasmania were likely to be different to those in Kings Cross.' The controversy that *Portnoy* had engendered offered an opportunity to get a reading of the public view. 'I didn't think it was for me to ban the blessed thing,' he recalled. 'The only way of testing the public attitude was to put the matter in the public arena and see what happened. That, I thought, satisfied the duty of the attorney-general.'[17]

Bingham was therefore untroubled by the summons issued both to Reid and to Ian Pearce, director and part-owner of one of Hobart's literary stalwarts, Fullers Bookshop. A plainclothes police officer named Philpott had visited Fullers on 2 September and, without disclosing his identity, asked Pearce to order him a copy of *Portnoy*.[18] Pearce had taken down his name and address, but admitted as he did so that he was uncertain whether they would receive the book at all. Nonetheless, a week later, a copy of *Portnoy* arrived in Philpott's mailbox along with an invoice from Fullers for $1.48. Philpott returned to the store on 10 September, paid for the book, and asked if he could buy another copy. 'We haven't got any left,' Pearce replied, 'but Millers might have some — they had them on the counter yesterday. I don't think they realised what they were selling. We have been taking orders and selling them surreptitiously.' Philpott left, checked Millers — which had no copies — and returned again the next day, along with another officer, to inform Pearce that charges might be laid against him.

It seemed that police had the matter sewn up. But the March 1971 committal hearing against Fullers went disastrously awry. Police magistrate Harold Solomon was profoundly unimpressed with the way police had handled the matter. By their own admission, Pearce's agreement to sell the book to Philpott was noncommittal at best. 'That incident was of no more than an exploratory nature,' ruled Solomon. 'Comparable to a case where a man says, for example, to a bookseller, "If you ever come across a copy of West's *History*, keep it for me, will you?"' He dismissed the summons: 'There is no case to go to a jury.'[19]

But Reid was a different matter. Expecting to be charged with a misdemeanour, he had been shocked to find that he was charged with offences contrary to section 138 of the criminal code. A nervous Reid approached Mervyn Everett QC, the shadow attorney-general in the Tasmanian Labor Party, to ask for help. Everett agreed to represent him. At the committal hearing, evidence given by two police officers showed plainly that Reid had sold the book. That was enough. Notwithstanding John McLaren's appearance on the stand to testify to the literary merit of *Portnoy's Complaint*, Reid was committed to stand trial in April in the Tasmanian Supreme Court.[20] He showed up to that hearing heeding the only advice that Everett had given him: 'John, just make sure you look neat and clean right down to your underpants.' It was a bewildering experience, underscored by the Dickensian atmosphere and surreal twists of everyday life: in the convict-era courthouse, Reid trooped up the dark stone stairs from underground and into the dock, only to find that the judge's clerk was a friend. 'This was Tasmania, after all,' said Reid. 'So, when Bill asked me to confirm my name, he was smiling at me!'

Then there were the proceedings. Upon hearing the charges and checking the court file, the judge pointed out to the prosecution that Reid had not been selling the book for any gain. All the profits were going to ABSCHOL. 'I don't see that there is much of a case,' the judge said airily. 'Adjourned — *sine die.*'

He rapped his gavel and disappeared into his chambers. Reid had not been found guilty, nor had he been found not guilty. The case had been adjourned without a date being fixed. Though it was possible for it to be taken up again, the matter was, for all intents and purposes, over. Reid, who had found himself querying the judge's Latin pronunciation, was shocked, thankful, and completely at a loss as to what to make of it.[21]

* * *

Such halting court action and token sentences were now becoming ridiculous. And there were signs that the saga was not over: as Penguin had foreshadowed after the November trial, the company successfully applied to the Victorian Supreme Court to have Ross's finding reviewed.[22] The company argued that Ross was 'wrong in law' to declare *Portnoy* obscene: he had failed to consider the meaning of the term within the meaning of the *Police Offences Act*, had 'misdirected himself', had 'wrongly accepted' submissions, and had taken into account 'extraneous and irrelevant matters'. The appeal grounds included Ross's failure to hear expert evidence about the book's capacity to deprave or corrupt a particular class or age group of people, but what Penguin believed was its 'best bet' was Ross's finding that *Portnoy* had literary merit. With that finding, their appeal argued, he should not have declared the publication and distribution of the book unjustified.[23]

That hearing, in March 1971, did not exactly go to plan. 'Our Supreme Court appeal was short-lived,' Michie wrote to Graham C. Greene, afterwards. 'The judge had very strong views on the subject and gave our barrister a mauling. We have now moved for a full bench hearing, which gives us three judges. This should be listed for August.'[24] Another trial against Penguin, with all the embarrassment and mirth of the first, beckoned.

This prospect led some observers to question whether there would be another trial in New South Wales. Most thought so, although attorney-general Kenneth McCaw seemed to suggest not when he was asked about the matter on 16 February.[25] Notwithstanding that the Crown's costs had reached $4,000, Eric Willis was firmly of the view that the case should be retried. 'There should be another trial,' he wrote on 17 February, 'so that a jury of representative citizens (not just one person) can decide whether this book may be published.'[26]

A meeting that same day gave the Crown's prosecutor an opportunity to have his say. Speaking in his chambers with officials from the Crown solicitor's office, Kenny gave verbal advice recommending that a further trial be held. There was no reason to not adhere to the ordinary procedure in criminal cases, he said.[27] Moreover, his personal opinion was that if a second trial were not held, the government would be 'extremely weakened so far as action against any future publications was concerned'.

However, Kenny said that he could make no promises about the outcome of a second trial. It was 'most likely' that the jury would split, and 'quite probable' that disagreement could result in another no-verdict. Kenny was hedging his bets, expressing no great confidence: 'He felt the prospects of conviction were not great,' wrote one of the attendees. Kenny's frustrations with the nature of the case were also clear:

Mr Kenny stated that the weight of evidence on literary merit, as opposed to the non-rebuttal of such evidence by the Crown, was a problem but he felt certain that there must be a person or persons in the community of academic standing who could give evidence for the Crown on the literary merit angle. In this regard he was looking for persons who could draw a distinction between 'skill in writing' and 'literary merit'. The Instructing Solicitor would be endeavouring to locate such witnesses and the Department will be providing any assistance possible.[28]

Should the jury fail to agree on a verdict for a second time, Kenny said that he 'could not see how any further legal proceedings could be pursued'. Despite Kenny's pessimism, what settled the matter was his advice that there were no legal barriers to a second trial, and the political need for the government to look strong. The decision was made 'on the spot'. A second trial would go ahead.

But the publicity and the public consciousness of censorship were having an effect. On 1 March, while confirming that there would be another trial against Angus & Robertson, Eric Willis stated that he had decided a jury should determine whether or not the book was obscene. 'What I have done,' he said, 'is to let twelve ordinary Australians, chosen at random as representatives of New South Wales, decide whether publication and distribution of this book should be permitted or prohibited.' This was not, however, his preferred course of action: he would have preferred to decide himself whether *Portnoy's Complaint* was obscene, he said. But, as he also told the press, if he had exercised this option he would almost certainly have been accused of making a 'one-man decision'.[29]

Penguin, keeping in touch with Angus & Robertson and Allen Allen & Hemsley, hoped that Willis's decision could be reversed: 'There is a possibility that the Crown will not pursue the matter,' Michie wrote.[30] Angus & Robertson and Allen Allen & Hemsley did their best to convince the state government to drop it. On 10 May, the firm filed an application for proceedings to be dropped; the next day, it sent a letter to the attorney-general, Kenneth McCaw, arguing that the result of a second trial would be the same as the first. The jury at the first trial had been representative of the community; should another jury be empanelled, it would surely reach a similar conclusion. The firm noted that *Portnoy* had received widespread acceptance among the public and among critics, in Australia and overseas, and pointed out that the cost of further proceedings was clearly inordinate. The cost to Angus & Robertson for the first trial had been $10,000, the firm said — yet the maximum fine for a first offence on the obscenity charges was only $500. What would be the point of a further trial?[31]

Angus & Robertson chairman Gordon Barton echoed these arguments. He rang McCaw directly to seek a stay of proceedings, and managed to arrange an appointment with Willis to lobby him face-to-face. 'I have been anxious to see you with a view to avoiding, if possible, a second hearing, with its attendant inconvenience and expense, of the *Portnoy* trial,' he wrote subsequently. McCaw had turned Barton away while the application was considered; upon realising that his appointment with Willis was fixed for the same day as the trial was to begin, Barton followed up with Willis by sending letters to his home and office, seeking a meeting at any time of the day or night. 'This is to ask, as a matter of urgency, if you would consent to an adjournment of the trial pending our discussion and your decision.'[32] But upon realising what Barton wanted, Willis, too, cancelled their meeting. 'Had I known [the] purpose of visit earlier I [would] not [have] made appointment,' he grumbled.[33]

McCaw sought Kenny's response to the application for a No Bill. The prosecutor was dismissive, curt. Nothing had changed since February, he wrote from his chambers, and Allen Allen & Hemsley's application raised no matter that would cause him to alter the advice he had given. The trial should go ahead.[34]

That sealed it. Immediately upon receiving Kenny's advice, the undersecretary for justice sent Allen Allen & Hemsley a letter. 'The Attorney-General, having carefully considered all the circumstances and the evidence available, has directed that the case against the above-named [Angus & Robertson Ltd] proceed to retrial.' Then, almost snarkily, the letter went on, 'As you are aware, the retrial of this matter has been listed at Sydney Quarter Sessions on 18th May 1971.'[35]

Allen Allen & Hemsley was aware: 18 May was the next day.

CHAPTER 15

A cloistered and untried virtue

When the next *Portnoy* trial began in the Taylor Square court-house, at ten o'clock on Tuesday 18 May, Deane and Masterman reappeared for the defence, with Hugh Jamieson instructing.[1] After qualifying as a solicitor and practising for one day, David Marr had left the law to travel and begin a career in journalism, leaving Malcolm Oakes to take his place. Twenty years old and an articled clerk with Allens, Oakes had played second fiddle to Marr at the first trial, but his involvement this time was to be much greater — beginning with jury selection.

As proceedings got underway, Deane asked Oakes to tug on his gown if he believed there should be an objection to any potential juror. Oakes duly watched as the jury was selected. It was mostly men who were selected — but then came a woman with well-coiffed hair, dressed in a dark two-piece suit. Oakes immediately thought: *Mrs North Shore*. Not a good candidate for judging the literary merit of a rather hung-up Jewish New York youth with unusual masturbatory habits,' he remarked later. He therefore tugged Deane's gown. Deane objected, and the woman was asked to step down.[2]

Later, she came up to Oakes. Why, she asked, had they objected to her? She was the secretary of an anti-censorship league, she said. She would have been a locked-in vote for acquittal.

Oakes could only shrug off the missed advantage. If he could not pick out a favourable juror, he joked, perhaps he was not cut out for the criminal law.

The excitement of the first trial was not to be repeated at the second. There were regularly gaps in the public galleries. The witness list was shorter. The big witnesses — Patrick White, in particular — would not be appearing. Margaret Harris, who had agreed to testify again, recalled that there was a sense that the whole affair was now redundant: 'In the second trial, by then, it was flogging a dead horse.'[3] It seemed that the stakes were now lower. With victory in Western Australia, a stalemate in Tasmania, and the token fines imposed in Victoria and the Northern Territory, *Portnoy* had opened a schism across the country. And while the book was not free for purchase in New South Wales, the stakes were now much higher for the prosecution than for the defence. Another no-verdict result would be as effective as a not-guilty verdict for Penguin and Angus & Robertson: there was barely the scintilla of a chance that a third trial would be pursued if the result again was a no-verdict. For the prosecution, however, either of these would be a disaster, a complete failure. The prosecution *needed* a guilty verdict.

The acuity of that need prompted the New South Wales government to add another charge to the indictment: that, in addition to selling an obscene publication, Angus & Robertson — by virtue of owning Halstead Press and printing *Portnoy* for Penguin — had published an indecent publication as well. It was a backup: if the prosecution could not convince the jury to convict Angus & Robertson of selling an *obscene* publication, it might be able to convince it that it was guilty of the lesser offence of publishing an *indecent* one. The additional charge provoked consternation from Deane. He lobbied to have it dropped. 'The Crown should be required to elect which charge it wishes to proceed with,' he argued. 'It cannot proceed with both.'

Justice Phillip Head QC MBE agreed to stress the difference between the two, but refused to force the Crown to choose. A decorated legal officer who had been held prisoner by the Japanese during World War II, Head was a former common law silk who had been raised to the bench in 1964.[4] Thin-lipped and high-browed, he had a careful, formal, and rigid manner and little patience for the kind of lengthy debates that Goran had allowed in February. This lack of patience would be exacerbated by a painful skin disease he was enduring that forced him to wear green protective gloves and to cover his face with white ointment. He would repeatedly intervene to circumvent the testimony of witnesses and to reprimand counsel for laughing. All this would make the trial heavy-going.

The opening stages of the trial were brisk. After Deane's submission, Kenny opened, decried *Portnoy's Complaint* and its blatant obscenity, and sought to reduce the trial to one question: 'You are only concerned [with] whether this book is acceptable in the community.'[5] Kenny called Mitchell and Quill to the stand, quizzing both about their visit to Angus & Robertson and their return the next day. Conscious of the weaknesses of the police evidence from the first trial, he skated lightly over the sixteen-year-old schoolgirl; Deane, cross-examining, worked hard to draw it out again while politely making much of the inconsistencies and fortuitous instances of the detectives' visit and record keeping. He put to them, again, his proposition that the schoolgirl was a figment of their imaginations. Both, again, denied it.

Then Deane opened the defence case. *Portnoy's Complaint* was a work of high literary merit. 'We will defend ourselves loud and clear,' he said. 'This is not a written collection of dirt from a lavatory wall compiled for the sake of dirt — it is a work of literature.'

Angus & Robertson's reputation and character was at stake. The company had sold the book in a responsible way. 'We will call evidence to show that Angus & Robertson sold a work of literature, without extending any invitation or enticement.'[6]

The court adjourned so that the jury could begin reading *Portnoy* before it was sent home. On Wednesday, the jury read; on Thursday, Head was sick, and proceedings were adjourned for that day and the next so that he could have the weekend to recover.

Court resumed on Monday 24 May. While waiting for a tardy jury member to arrive, Kenny sought to repeat his luck from the first trial, and put it to Head that the defence witnesses should not be allowed to testify to *Portnoy*'s literary merit. 'This is not a matter for experts at all,' he argued. Again, his argument was simple: the existence of literary merit in *Portnoy* was for the jury to determine. Therefore, witnesses should only be allowed to express views about the criteria for identifying literary merit. Moreover, Kenny went on, Head should select the rules that the jury could use to determine whether that merit existed.

Head was surprised, but said that he had intended already to rule that literary merit described a 'written composition which has worth or excellence on account of its qualities of form, style, or expression'. Witnesses would be restricted to saying whether a book had worth or excellence on these points — and these alone, he said. Functional though Head's definition was, it was also a highly restrictive way of discussing literary merit. But Kenny was not satisfied with the advantage this gave him. He further argued that, in light of Head's intentions, whatever defence witnesses said would be only their opinion — and therefore should not be heard. To Head's suggestion that medical doctors, too, when testifying, merely expressed an opinion, Kenny scoffed.

'A doctor is in a particularly skilled position *vis-a-vis* the jury as compared with the jury in this situation,' he said, 'because he [the doctor] is a man who is skilled in diagnosis, he is skilled in taking the relevant from the irrelevant in the sense of observable phenomena. He can look at a man and he will see things that a person not skilled in diagnosis will not see, and he knows what will follow.' The literary experts, however, were doing something that anyone could do: 'The jury *can* read.'

It was an unconvincing submission, not in the least because it flew in the face of standard practice in obscenity cases, but it was wholly of a piece with Kenny's determination to obtain every advantage he could. Head decided not to make a ruling. He preferred to play it by ear, he said, and deal with the question as it arose. Then, noting that the final juror was still missing, Head ordered a policeman to fetch him, and adjourned the court.

* * *

It took until two o'clock for the juror to arrive and the hearing to get underway. The defence first called Ronald Dingley. Deane led Dingley efficiently through his evidence — through the circumstances in which Angus & Robertson had sold *Portnoy*, the restrictions that had been placed on the sale, and whether he had seen any schoolgirl in the store. 'I did not,' Dingley said.

Paul Grainger followed, and repeated his testimony from the first trial. Kenny barraged him with questions, but found the young man immovable. He gave up his questioning in short order. It did not escape the defence's notice that Kenny asked no questions about whether Grainger had sold the book to a schoolgirl: plainly, the prosecutor had calculated that repeated denials of the allegation would be sure to have an impact on the jury.

Then there was a new witness: Helen Watkins, an assistant with Angus & Robertson who had been aiding Grainger on the paperback counter when *Portnoy's Complaint* went on sale. Nervous, hesitant, and upset that she had been called to appear, Watkins nonetheless buttressed Angus & Robertson's defence that it had been responsible when selling the novel: she confirmed what Dingley and Grainger had said. As the defence had intended, the emphatic testimony of the three Angus & Robertson witnesses, right at the start of their defence, all but banished from the trial the spectre of the sixteen-year-old schoolgirl.

Harry Heseltine came to the stand. The effect of Head's restrictions on what literary experts could speak to became palpable immediately. Deane had to ask Heseltine his opinion of the quality of *Portnoy's Complaint* 'insofar as form is concerned', what it was insofar as 'the style' was worth, and what should be said about *Portnoy* in terms of its 'expression'. Heseltine answered these questions, but added that humour was a central feature of the novel and should be discussed — particularly since it related to form, expression, and style. Thus he returned the next day, 25 May. From the humour, Heseltine moved to justify the voice and language of the book. He pointed out that Roth had given his narrator a voice just as Mark Twain had to Huckleberry Finn, and that the direct, coarse language of the novel was necessary to create Portnoy as a character.

Deane went patiently through all of this, but the crucial point was at the end: 'What is your opinion on the question whether the book *Portnoy's Complaint* is a work of literary merit?'

Kenny objected, but Justice Head allowed the question. 'On each of these tests — the test of style and the test of form and of expression,' said Heseltine, 'I believe Philip Roth's book *Portnoy's Complaint* to be a considerable work of literary merit, of demonstrable merit.'

In cross-examination of Heseltine and the witnesses who followed, Kenny was even more ferocious than he had been at the first trial. He scorned, badgered, nitpicked, and barked. He sought to fog up the clarity Heseltine had brought, to mess up his categories. He asked if form and content were different matters. Are they, he asked. Do you regard style and form as one and the same? When you say the form has merit, do you mean that the use of language by the author has merit?

Heseltine corrected the prosecutor's confusion of Roth with

Portnoy ('No, it was the explicit description of *Alexander Portnoy*'s recall of sexual acts'), and met Kenny's sarcasm with his own ('You profess to have some legal knowledge, do you?' Kenny asked. 'No,' said Heseltine, 'but I assumed that is what this trial was about.') Their most contentious exchanges came during questions over a writer's freedom.

'Do you believe in literary censorship?'

'I think not.'

'Your point of view is from a social point of view [that] an author should be free to write about any subject which he, the author, selects?'

'My point of view would be that of John Milton, the great moralist.'

'Is that what you say?' said an unimpressed Kenny.

'My point of view coincides with John Milton's: "I cannot praise a cloistered and untried virtue,"' Heseltine said. 'That is from the *Areopagitica*.'

Kenny pushed him once more: 'I will ask you to answer it.'

'I have,' said Heseltine, 'in the words of Milton, which I make mine.'

Margaret Harris followed. By its use of form, style, and expression, she said, *Portnoy's Complaint* presented its protagonist in a manner that was convincing and moving: it was a work of 'distinct literary merit'. The subsequent fusillade from Kenny demonstrated his opinion of this argument: the thin veneer of literary merit she perceived in the use of the first-person narrator, he suggested, was simply a way for Roth to include obscene material. After all, he went on, other writers had explored the same issues as *Portnoy*, and they not gone into the 'detailed description of sexual acts'.

The defence objected on grounds that Kenny was comparing *Portnoy* with other books, and Kenny quickly withdrew. Doubtless he was aware that it might open the door for the defence to make comparisons themselves. But he continued to push for an admission that subjects could be explored without the explicit sexual material included in *Portnoy*. 'If that skilful novelist's view of the situation of mid-twentieth century man did *not* involve his mid-twentieth century man's sexual history and emotional make-up,' said Harris, cautiously, 'perhaps he could.'

To all this, Kenny became frustrated: 'Perhaps you could answer yes or no,' he barked. He was sarcastic, contemptuous: 'What is central [to the novel] is that he masturbates?' He reprimanded her: 'I did not ask you about the approach of other people to reading, did I?' Malcolm Oakes, watching and hearing this, at times felt uneasy: it was as though Kenny was beating up on a younger sister. But he also thought that it had the effect of alienating the jury. 'Cross-examination is a delicate business,' he said later, 'and can turn sour on the cross-examiner.'[7]

Kenny had more success with William Priest, an English teacher at Ryde High School, who came next to the stand. Priest found it difficult to stay within the bounds of the definition of literary merit that Head had imposed. His repeated forays beyond it prompted objections from Kenny and interventions from Head that, inevitably, sapped Priest's confidence and clarity, making him scattered and hesitant. Deane carried him as best he could, but the man was nervous. 'I am sorry, I have lost the thread of that sentence,' he said at one point. At another, he exclaimed that he would answer the question as a schoolteacher, then — 'No, I am sorry, I must answer as a critic of this book, as an analyst of this book.'

Finally, Deane got him to the crucial question, but even here Priest could not answer with the necessary certainty and clarity. Did Priest think *Portnoy's Complaint* was a work of literary merit?

'There is no question in my mind as to the worth of the novel,' Priest replied. 'I accept it implicitly because I have measured it against criteria that I apply to any work of art or any, in this case, work of literature.'

'What do you say is your opinion to the worth of this book as a work of literary merit?'

'My opinion is a very high one.'

It was close, but not clear enough. Deane asked again: 'Do you say it has or does not have literary merit?'

'It has decided literary merit, yes.'

Kenny's manner with Priest was decidedly calmer than with Heseltine and Harris. Citing his statement that he had measured *Portnoy* against the criteria that he applied to any work of art, Kenny asked to know the first criterion. Then he asked to know the second. Priest floundered. He stammered, said that he did not understand the question, asked for more information. Kenny remained reasonable, even gentle. 'I am asking you to tell these gentlemen [of the jury],' he said, 'so that they may know, what were the criteria which you referred to when you said you measured it [*Portnoy's Complaint*] against criteria which you apply to all works of art. That is what you said?'

'I am attempting to answer the question, yes,' said Priest. 'Am I [being] irrelevant?'

'Yes, I suggest you are,' said Kenny. 'Could you just tell us what are the criteria?'

But Priest could not. He could not speak of literary merit without overriding Head's definition, prompting yet another intervention from Head: 'You may or may not like that ruling, but it is the ruling I have given and it is the ruling I propose to maintain.'

It did not get any better. When Priest confirmed that one ground for *Portnoy's* literary merit was its use of allegory, and explained that he had seen this after reading it for a second time, Kenny asked if it was likely that a first-time reader would miss it. What about a second-time reader? And a third?

Priest could not overcome his problems with the definition of literary merit as imposed by Head. 'They all overlap,' he said, at one point. 'Form, style, and expression — I would never use these terms to a class. They are terribly obscure, and what one must find are terms that clarify the issues, with due respect.' But when invited to offer definitions of those terms, and to speak within those definitions, Priest could not keep them straight, kept getting led to questions that he found difficult or problematic. It was a small mercy when the lunchtime adjournment ended his time with Kenny.

Deane sought to repair the damage by keeping Priest on the stand, and asking him to detail the meaning of *Portnoy* at the allegorical level. This time, Priest delivered. He argued that the deeper meaning of the novel lay in the historic and ethnic treatment of Jews. The constipation that afflicted Portnoy's father was symbolic of this meaning. 'Roth is saying all Jewish fathers are constipated by their traditions, by their religious beliefs,' said Priest. 'Likewise with the mother. She has a hysterectomy. The sterility which results from that again is Roth's way of saying of all Jewish mothers [that] they are spiritually sterile, physically sterile … The physical impotence of Portnoy, coming at the climax of the novel, is one of Roth's ways — and there are several ways — of saying, "Here is the end product of a union between a morally constipated [father] and a spiritually sterile mother."'

It was astute, credible, and convincing — and Head stomped on it the moment that Priest had finished: 'This might be the meaning of the book,' he rumbled, 'but it is not the form.'

Maureen Colman followed. The manner of her testimony was not to Head's liking. When, during a discussion of the humour in *Portnoy*, Colman began reading a passage aloud, Head interrupted to say that she was not an actress and was in a court of law. George Masterman, who was leading Colman's examination, diplomatically requested she read without an American accent.

'I did not say anything about accent,' Head growled. 'I said acting and not reading.'

'Would you continue in a flatter voice?' said Masterman.

'If I might just say,' Head interrupted for a third time, 'a *normal* voice.'

Colman thought little of this. The book was designed to mimic the spoken word, and to draw forth a certain style of reading. Head's attempt to stop that, she said later, was silly: 'If you are going to read a bit of dialogue from a novel — for heaven's sake!

— are you not going to give some indication of what the character is saying?'[8]

Colman was unperturbed by the glowering presence at the bench and the barrage of scorn that Kenny launched in his cross-examination. She had been through it before. To all his questions about the instances of sex, she maintained a resolute line: it was funny.

Barbara Jefferis appeared next. She had no trouble with the restrictions that Head had imposed on witnesses, nor with answering the crucial question: was *Portnoy's Complaint* a work of literary merit? 'How would you classify it — small literary merit?' Deane asked. 'Large literary merit?'

'Very considerable literary merit,' she replied.

Kenny's cross-examination was short, contained. He tried to muddy Jefferis's praise of Roth's writing by muddying the distinction between *style* and *expression*, suggesting that both were a question of 'the use of words', but Jefferis was too sharp for that: 'It does seem to me to include some sort of concept of the quality of his thoughts as well.' There needed to be an acknowledgement both of the capacity to link words together on the page and the capacity to pick those words that would express the idea an author wanted expressed, she argued.

Just as with Margaret Harris, Kenny sought to badger Jefferis to admit that the subject matter could have been developed and delivered in any kind of way: 'Some [writers] would describe sexual acts in detail, some would not?' Was it her view that an author is entitled to develop a subject in any way he or she sees fit?

'Yes, I think so,' Jefferis said.

* * *

When Jefferis retired, the defence's case was closed. As with the first trial, Kenny sought to offer no case in reply: once again, the Crown had been unable to find any witness who would testify that

Portnoy's Complaint possessed no literary merit.

This was a boon to Deane, who made much of the point in his closing address the next day. Kenny had offered no case-in-reply to the defence witnesses — all of whom, Deane added, were of high standing, even Mr Priest, who was perhaps not 'good at going into the witness box and saying what he wanted to say'. Nor had Kenny ever put it to the defence witnesses that *Portnoy's Complaint* was without literary merit. Not once. His cross-examination was about checking credit, Deane said: 'You heard the evidence that was given on this point yesterday. It remains uncontradicted.'

Deane revived the spectre of the schoolgirl and scoffed at the evidence about her. He was unequivocal that *Portnoy* was neither indecent nor obscene. 'You have read this book, you have had it in your possession, and you have taken it home,' he told the jury. 'Do you really think it could corrupt or deprave anyone?' Moreover, aware of the adverse reaction to Kenny's argument, in the first trial, that *Portnoy* could deprave and corrupt the young, potentially even incite them to rebellion, Deane emphasised the restrictions on who could purchase a book and read it. 'If you are old enough to fight and die for your country,' he said, 'you are old enough to be thought of as an adult when it comes to reading a book.'[9]

Deane emphasised the pitiableness of Portnoy, reading aloud a passage that described Portnoy's vision of an idealised family life. He also made fun of Kenny's arguments. To the prosecutor's suggestion that buyers could pass the novel on to others, Deane laughed. Could Angus & Robertson really make people sign a contract promising to not do so? He mocked the prosecutor's suggestion that only readers with a tertiary education would be able to understand it. Should there really be some 'elite' who could read the book, but not others? 'That the man with the tertiary education,' asked Deane, 'is entitled to drink in the streams of literature, but the man without it is not to be allowed the same benefits?'

Kenny used that image for the opening salvo of his reply. After reading passages — of Portnoy masturbating in the bathroom, of

Portnoy masturbating after dessert — he stopped. 'My friend Mr Deane used the wonderful phrase "drink of the streams of literature",' he sneered. 'It would be a rather unpleasant draught if *this* is to represent the stream of literature. Do you really think that this is the stream of literature, or do you think it is the stream of filth?'

Kenny told the jury to forget their individual views and become the guardians of community standards: 'What you are there to do — and there is no better tribunal to do it — is to apply not the standards of you personally, but the standards of the community from which you come.' He rubbished Angus & Robertson's restrictions on the sale — 'If it did exist, it was completely ineffectual' — and pooh-poohed the testimony from the literary experts, especially Priest. 'As an expert witness, he was something less than adequate,' Kenny said. His evidence was 'embarrassing'.

The defence of literary merit was 'not conclusive', and to say that literary merit justified allowing a book into circulation was to give writers an awesome power. All they would need was 'a little skill with the use of words, a little skill with the formulation with some sort of a plot', and writers could write whatever 'filth' they wanted. 'Gentlemen, in the circumstances,' Kenny finished, 'I would suggest that you would without hesitation come to the conclusion that the Crown has proved and proved resoundingly that the sale of this book is not justified in this day and age in this community.'

The judge's summary was hostile to the novel at the heart of the trial. Head encouraged the jury to look at individual passages in *Portnoy* and determine whether they ruined the book. 'Are there so few rotten apples in the barrel that the remainder can be eaten and enjoyed as a wholesome fruit, or are there so many rotten apples and so distributed that all the fruit is tainted and the lot must be discarded?' He downplayed the defence witnesses, told the jury that they alone were the ones to determine literary merit: 'You are not bound to accept any opinion, just as you are not bound to accept any evidence'. He dismissed as irrelevant the novel's subject matter, scorned the supposed humour of masturbation and constipation, and told the jury that they were charged with protecting society's morals: 'Well, gentlemen, it is not the degree of civilisation we are concerned with except in so far as civilisation is reflected in a normal, decent standard of morals.' Discussing the circumstances of the sale, Head directed the jury that *Portnoy's Complaint* could not be sold if the Crown had proved that 'in all the circumstances of the particular case' the sale was not justified.

Eventually, he concluded with a reminder of the jury's responsibilities. 'You are dealing here with offences charged under an Act of Parliament, of the New South Wales Parliament. You are taking a major part in the administration of the law. You are not concerned with the rights or wrongs of book censorship or any similar social question of what should or should not be.'

Immediately upon the jury's departure, the defence requested amendments to Head's summing-up, especially to his comments on the humour and four-letter words in *Portnoy*. 'Your Honour should not have directed the jury in those terms,' said George Masterman. '... Your Honour used the expression "four-letter words — dear oh dear, I suppose that is one description of them". I would respectfully submit Your Honour ought not to have made that comment of them.'

But Head accepted none of this. His comments were 'inconsequential', he said, and his discussion of the subject matter in the determination of literary merit was a 'grammatical' reading of his comments.

And so they waited.

* * *

The jury went to the small room off from the courts to consider its verdict. But, after a few hours, they sent a message to Head. There was no way they were going to agree to a verdict, they said. Could they return a no-verdict result yet?

Head told them to keep going. They were required to deliberate for a minimum of seven hours, and they would fulfil that minimum. The jury's response to this was to ask the court officer for two packets of cards.[10]

Finally, at six o'clock, after six hours of deliberation and play, the jury was allowed to return. Justice Head addressed the foreman: 'Earlier this afternoon I received a message that the jury could not agree … Are you still in that position, that you have not agreed?'

'Yes,' said the foreman. 'Your Honour, I don't think there is any possible chance.'

It was the same result as before: no verdict. This time, however, there was no lamenting the outcome, no thanks to the jury for its work, no attempt to cover the embarrassing absence of a resolution to a matter that had now gone on for too long, that had cost too much, that had had so much riding on it.

Head discharged the jury, and did the only thing he could do: 'I remand the accused for trial at such time and place as the attorney-general may appoint.'

Would there be a third trial? After two attempts and no resolution in either, would the Crown try again?

As they left that evening, the defence team knew that if they had not won outright, they had almost certainly won the bigger battle.

CHAPTER 16

Paper tigers

The backdown took less than twenty-four hours. On the morning of 28 May, the day after the trial's conclusion, the New South Wales attorney-general, Kenneth McCaw, announced that the case against Angus & Robertson would go no further. 'Proceedings are therefore at an end.'[1]

But there was no word on the charges still listed against booksellers James Thorburn, Bob Gould, and four other sellers. Would they be pursued? The Crown solicitor's office wrote to Eric Willis to clarify the matter. Willis, however, was overseas, and it took until 7 June for him to send word. Regret coloured his note: there was 'no alternative' to dropping all charges against the remaining *Portnoy* sellers, he wrote. 'The A+R prosecution was the test case.'[2] With the second failure to secure a conviction, it was all over.

The New South Wales decision forced the federal government to move. On 15 June, Don Chipp announced that *Portnoy's Complaint* would be removed from the list of banned books. In light of the inconclusive court action, he said, the import ban that

Customs had placed was not sustainable. 'The decision has been taken because the Australian edition of the book is now freely on sale in three States and in the Australian Capital Territory. It would be absurd, in the circumstances, to maintain the prohibition on the imported edition.'³ The telegram went out to Customs offices across the country: 'IN ACCORDANCE WITH MINISTER'S PRESS STATEMENT IMPORTATION OF PORTNOY'S COMPLAINT MAY BE ALLOWED.'⁴

It was an ignominious defeat, and it left the censorship regime reeling. The agreement on uniform censorship was in tatters. Crucial flaws in the state-based legislation had been exposed and exploited. Publishers, booksellers, writers, and artists were emboldened and defiant. Alongside the backdown on *Portnoy*, Customs' wilting powers saw it remove the bans on ten other titles, including Norman Mailer's *An American Dream* and *Why Are We in Vietnam?*⁵

If Penguin's staff had needed any further proof that publishing *Portnoy* would effect change, this was it: it had, in every sense of the word, succeeded. They were elated. Michie, Froelich, and Hooker were triumphant. They felt satisfied, vindicated. 'We took a risk and it came off,' Peter Froelich said later. 'I felt good about that.'⁶ Hilary McPhee recalled the same feeling. 'Penguin had sold a lot of books. In the public's eye, they [Michie, Hooker, and Froelich] were heroes.'⁷ From London, Graham C. Greene cabled Michie and Hooker: 'Congratulations on a great victory.'⁸ Hooker wrote him back: 'Taking New South Wales is a triumph.' Then, referring to the still-pending appeal against Penguin's conviction, he added: 'If we take Victoria (doubtful) we'll have run 'em out of town.'⁹

This would not happen — not exactly. On 31 July, Penguin's board decided to approach the Victorian government to seek 'some compromise' over its appeal. With *Portnoy* removed from the banned list, the government had to move: it grudgingly agreed that that *Portnoy* could be sold to people aged eighteen and above.¹⁰ But it was not about to back down completely. It continued to insist that the 414 copies of *Portnoy* that police had seized in 1970 be destroyed. This was petty and silly, and Hooker insisted, just as obstinately, that he be there to see it happen. But in October 1972, when it finally came time for the books to be incinerated, Hooker was amused to attend the destruction and find that all the copies had disappeared — likely pilfered and sold by the police.[11]

Other state governments remained intransigent. A week after Customs rescinded its ban, Tasmanian attorney-general Max Bingham warned that nothing had changed in his state: anyone offering *Portnoy* for sale would be prosecuted. That prompted derision and laughter. Shadow attorney-general Mervyn Everett, who in March had defended John Reid for selling the book, lampooned the announcement. 'Tasmania will be a laughing stock,' he said. '... The attorney-general's latest decision will do nothing to enhance the reputation of Tasmania in literary circles, nor will it be approved by Tasmanians who still regard themselves as part of the Commonwealth.'[12]

But Bingham was impervious to the laughter. 'The legal difficulties which caused recent prosecutions [of John Reid and Ian Pearce] in respect of this book to be abandoned,' he said, 'would not necessarily arise on any future occasion. In this event, any proceedings would be taken to their conclusion.' He had been guided by the advice of the National Literature Board of Review, he said, and 'nothing, in my opinion, has occurred which has changed the status of the book in Tasmania at all'.[13] Bingham insisted later that his resistance did not arise from a particular moral standpoint on *Portnoy* — although he doubted that he would 'have gone to the barricades' for the book. His comments were instead the natural consequence of his position that it was Tasmania's prerogative to determine what should be distributed within its borders. 'Tasmania is its own state,' Bingham argued later, 'and it had the right to maintain its own laws and determine them. Any attempt to bind Tasmania unjustifiably to a decision made in Canberra was not popular with me — nor, I think, would it be to many Tasmanians.'[14]

Bingham's colleagues did not disagree. Approached by

intermediaries working on Graham C. Greene's behalf, Tasmanian chief secretary Kevin Lyons — an independent in coalition with the Liberals, who also served as deputy premier — confirmed that any vendor of *Portnoy's Complaint* would be prosecuted under the state's criminal code 'in order to obtain a jury decision on the question of whether or not it is an obscene publication. I would point out,' Lyons added, 'that a conviction has been obtained in a prosecution relating to this book in Victoria and that juries disagreed twice in New South Wales about it.'[15]

Officials within the Department of Customs groaned when they heard of Bingham's position. 'All has been quiet since [*Portnoy's*] release, except in Tasmania,' recorded one official. After the announcement that Tasmania would maintain its ban, Chipp had agreed to talk to Bingham 'to quieten him down'. But Bingham's willingness to respond to Everett in such absolute terms, Customs thought, had been silly. With their own role in the matter now at an end, Customs officials wished simply for *Portnoy* to go away. 'It seems to me he has dug a ditch for himself and will not be able to back down gracefully,' wrote one official. 'However, it seems of local interest only — I think everyone else is heartily sick of *Portnoy's Complaint*.'[16]

But Bingham was not alone. Upon enquiry, the assistant administrator in the Northern Territory, M.W. McDonald, advised that any decision to import and sell *Portnoy* should be made in consultation with a legal adviser. 'But the Northern Territory Police will take such action as they see fit,' McDonald added, 'should they detect breaches of section 57 of the *Police and Police Offences Ordinances* 1923–1971.'[17]

Queensland, too, proved to be unamenable. Notwithstanding that the state Literature Board of Review had decided against placing an explicit ban on *Portnoy* in 1971 — declaring that it was refraining 'from entering the field of serious literature' — police had seized copies from the People's Bookshop, on Brisbane's Brunswick Street, and the government had pressed ahead with legal proceedings against proprietors Bill Sutton and Vincent Englart. But those proceedings were stalled more than a year later, meaning that efforts to ascertain *Portnoy*'s legality were frustrated. Officials from the state government told Graham C. Greene's contacts that the matter against Sutton and Englart was *sub judice*, and that no comment or clarity on *Portnoy* could be offered.[18]

Sutton, a self-proclaimed 'shearing-shed anarchist', had taken over the People's Bookshop in the 1960s, and had stocked it with an enormous range of literature, music, poetry, and art. Much of it was socialist and communist in bent, and the clientele that visited were similarly inclined. The historian Humphrey McQueen, for example, purchased *The Modern Prince* — Antonio Gramsci's commentary on Machiavelli — from the People's Bookshop, and used it while writing *A New Britannia*.[19] Sutton was avowedly anti-censorship and adept at winning allies to his cause. As the case over *Portnoy* dragged on, with adjournments aplenty, he solicited donations for his defence in the Communist Party–owned *Tribune* and from the Right to Read movement in Melbourne.

It took until the middle of 1972 for his case to be resolved. In the Brisbane Magistrates' Court on 3 May, Magistrate E. Martin cut short the first day's proceedings to read *Portnoy*. The next day, Martin declared his finding that the book was obscene. He had found it 'filthy', and was disgusted by the continued references to 'gross sexual perversion'. 'Anybody who does not think this book is filthy is not,' he said, 'in my opinion, in step with the community so far as decency is concerned.' He found Sutton and Englart both guilty.

Sutton and Englart's lawyer argued that the penalties for the offence should be nominal, and was given leave to call evidence to support that argument. The defence had four witnesses, all from the University of Queensland. First was Professor Peter Edwards, who said *Portnoy* was not just about sex, and that, while funny, it was also a very moral work: 'It is of such quality that I have set it for a group of postgraduate students to study.' English lecturer

Rev. John Strugnell said *Portnoy* was a 'serious book', and lecturer Leon Cantrell argued that it was comedic but also 'immensely serious'. The last witness, solicitor Ron Finney, showed the court various pornographic books that he had bought at random in other Brisbane bookshops: they emphasised sex and violence, he said, without making any serious moral point, as *Portnoy* did.

Martin appeared to listen only because he had to. When they were done, he fined Sutton $20 — half of the maximum possible penalty — and ordered the seized copies destroyed.[20]

The fine was token, the number of copies small, and Sutton could see the wry side of the matter. A budding writer and member of a realist writers' group in Brisbane, Sutton used the trial as basis for his satirical fable, 'The Goodlooking Bookseller and the Ugly Society', in which the eponymous bookseller is charged for selling *Portnoy's Complaint*. The matter does not upset him. He has stocked the novel with a plan to eventually sell it to police and be brought before the courts. He is 'not fooled by the propaganda that he lived in a free country' — especially in the 'city of the Winding River', in the state of 'Banana-land', where 'Kama Sutra Joe' is premier, and the government looks after its mates. He is, however, curious about why he is being prosecuted, and so asks a friend, Professor Harry Edwards, for an explanation. 'If the capitalist can control you sexually,' Edwards tells him, 'then they have you by the balls politically.'

The trial unfolds much as it did to Sutton, but the Goodlooking Bookseller is undeterred. When a moral panic breaks out over another book — this one, small, red, and intended for children — he decides to stock and sell it, as well.[21]

* * *

The Little Red Schoolbook was the work of Danish schoolteachers Søren Hansen and Jesper Jensen. A compilation of frank, calm advice on a gamut of topics for adolescent children — sex, drugs, alcohol, politics, authority, and independence — its benign name was nonetheless all out of sync with the controversy that it aroused all over the world. It was banned in France and Italy, denounced by the pope, and became the subject of a long-running obscenity case in the UK that went, eventually, to the European Court of Human Rights.

In Australia, the book caused considerable angst. Referred to the National Literature Board of Review in July 1971, Customs held off on an explicit decision on whether to ban it until the following year. In the interim, activists smuggled the book into Australia, and began to circulate a domestically printed edition — notably, under the auspices of 'Thor'. Despite this, Customs continued to explore whether it could ban the book. But Chipp rapidly came to realise that a ban would not work. Even if the matter of the domestic edition were set aside, the book's content just did not justify banning. The book did not advocate drug use. Its discussion of sex was frank but far from pornographic — a crucial problem, if Customs was to try to invoke Regulation 4A. The book did warn young readers not to trust adults — 'All grown-ups are paper tigers,' it declared — but this was not firm ground for a ban.[22]

Conservative-minded MPs in the government nonetheless became increasingly critical. Partly stemming from the acrimony that had suffused the Liberal Party since John Gorton had been deposed from the prime ministership and replaced by his deputy and foreign minister, William McMahon, in March 1971, the controversy over *The Little Red Schoolbook* also pointed to the desire among some MPs for the government to continue to be the guardian of the nation's morals and virtue. John McLeay, the assistant minister assisting the minister for civil aviation, said that allowing the book would undermine morals among schoolchildren; government backbencher and malcontent Les Irwin bleated that it could lead young people into 'misbehaviour'.

This noise and fuss prompted McMahon to call Chipp and tell him to change the decision. When Chipp refused, McMahon told him that the matter would go to cabinet — and that he would be forced to change the decision. Over the weekend that followed, Chipp heard that McMahon was backgrounding the press on the matter, boasting that cabinet would override Chipp. Chipp decided to raise the stakes. Calculating that McMahon could not afford a resignation ahead of the election due that year, he decided to call the prime minister's bluff: Chipp spread the word that, if he were forced to reverse the decision, he would resign.[23]

At cabinet on the morning of 18 April 1972, *The Little Red Schoolbook* matter was at the top of the agenda.[24] Chipp was blunt when he made his case. The advice from his department was clear. As there were no grounds for banning the book under the *Customs Act*, any censorship would have to be political. The advice he had received, he said, including from educationists, was against banning. 'Beyond that,' he went on, 'the practical point is that the book is here and being printed. So there is no opportunity, in reality, to ban the book.' Moreover, any such ban would doubtless have been appealed — just as any ban cabinet sought now would be appealed.

McMahon's retreat, in the face of Chipp's well-publicised threat and his argument, was quick and ignominious. 'I have read only one chapter [of *The Little Red Schoolbook*],' he said, 'and I found it unbelievable — I didn't read further.' He accepted Chipp's position that there should be no ban on the imported edition. 'On practicalities and on law, we could not sustain a ban. So the minister's position is sound.'

The ministers who spoke afterwards grudgingly agreed, but their comments underscored their view of censorship as a way of maintaining morality in the community. Peter Nixon, the minister for shipping and transport, said *The Little Red Schoolbook* was 'in very bad taste, ludicrous and disgusting', that its section on sex 'justifies banning', and that the 'subversive slant' in its discussion of the school system was not appropriate — but also admitted that Chipp's case was sound. The minister for education, Malcolm Fraser, grumbled that the book 'undermined family and society', but also conceded that Chipp's position was correct. Ian Sinclair, the minister for primary industry, made no secret of his dislike for the book, but emphasised, repeatedly, that Chipp was in the right and that the government should stand behind him.

There was no room for manouevre. A ban would not be instituted. The only action that the government could take was to have Fraser exercise his 'influence and authority' to prevent the book being distributed to schools.[25]

It was a desultory attempt, made at the last gasp, to reassert the powers of the censors to shape the country's morals — and it was, almost immediately, snuffed out. The state governments almost as a whole decided not to prosecute the publisher of a domestically produced edition; Bill Sutton openly invited prosecution from the Queensland state government for stocking and selling it; and Wendy Bacon — still fighting against the censorship regime — led university students across the country in a protest against the restrictions on the book by handing out copies to schoolchildren.

As the year wore on, with the Liberal government limping towards an election that it knew it was almost certainly going to lose, further acts of defiance emerged. The most notable of these was Angus & Robertson's decision, late in November, to publish a domestically printed edition of *Beautiful Losers*, the second novel written by Leonard Cohen before his switch to music. Originally published in 1966, *Beautiful Losers* had been almost immediately banned by the Commonwealth's Literature Censorship Board for its focus on sexuality, its profanities, and its depiction of sex and drug-taking.

The mixed results of the *Portnoy* trials had led the book's UK publisher, Jonathan Cape, to approach the National Literature Board of Review for a reconsideration of the ban — but they were rebuffed. Angus & Robertson thus decided to publish it in the same way that Penguin had published *Portnoy*, but this time restricted the number of copies to 3,000, and produced it as a hardcover priced at a relatively expensive $4.95.

Richard Walsh, who had been appointed publisher at Angus & Robertson by Gordon Barton after his success in running *Nation Review*, was forthright about the reasons for publishing and the impunity with which the company was operating.[26] 'Basically,' he said, 'we believe this is a very fine book, which should be published and read. A confrontation with the censor is only a very secondary motive. All we want to do is get the book on the market, and achieve some steady sales.' And although police came to Angus & Robertson's new premises on Pitt Street on the first day that *Beautiful Losers* was available, and purchased copies — all in front of the press — Walsh was not cowed.[27] Angus & Robertson did not seriously expect to be taken to court, he said. 'Not after *Portnoy*.'[28]

If the company were taken to court, however, it would fight. 'We felt there had to be a confrontation over censorship,' Walsh said later, 'with *Beautiful Losers* if need be. And when the state saw how strong we were — particularly having Gordon Barton, who was rich and willing to spend money to defend it, to go on a crusade for it — they backed off. They had lost the war on *Portnoy's Complaint*. They had lost the war on *Oz* and *Tharunka*. And they decided to turn their attention to other matters.'[29]

Angus & Robertson did, however, decide to withhold the book from sale in Western Australia, largely because it could not judge the effect of the changes that had been made to the state's *Obscene and Indecent Publications Act* in the wake of the failed case against Joan Broomhall. Although those changes had been made with the express aim of targeting 'certain magazines' and not '*bona fide* writers', there was sufficient concern from Angus & Robertson that a prosecution could follow if they distributed the book in Western Australia. Their decision to withhold it from sale was embarrassing; according to one Perth journalist, people in the state were 'writhing' from the knowledge that they were being bracketed with Queensland in the censorship fights.[30]

But then there was the election, on 2 December. The Labor Party, led by Gough Whitlam, with his promises in healthcare, education, taxation, and the arts, won office — and, in a series of swift decisions, began to dismantle the book censorship regime. On 19 December, responsibility for censorship was transferred to the Department of the Attorney-General. From then on, it was no longer the remit of the Department of Customs to search luggage bags for banned literature; nor was it up to the department to determine whether material should be banned. The days of acting as a protector of the nation's virtues and morality were over.[31] As the subsequent advice to Customs officers had it, 'The customs role in censorship matters will … progressively diminish.'[32]

It was the moment where everything changed — punctuated, perhaps fittingly, by the Whitlam government's decision that same month to allow into Australia the Warner Bros.' film adaptation of *Portnoy's Complaint.*

CHAPTER 17

Stories of Australian censorship

A year after the *Portnoy* trials ended, John Hooker went to the US and met the man whose book had spurred the whole affair. Philip Roth had not resiled from controversy in the three years since he had published *Portnoy's Complaint*. He had since published a caustic and satirical *roman à clef* of US president Richard Nixon, *Our Gang* (1971), and a surreal homage to Kafka, *The Breast* (1972). But he had grown weary of the notoriety that *Portnoy* continued to attract — to the point that, during the fight over his novel in Australia, he had allowed his agent to say only that he was 'amused' by the whole affair. Thus, at Hooker's explanation of what had happened, Roth deadpanned: 'I suppose, after me, all the shits came in?'[1]

There was something to this, as Hooker acknowledged. In its efforts to reform the censorship system so that adults could choose what they wanted to read and view — whittling the list of banned books down to zero, and declining to use section 4 of the *Customs Act* to ban books and launch prosecutions — the

Whitlam government all but did away with the controls that could keep publications out of Australia. In light of this, the state and federal governments had to negotiate an agreement to provide a new approach to writing that claimed no literary or artistic merit — that is, to pornography. The agreement they reached shifted the onus of regulations onto the point of sale. Imported and domestically produced works would be classified by the federal government according to agreed-upon guidelines, and those works would be subject to restrictions on how they could be displayed and sold. The aim was to simultaneously ensure the freedom of access to material for adults, to protect children, and to prevent public offence.

Along with the growth of the American pornography industry and the proliferation of domestic publications — made possible by continued innovation in printing technology — the result was a dramatic increase in the availability of and demand for pornography in Australia. By 1974, the New South Wales government was complaining that Sydney had been 'flooded' by pornography.[2] The shits, as Roth had suggested, had certainly come in. Those who won most from the censorship fights, Richard Walsh said later, were the producers of pornography: 'They were the ones who took advantage, and got the most advantage.'[3]

There were attempts to stem the tide. The Queensland Literature Board of Review sought to step in where the federal government had retreated, and set about prohibiting an increasing amount of material. It banned ninety-three publications in 1972–73, sixty-seven in 1973–74, eighty-two in 1974–75, and eighty-six in 1975–76. In its annual report for 1973–74, in a section titled 'A Nation of Voyeurs', the board argued that its prohibitions had nothing to do with the individual's freedom to read:

> The author of this stuff will always be with us: those who publish on lavatory walls are in essence urged by the same zeal. The pedlar, however, of all this whether he emerges from the lavatory

or some gilded lair, must be restrained from using the magnificent
services of printing, publication, and distribution to present to all
of us (and there is none of us immune from these depravities), the
degradation of humans taking their sex as animals.[4]

Other states established their own classification bodies, or
gave to existing ones more generous powers. The Victorian State
Advisory Board, for example, was established with powers to classify
printed material in the same manner as films were; in New South
Wales, two years after a failed attempt to reform obscenity law in
1973, the government passed the *Indecent Articles and Classified
Publications Act*, establishing the Publications Classification Board,
which was tasked with advising the chief secretary on the category
of publications.[5] A restricted publication could only be sold to
people aged eighteen and over; a direct-sale publication could only
be sold via mail order or after an unsolicited request from a person
aged eighteen and over. It was of a piece with attempts to regulate
the display, advertising, and sale of sexual material — not to ban
the sale itself.

Censorship, in effect, was reconfigured as a process of classification, with availability, display, and ratings all used to inform
the prospective reader or viewer of the nature of the material. The
arguments for the continuation of censorship evolved alongside
this shift. In addition to his criticism of the proliferation of pornography, Peter Coleman came to argue that censorship was necessary
if a society was to have any way of expressing its disapproval: it was
a way of labelling, of alerting the public to disreputable material.
As he put it, pithily, to censor material in this way was to censure
that material.[6]

This shift in the censorship debate left literature behind.
Within three years of the unprecedented series of court trials and
legal action, books such as *Portnoy's Complaint* no longer bothered
anyone. For all the heat and passion that it had aroused, *Portnoy*
was essentially different from the 'cheap, filthy, tabloid-type

publications' that now proliferated, one NSW politician remarked. The difference was in the way that sex and 'filth' were depicted. It was the difference 'between the pictorial and the manuscript', between the image and the printed word.[7]

Efforts to protect the community — through restriction and quarantine — were thereafter directed towards images, and controversy over censorship moved to magazines and films; and then, in time, to videos, video games, and material accessed via the internet. And although there were still occasions when it became a matter of contention, writing and reading in Australia were, for the most part, no longer subject to acts of censorship.

For writers and readers, the end of book censorship was a profound change. The poet Nancy Keesing, who had testified on behalf of *Portnoy's Complaint* in the first trial in New South Wales, later commented that censorship's disappearance was 'the greatest and most beneficial change' to writing in her lifetime.[8] Yet memories of it faded quickly, slipped easily into the past. Like the experiments with Prohibition, what remained was disbelief that censorship had ever been real. It seemed absurd, a joke. 'That ever so many books could have been put on any one list, and people told that they were not to read them,' Peter Cowan commented later, 'seems to be like something out of science fiction.'[9]

But for the laws of libel and defamation, the 'literary onanisms' that Arthur Angell Phillips had lamented in 1969 were now at an end. Reading would come to be regarded as a means of education and self-improvement, not corruption or depravation. Writers had the freedom to explore their ideas in whatever way they wished, to use the words that they saw fitting, to depict the whole spectrum of life, without fear of censure or imprisonment. Publishers could accept and print material without fear of prosecution. Booksellers and librarians could order books and place them all on the shelves, holding nothing under the counter, fearing no visit from the Vice Squad. And readers coming to explore the literary world could wander, browse, and read without limit.

* * *

The downfall of the censorship regime was a hard-won moment that came after a long campaign of opposition. Over the decades, there had been authors tried, shamed, fined, and — in the case of Robert Close — imprisoned for their work. There had been activists who had openly defied the censorship regime: from Leon Fink and Alex Sheppard, to the crew and organisers of *American Hurrah*, to Dennis Altman and his copies of *Totempole* and *Myra Breckinridge*, to Wendy Bacon and Frank Moorhouse. There had been the editors, writers, and printers of *Oz*, of *Tharunka* and its spin-offs. There had been booksellers who had nourished the opposition to censorship by selling illicit volumes from under their counters. There had been publishers and printers who had typeset and published banned works at considerable risk to their livelihoods and liberties. There had been academics and critics who had continued to argue and to agitate, to question and to criticise. Over successive decades, the actions of these protagonists ensured that the grounds for opposition to censorship were always fertile.

The publication of *Portnoy's Complaint* had been made possible by that long opposition. Penguin's cultural pride in publishing *Lady Chatterley's Lover* in the UK, and its burgeoning publishing program of vibrant and culturally engaged Australian works underscored the company's motivation to publish *Portnoy*. With improvements for scale, Penguin followed the model that Fink and Sheppard had provided when they published *The Trial of Lady Chatterley* in 1965. The support that Penguin received from booksellers and activists was of a piece with the ongoing opposition of those booksellers and activists to censorship. The press coverage that *Portnoy* attracted was predicated, in part, on knowledge of the censorship controversies of the past: their spectacle, their sound, their fury. The public's uptake of the novel — buying it in numbers large enough to make it a bestseller many times over, in barely a month — stemmed from the notoriety, merit, and 'buzz' that surrounded the novel. The willingness of writers, academics, and experts to testify to the excellence and worth of *Portnoy* emanated from the common-felt duty among the literary community to see censorship gone.

Where the publication of *Portnoy's Complaint* figures most in the history of the end of book censorship is in its scale and scope. It was an unprecedented undertaking. In all the opposition to censorship in Australia, no other act of defiance was as bold. It was the first occasion where one book was used to test every channel of the Australian censorship system. It was an expensive, deliberate, and highly publicised affront to the censorship authorities, conducted within view of the public and — by its sales and its press coverage — with the support of that public, too. In circumventing the Department of Customs, and evading, with mixed success, the various state governments, *Portnoy's Complaint* exposed them as near powerless and out of touch, trying to shield an increasingly mature people from the supposedly corrupting story of a man tormented by and obsessed with his mother and his penis.

Penguin's decision to invite prosecutions in states across the country magnified the impact of the book's publication and the importance of the challenge it represented. It became a supreme test case. No other work published to defy the censorship regime was the subject of so many court cases in Australia, nor in so many jurisdictions. As it turned out, those trials exposed crucial flaws in the censorship system and in the rationales put forward by advocates for its continuation. For all the polling that Arthur Rylah and Eric Willis brandished, pointing to support within the community for censorship, the trials revealed a far more nuanced picture. Support for censorship was not monolithic, and though the opposition to it was not perhaps yet a majority of the population, as Geoffrey Dutton had claimed in 1970, there was nonetheless a sufficiently large opposition to make change almost certain.[10]

In the aftermath of the *Lady Chatterley* trial in the UK, much had been made of the suggestion that England in the 1960s was like Disraeli's two nations: no intercourse or sympathy between them; each ignorant of the other's habits, thoughts, and feelings; formed by different breeding and ordered by different manners.[11] The same might be said of Australia's community standards during this period. Plainly, the great number of people who purchased *Portnoy's Complaint* did not believe it contravened those standards. The varying verdicts in the court trials, meanwhile, suggested that there was no uniformity in those standards, even among those tasked with determining them. Magistrates and judges made markedly different decisions: even when proclaiming their disgust with *Portnoy's Complaint* and finding defendants guilty, they accepted that there was more to the work than that disgust alone. The twenty-four men empanelled in the two juries in New South Wales were ostensibly representatives of the community — but they, too, could come to no agreement.

The trials also exposed the inadequacy of the censorship laws to deal with works that simultaneously triggered bans and the exemptions from those bans. The flowing stream that was supposed to separate high culture and low, that ran between literature and filth, as Kenny put it in the New South Wales trial, was, in *Portnoy's Complaint*, muddied. Was it obscene, or a work of literary merit? Was it both? Which was the more important?

These questions were both a diversion and a paradox. As the historian Barbara Sullivan was to later point out, even if *Portnoy's Complaint* could have been neatly placed onto one side or the other, there was no longer any agreement that this was the basis on which it should be censored.[12] The argument pursued by Wendy Bacon and her fellow writers in the pages of *Tharunka* and its variants — arguing not for obscenity redeemed by literary merit, but rather obscenity, in no need of redemption, as a valid and useful language on its own — had exposed the artificiality and class dimensions of that separation. Why should obscenity require some kind of literary merit? What even was that, but a way of treating some books differently from others? The *Portnoy* trials not only helped to unsettle the ambit of the term *literary merit*, but also that of *obscenity*.[13]

'*Portnoy's Complaint* was a very good case [to run],' Bacon said later. 'It was respectable and literary, but also very explicit. It wasn't a run-of-the-mill literary defence. It was unique.'[14] In some ways, the novel proved what they had argued: obscenity could be its own, vital subject (as Roth had said, obscenity is 'very nearly the issue' in the novel), just as worthy as 'literature'.[15] It won an agreement, widespread if not always wholehearted, that art could explore the obscene. In 1982, when controversy erupted over Juan Davila's *Stupid as a Painter*, his tableau of flesh and fluid, New South Wales premier Neville Wran immediately ruled out police action: 'I do not think art has got anything to do with the Vice Squad.'[16] Such a statement would have been unthinkable a decade earlier.

In another vein, *Portnoy's* subject matter insidiously paralleled the arguments for censorship: just as the solitary act of masturbation was supposed to be dangerous for the masturbator, so was reading supposed to be dangerous to the reader. *Portnoy's Complaint* showed that argument to be profoundly flawed.

As the foundations and the ambit of censorship became increasingly untenable, the trials of *Portnoy* helped to bring to light a crucial point: the state's efforts to position itself, through government, the bureaucracy, and the judiciary, as the guardian of public morals and virtue. This role was not passive. In guarding morals and virtues, it also shaped them, categorising and delineating what was acceptable and what was not. But where the public had once been willing to accept that guardianship, it was no longer willing to do so in the 1960s and 1970s.

Censorship could not coexist with the debates that activists and writers were forcing on sexuality, power, education, gender, and discrimination. And notwithstanding that these debates and their results would be an enduring source of controversy, censorship would never be as accepted as it once was. By the 1970s, the long-running campaigns and protests against it had flowered and found recognition in the platform of Whitlam's Labor Party. And when that party came to power, to give effect to changes that had already been underway for years, the censorship of books was all but over.

Julie Rigg would not be able to write her book about the *Portnoy* affair. Life got in the way.[17] But the initiative and courage shown by Penguin — in particular, by Michie, Hooker, and Froelich — would not be forgotten. The demise of censorship became an essential part of the realisation of their ambitions for Australian literature and publishing. They understood its significance: Penguin Australia went from strength to strength. It was no longer a clearing house for a British publishing program. It developed a vibrant list of culturally engaged Australian works — more and more of them original titles — that sold well in Australia and abroad. The significance of *Portnoy* in accelerating this was not to be understated.

When *Portnoy* was published, Peter Coleman sensed that it would be significant. Writing in the *Bulletin* a few days afterwards, he declared that the story of *Portnoy*'s publication would be 'an important one in the story of Australian censorship'. Matters had already begun to shift: the agreement for uniform censorship had already been shattered. Don Chipp was raising the stakes, declaring the return of the 'dark ages'. Coleman was less worried. It was a 'revival of enlightenment', he wrote. 'There should be more of it.'[18]

More enlightenment would come. The end of censorship was not far off. And *Portnoy* would play a significant role in bringing about that end. As Graham C. Greene wrote to Michie only a few months later, after the first *Portnoy* trial in Victoria: 'You have certainly won a great moral victory, and I cannot believe that the censorship situation in Australia will ever be quite the same.'[19]

Acknowledgements

This account has drawn on an array of published, unpublished, archival, and interview-based material. The most crucial of the published works are Nicole Moore's authoritative history of Australian censorship, *The Censor's Library*, and Geoffrey Dutton's *A Rare Bird*, a history of Penguin Books Australia. I am indebted to these works and their authors.

I am also in the debt of those who spoke with me about Penguin Books, Philip Roth, *Portnoy's Complaint*, the trials, and censorship in Australia: Wendy Bacon, Blake Bailey, Reginald Barrett, Sir Max Bingham, Penelope Buckley, Stephen Charles, Hal G.P. Colebatch, Maureen Colman, Dennis Douglas, Sam Everingham, Leon Fink, Peter Froelich, Lucy Frost, Paul Grainger, Jennifer Gribble, Peter Grose, Margaret Harris, Nicholas Hasluck, Harry Heseltine, Tom Hughes, Stuart Kells, Brian Kiernan, Joanne Lee Dow, David Marr, Joan Masterman, Hilary McPhee, Meredith Michie, Nicole Moore, Malcolm Oakes, John Reid, Julie Rigg, Bob Sessions, Jeff Sparrow, Brian Stonier, Jennifer Strauss, Ian Viner, David Walsh, Richard Walsh, Charles Waterstreet, and Charles

Wooley. For their help, kindness, patience, and generosity, all are due my considerable thanks.

I wish to thank those who gave me permission to access and reproduce from public and private archival papers and photographs: the family of Geoffrey Dutton, the family of Graham C. Greene, the family of John Hooker, Hilary McPhee, Freya Michie, Matthew Michie, James Michie, Julie Rigg, the family of Frederick Osborne, the estate of Philip Roth and the Wylie Agency, the family of A.W. Sheppard, the estate of Patrick White, the New South Wales State Archives, the New South Wales District Court Registry Office, the Penguin Random House Archive, and the Penguin Archive. I also wish to thank Catherine Reade, of Fairfax Pictures, and Kevin Davis, of Newspix, for their aid in unearthing some of the photos used in this book.

I wish to thank the efforts of staff at various libraries, archives, and institutions. In particular, I thank staff at the National Library of Australia, the National Archives of Australia, the Library of the University of Canberra, the New South Wales State Archives, the State Records Office of Western Australia, the State Library of New South Wales, the Penguin Archive at the University of Bristol, and Ceri Lumley of the Special Collections section of the Penguin Random House Archive at the University of Reading.

This book received invaluable support, in the form of a grant, from ArtsACT: I thank the team and the government that affords this vital support for writers and artists in the Canberra region.

This is the second book that I have been honoured to publish with Scribe. I wish to thank Henry Rosenbloom and his team for their fine work, support, and expertise.

I could not have written this book without the generosity and all-round forebearance of my colleagues, my friends, and my family. For their generosity and advocacy, I am indebted to colleagues at the University of Canberra — including, but not limited to, Shane Strange, Katie Hayne, Tony Eaton, and Jen Webb — and to colleagues and friends further afield, especially Professor Nicole

Moore, of UNSW Canberra; Professor Matthew Ricketson, of Deakin University; and Professor John Nethercote, of Australian Catholic University, who read over the manuscript and made valuable suggestions and comments.

My parents continue to be soundly supportive, loving, and interested, in spite of the 'slipshod' language of this book: I thank them. My wife, Kate — who has seen too many weekends and evenings disappear with my head in a book or archive box — has throughout it all been patient, generous, loving, and encouraging: I thank her from the bottom of my heart, and look forward to repaying the enormous debt I owe to her.

Finally, this book is for my siblings — Sean, Siobhan, and Liam — for their good humour, their longstanding encouragement, and their love.

Notes

Chapter 2: In the national interest

1   This chapter draws on Nicole Moore's authoritative history of censorship in Australia (2012) and Deana Heath's pre-eminent exploration of the role played by racial and imperial ideologies in the formation of the censorship regime in Australia (2010).

2   Heath, in Lyons and Arnold (eds), 2001, pp. 69–82. As Heath points out, there is a strong racial dimension to censorship policy: what was virtuous and moral was inevitably also homogenous and white.

3   'Prohibited books', *Herald* (Melbourne), 13 September 1901, p. 1.

4   Smith, *House of Commons Hansard*, 8 May 1888, vol. 325.

5   Heath, 2010, pp. 101–07.

6   'Melbourne, Saturday', *Age*, 17 July 1889, p. 8.

7   *Daily Telegraph* (Melbourne), 30 July 1889, cf. Coleman, 1963, pp. 4–5.

8   On the stand, Professor Edward Morris of the University of Melbourne would prompt considerable laughter from the public galleries when he said that, after reading the books, he felt he 'needed a bath', that his 'moral tone' had not been lowered because he had been 'on guard' while reading the books, and that only time could tell whether he had fallen from his 'high estate'. See Day, 1996, p. 104.

9   'Prohibited literature', *Daily Telegraph*, 21 September 1901, p. 9.

10   Coleman, 1963, p. 12.

11   *1904 New South Wales Royal Commission on the Decline of the Birth Rate
     and on the Mortality of Infants in New South Wales Report*, vol. 1, p. 32.

12   Heath, in Lyons and Arnold (eds), 2001, pp. 69–82. Justice Windeyer
     ruled in 1888 that information about birth control was not obscene.

13   General order 978, in Coleman, 1963, p. 20. H.N.P. Wollaston would
     write in 1904 that 'the question of what is indecent is so largely a matter
     of taste that no definition can be given which is entirely satisfactory to all
     minds'. See Wollaston, 1904, pp. 35–36.

14   Marr, 2008, p. 464.

15   'Trade and Customs: the interesting history of a great department', *Life: a
     record for busy folk*, Melbourne, 15 November 1907, p. 446.

16   Heath, 2010, p. 95.

17   Garran, 1958, p. 221.

18   Moore, 2012, p. 73.

19   Ibid., p. 77.

20   See, in particular, Barnes, 2014, pp. 75–93.

21   Norman Lindsay, 'Norman Lindsay loses his temper at last with
     officialdom', *Smith's Weekly*, 31 May 1930, p. 8.

22   'Banning a book', *Argus*, 19 January 1933, p. 8.

23   'Books and morals', *News* (Adelaide), 18 January 1933, p. 4.

24   'Brave new world', *Herald* (Melbourne), 9 February 1933, p. 14.

25   'Censorship of Books', Cabinet decision, 9 May 1933, Papers of Thomas
     White, National Library of Australia (NLA) MS 9148.

26   'Book censorship: Advisory Board's duties', *Sydney Morning Herald*
     (*SMH*), 14 July 1933, p. 12.

27   Barnes, 2014, p. 78.

28   For background on Ball, see Koyabashi, 2013, pp. 35–38. For an
     authoritative account of the league's activities, see Barnes, 2014,
     pp. 75–93.

29   Sendy, 1983, p. 68.

30   W. Macmahon Ball, 'Book censorship', *Age*, 16 February 1935, p. 23.

31   White to Jieland, 5 September 1935, Papers of Thomas White, NLA MS
     9148.

32 It also stirred his combative side. White pushed back, hard, on critics in the press; he claimed that the Book Censorship Abolition League was disingenuous about its aims and that it wished to allow the proliferation of indecent and obscene material — that is, pornography. He quoted inaccurate figures about the instances of censorship, and conflated works that had been banned for indecency with works that had been banned on grounds of sedition. Interspersed with this were some credible arguments for a degree of censorship. The most compelling was that the Commonwealth's withdrawal from censorship would result in inconsistent application of censorship across the country, as each state would deal with works differently; moreover, this argument ran, any move to liberalise the importing and distribution of political works would allow obscene works, too.

33 Martin, 1993, p. 202. For a further example of Menzies' liberalism on these questions during this interwar period, see the minutes of his 9 November 1937 meeting with leaders of the Council for Civil Liberties. Calling him 'a liberal influence' in the cabinet, those leaders would ask Menzies for help removing postal restrictions on the circulation of a Yugoslavian newspaper, and debate with him the provisions of the *War Precautions Act* that allowed the prosecution of individuals for inciting the overthrow of the government; see National Archives of Australia (NAA): CP450/7, 284.

34 Lyons, *Commonwealth Parliamentary Debates* (*CPD*), vol. 150, 22 May 1936, p. 2243; Douglas, 2002, pp. 150–51.

35 Sir Robert Garran was appointed to this position. For Garran's views on censorship, see Garran, 1958, pp. 391–94; for criticism of Garran's work, see Moore, 2012, pp. 33–35.

36 Fisk to Wilson, 8 September 1941, NAA: C4480, 23.

37 Wilson to Harrison, 9 September 1941, NAA: C4480, 23.

38 Hasluck, 1997, pp. 61–65.

39 Harrison, 16 September 1941, annotation to Fisk to Wilson, NAA: C4480, 23.

40 'Joyce too much for Mr Hughes', *SMH*, 22 September 1941, p. 9.

41 'Harrison's hair stood on end', *Sun*, 19 September 1941, p. 4.

42 Payne, 1980, pp. 30–31.

43 Fullagar J, 1948, 'R v. Close', *Victorian Law Reports*, p. 467. Fullagar's writing on context and the existence of community standards would be cited internationally.

44 Iliffe, 1956, p. 134.

45 Kennedy to Allen, 16 May 1945, NAA: A3023, folder 1945/1947.

46 'Best-selling American novel banned', *SMH*, 1 August 1945, p. 3. Winsor would be profoundly unimpressed with this. 'I don't care whether Senator Keane likes my book or not,' she said, after she was informed of the ban. 'Apparently, he does not like English history. I don't make English history. The English did it first. I only wrote about it. When a reporter writes a murder story, you don't hang him for murder.' See 'Author critical of Sen. Keane', *SMH*, 4 August 1945, p. 3.

47 Kennedy to Dedman, 1 May 1946, NAA: C4480, 23.

48 Fred Osborne, interviewed by Ron Hurst, NLA Oral History, TRC 4900/108.

49 'Transport Publishing Company Pty Ltd et al v Literature Board of Review', 1956, HCA 73, 99 CLR, pp. 111–31.

50 Page, 1970, p. 127.

51 Peter Cowan, interviewed by Stuart Reid, October 1991–August 1992, NLA Oral History, TRC 287, pp. 9–10, 46.

52 Pamela Williams, in Rigg and Copeland (eds), 1985, p. 61.

53 Meere to Henty, 30 May 1957, NAA: C4480, 23.

54 Meere to Henty, unspecified date, July 1957, NAA: C4480, 23.

55 For a detailed account of the ban of *The Catcher in the Rye*, see Nicole Moore, in Dalziell and Genoni, 2013, pp. 181–87.

56 Dutton, 1994, p. 373; 'Book not banned', *Canberra Times*, 26 September 1957, p. 1.

57 'Censorship by customs clerks should end', *SMH*, 21 September 1957, p. 2.

58 Henty, *CPD Senate (Sen.)*, vol. 11, 25 October 1957, pp. 815–16.

59 Henty, *CPD Sen.*, vol. 12, 14 April 1958, pp. 577–80.

60 Coleman, 1963, p. 31.

61 Murray-Smith, in Dutton and Harris (eds), 1970, p. 84.

Chapter 3: Another country

1 'The James Baldwin banning', *Australian Book Review*, June 1963, vol. 2, no. 8, p. 122.

2 As Moore notes, Customs officials had been confiscating copies of *Another Country* for at least six months before the board recommended its ban in May 1963. See Moore, 2012, pp. 237–38.

3 Binns, 'Another Country' report, 27 May 1963, NAA: C4419, whole series.

4   Dutton, Wighton, and Harris, 'Open letter to Senator Henty', *Australian Book Review*, June 1963, vol. 2, no. 8, p. 122.

5   Muir, 1983, p. 186.

6   Ibid., p. 184.

7   'Freedom to read?', *Bulletin*, 28 March 1964, p. 7.

8   Richard Walsh argues that regulations forcing newspapers and magazines to be sold through newsagencies were a way to control those newspapers and magazines. The Newsagents Association of NSW and the ACT (NANA), dominated by the mainstream press companies, was never going to accept small, radical publications such as *Oz* and allow them to be sold in newsagencies. This forced *Oz* to have the paper sold on the streets. 'We had found another way. It was illegal,' Walsh says, 'but there really was no reason why we couldn't do it.' Author's interview with Richard Walsh, 15 May 2019.

9   Sullivan, 1998, p. 129.

10   Author's interview with Richard Walsh, 15 May 2019.

11   Author's correspondence with Peter Grose, 11 June 2019.

12   Richard Walsh, 'Twilight of sanity', *Oz*, no. 2, May 1963, pp. 4–5.

13   'Abortion', *Oz*, no. 1, April 1963, pp. 4–5.

14   Author's interview with Richard Walsh, 15 May 2019.

15   Neville and Walsh, 'Letter from editors', *Oz*, no. 5, December 1963, p. 5.

16   Neville, 1995, pp. 28–29.

17   Author's interview with Richard Walsh, 15 May 2019; Neville and Walsh, 'Letter from editors', *Oz*, no. 5, December 1963, p. 5.

18   Neville, 1995, p. 31.

19   'What a mock!', *Obscenity*, no. 2, p. 22.

20   'Oz in brief', *Tharunka*, 13 September 1963, p. 7.

21   *Oz*, no. 6, February 1964, p. 1.

22   'The judgement of Mr Locke', *Oz*, no. 14, October 1964, p. 9.

23   Richard Walsh, 'Twilight of sanity', *Oz*, no. 2, May 1963, pp. 4–5.

24   *Crowe v Graham*, 1958, 121 CLR 375, p. 394.

25   'Trial by jury in obscenity cases', *SMH*, 23 June 1967, p. 4.

26   Mackerras, in Clune and Turner (eds), 2006, pp. 387–99.

27   Evan Williams, 'The Chief Secretary once said Hell!', *SMH*, 4 October 1968, p. 2.

28   Willis, *New South Wales Hansard Legislative Assembly*, 28 September 1967, pp. 1773–79.

29   'Bill to prohibit reading under-16s', *SMH*, 18 January 1967, p. 1; 'Bill to force out "smut pedlars"', *SMH*, 29 September 1967, p. 5.

30 'Play ban theatre seeks advice', *SMH*, 26 July 1968, p. 4.

31 Anthony Blackshield, 'America Hurrah', *SMH*, 26 July 1968, p. 2.

32 Tasker, in Dutton and Harris (eds), 1970, pp. 39–44.

33 This account draws on Bacon, 2011; Moorhouse, 2007, pp. 5–35.

34 Author's interview with Wendy Bacon, 26 June 2019.

35 See *Tharunka*, 24 February 1970, pp. 3, 5; 3 March 1970, p. 10.

36 'Eskimo Nell', *Tharunka*, 18 March 1970, p. 32.

37 Frank Moorhouse would expand on this point, arguing that justifying the publication of material on the basis of its literary merit was, in effect, meeting the establishment — synonymous with the censors — on 'its own terms'. See Moorhouse, 1980, p. 9.

38 Author's interview with Wendy Bacon, 26 June 2019.

39 Wendy Bacon, Val Hodgson, and Alan Rees, 'Eskimo Nell', *Tharunka*, 18 March 1970, p. 3.

40 Moorhouse, 1980, p. 5.

41 'Tharunka obscenity charges', *SMH*, 18 August 1970, p. 10.

42 'Nun's habit fined', *SMH*, 13 February 1971, p. 8.

43 Wendy Bacon, 'Sex and censorship', *Lot's Wife*, 18 March 1971.

Chapter 4: The lady

1 Quinn to Comptroller-General, 11 October 1950, NAA: A425, 1964/8571. Expurgated editions were allowed into Australia; however, it appears that Customs did not retain an unexpurgated edition with which to compare those expurgated editions.

2 Cabinet submission no. 975, 'Unexpurgated editions of "Lady Chatterley's Lover" by D.H. Lawrence', 16 January 1961, and 'Notes on Cabinet submission no. 975', 10 February 1961, NAA: A4940, C3263.

3 Cabinet minute no. 1205, 'Unexpurgated editions of "Lady Chatterley's Lover" by D.H. Lawrence', 16 February 1961, NAA: A4940, C3263; Cabinet notebook, 'EJ Bunting, 6 February 1961–3 May 1961', NAA: A11099, 1/50. There are rumours that Menzies was most responsible for maintaining the ban on *Lady Chatterley*. Stephen Murray-Smith writes that Menzies was 'revolted by this story of the interpenetration of the working and middle classes' and that this spurred his involvement (in Dutton and Harris (eds), 1970, p. 86). Geoffrey Robertson (2019, pp. 66–67) cites a story from Frederick Osborne, then minister for repatriation, to the effect that cabinet had expected to rescind the ban after the UK trial, but that Menzies — declaring he had read the book and was 'not going to

allow' his wife to read it — insisted on the ban remaining in place.

4   Labor MP Les Haylen accused the government of being wary of antagonising the socially conservative Democratic Labor Party, whose votes Haylen suggested the government wanted in the Senate. See Haylen, *CPD House of Representatives (HoR)*, vol. 30, 8 March 1961, pp. 49–54.

5   Denham Henty, 'Press statement', 29 June 1961, NAA: D596, 1961/2081.

6   'The Trial of Lady Chatterley by RALPH, CH–Release in Australia', NAA: A490/1, C4178.

7   Kenneth Anderson, interviewed by Mel Pratt, NLA Oral History, TRC 121/90.

8   Sheppard and Buckley, it appears, knew each other through the Council for Civil Liberties, and had met in the mid-1950s while on a delegation to Cyprus. See 'Kenneth Donald Buckley — Volume 1', NAA: A6119, 479 Reference Copy.

9   A.W. Sheppard, interviewed by Ann Turner, NLA Oral History, TRC 2725.

10   Ken Buckley, interviewed by Ann Turner, NLA Oral History, TRC 3018.

11   Author's interview with Leon Fink, 6 March 2019.

12   Sheppard to Penguin, 10 February 1965, Papers of A.W. Sheppard, NLA MS 8029, Box 3; author's interview with Leon Fink, 6 March 2019.

13   '"Chatterley" book on sale today', *SMH*, 15 April 1965, p. 4.

14   Murray-Smith, in Dutton and Harris (eds), 1970, p. 87. Sheppard later claimed that Max Harris refused to take copies of *Trial* so he would not run the risk of prosecution in South Australia. Solicitor and novelist Keith Thomas, writing twenty-eight years after the fact at Sheppard's request on the matter, recalled calling on Sheppard to hear how *Trial* was going. Sheppard, who had received a letter from Harris, explained his refusal thus: 'It's not his show and he wouldn't get any kudos out of it.' See Thomas to Sheppard, 19 December 1992, Papers of A.W. Sheppard, NLA MS 8029, Box 4.

15   Sheppard to Rylah, 22 April 1965, Papers of A.W. Sheppard, NLA MS 8029, Box 3.

16   Sheppard to Anderson, 22 April 1965, Papers of A.W. Sheppard, NLA MS 8029, Box 3. Sheppard repeated his reminders about military rank: 'Not that it is really relevant, but I might state, to stress my sense of responsibility, that I served for the whole period of the last war, rose to the rank of substantive colonel, was awarded MC, and my enlistment number was NX 68 (which shows that I enlisted early!).'

17   'The ghost of Lady Chatterley', *SMH*, 13 May 1965, p. 2.

18 A.W. Sheppard, interviewed by Ann Turner, NLA Oral History, TRC 2725. Sheppard's letter to Arthur Rylah was similarly unsubtle. 'I am writing to you personally about the above matter,' he told the chief secretary, 'firstly because you might remember our meeting on more than one occasion in the mess of 2/14d Fd Regt., when I was AA and QMG NT Force, and would therefore believe me to be a responsible individual.' See Sheppard to Rylah, 22 April 1965, Papers of A.W. Sheppard, NLA MS 8029, Box 3.

19 'Action by police over sale of book', *SMH*, 5 May 1965, p. 4; A.W. Sheppard, 'Accustomed as we are …', *Nation*, 7 August 1965, pp. 21–22.

20 Flesch to Sheppard, 28 April 1965, Papers of A.W. Sheppard, NLA MS 8029, Box 3.

21 Sheppard to Flesch, 29 April 1965, Papers of A.W. Sheppard, NLA MS 8029, Box 3.

22 Cabinet submission no. 768, 'Literature censorship — publication in Australia of prohibited book "The Trial of Lady Chatterley"', May 1965, NAA: A5827, Volume 23/Agendum 768.

23 'EJ Bunting — Notes of meetings 5 May 1965–26 May 1965', NAA: A11099, 1/73.

24 Dutton, 1996, p. 73.

25 A.W. Sheppard, 'Why were these books banned?', Papers of A.W. Sheppard, NLA, MS 8029, Box 5.

26 *Commonwealth Government Gazette*, 26 October 1967, iss. 93, p. 5854.

27 Dunstan, 1968, p. 201.

28 'Single authority on literature censorship', 27 August 1964, NAA: A5827, VOLUME 12/AGENDUM 394.

29 'Cabinet notebook, notetaker EJ Bunting, notes of meetings 1 September 1964–7 October 1964', NAA: A11099, 1/69.

30 Blackshield, in Dutton and Harris (eds), 1970, pp. 17–18.

31 Altman, 1970, pp. 236–39.

32 Murray-Smith, in Dutton and Harris (eds), 1970, p. 85.

33 Author's interview with Joan Masterman, 11 February 2019.

34 Altman, 1970, pp. 236–39.

35 'Banned material in book', *SMH*, 19 February 1970, p. 9.

36 Phillips, 1969, pp. 508–13.

Chapter 5: A literary onanism

1   Roth, 2016 [1959], p. 173.

2   Roth, 2016 [1975], p. 203.

3   McDaniel, 1974, p. 22.

4   Roth, 2016 [1975], p. 204.

5   Ibid., p. 205.

6   Kleinschmidt, 1967, pp. 123–25. Literary scholar Jeffrey Berman was the first to make the connection between Kleinschmidt's article and Roth. See Berman, 1980; and Mosher and Berman, 2015, pp. 63–81.

7   Roth, 2016 [1975], pp. 29–36.

8   Roth, 1967a, pp. 104, 107, 191–93.

9   Roth, 1967b, pp. 385–98.

10 Roth, 1988, p. 155.

11 Roth, 2005 [1969], p. 1.

12 Ibid., p. 45.

13 Roth, 2005 [1969], p. 22.

14 Ibid., pp. 17–20.

15 Ibid., p. 134. There is also a strong hint that it is this same liver that is served when Portnoy's father invites to dinner a colleague named Anne, a Gentile with whom — Portnoy comes to believe — his father has been sleeping. Certainly, as Portnoy relates it, his father's discussion of the liver is overlaid with sexual innuendo and Judaism.

16 Ibid., pp. 57–60.

17 Ibid., pp. 36–37.

18 Ibid., pp. 258–68.

19 Roth, 2016 [1975], p. 19.

20 Roth, 2005 [1969], p. 274.

21 Brauner, in Royal (ed.), 2005, pp. 43–55.

22 Roth, 2016 [1988], pp. 156–57.

23 Albert Goldman, 'Wild blue shocker', *Life*, no. 58, 7 February 1969, pp. 52–57.

24 *Time*, 3 January 1969; 'The Roth book', *New York Times Book Review*, 14 July 1968; Raymond Sokolov, 'Alexander the Great', *Newsweek*, 24 February 1969, pp. 51–52.

25 Cerf, 1977, p. 256.

26 Steven Heller, 'Paul Bacon, bestseller', *Printmag*, 10 June 2015.

27 Josh Greenfeld, 'Portnoy's Complaint', *New York Times Book Review*, 23 February 1969, pp. 1–2.

28 Alfred Kazin, 'Up against the wall, Mama!', *New York Review*, 27 February 1969.

29 'A sex novel of the absurd', *Time*, 21 February 1969, pp. 66–67.

30   Tony Tanner, 'Surfeit of oysters', *Spectator*, 18 April 1969.

31   Christopher Wordsworth, 'Leading a goy life', *Guardian*, 17 April 1969.

32   Avishai, 2012, p. 5.

33   Cooper, 1996, pp. 110–11. Irvinge Howe would, in 1972, add to the pile
      a more serious criticism of *Portnoy*, arguing that it spoke to a 'yearning
      to undo the fate of birth'. He asked: 'Who, born a Jew in the twentieth
      century, has been so lofty in spirit never to have shared this fantasy? But
      who, born a Jew in the twentieth century, has been so foolishly in mind
      as to dally with it for more than a moment?' See Howe, 'Philip Roth
      reconsidered', *Commentary*, December 1972.

34   Roth, 2016 [1975], pp. 15–16.

35   Ibid., pp. 16–17.

36   Salman Rushdie, 'Salman Rushdie discusses *Portnoy's Complaint*', BBC
      Video, 3 June 2018.

37   Atlas, 2019.

38   David Remnick, 'The fierceness of Philip Roth', *New Yorker*, 15 May
      2000.

39   Burgess, 1984, p. 106.

40   Roth Pierpont, 2014, p. 53.

Chapter 6: Regulation 4A

1   J.O. Sullivan, 'Publication for Review', 19 March 1969, NAA: A425,
      72/4378.

2   'Commonwealth of Australia: Minute Paper: Proof Copy', 28 March
      1969, NAA: A425, 72/4378.

3   J.H. Richards, 'Publication: Portnoy's Complaint by Philip Roth',
      31 March 1969, NAA: A425, 72/4378.

4   Chief Inspector to the National Literature Board of Review members,
      18 April 1969, NAA: A425, 72/4378.

5   Among the changes amid the agreement for uniform censorship was a
      decision to bring state representatives onto the National Literature Board
      of Review who were not necessarily experts in literature. Mulholland,
      for example, was a Queensland housewife who had served on the
      Queensland Literature Board of Review; Lloyd O'Neil was a publisher;
      and Marie Neale was an education and child-welfare academic.

6   Una Mulholland to Lloyd O'Neil, n.d.; H.C. Chipman to O'Neil,
      3 March 1969; M.D. Neale to O'Neil, 1 June 1969; Lloyd O'Neil to E.R.
      Bryan, n.d., NAA: A425, 72/4378.

7   R.M. Keogh to Malcolm Scott, 11 June 1969, NAA: A425, 72/4378.
    Regulation 4A of the Customs (Prohibited Importations) Regulation
    applied to all publications that described, depicted, expressed or
    otherwise dealt with matters of sex, drugs, crime, cruelty, and/or violence
    in a way that offended standards of morality and decency.

8   Gordon to Customs CBA, 24 June 1969, NAA: A425, 72/4378.

9   '"Portnoy's Complaint" appeal plan', *SMH*, 28 June 1969, p. 1.

10 Greene, in Roger Louis (ed.), 2008, p. 217; Sherry, 2005, p. 45; Young, 1976.

11 Harrap to Askew, 27 June 1969, 'Correspondence relating to the export
    to Australia of *Portnoy's Complaint* by Philip Milton Roth', JC 118/2,
    Jonathan Cape Archive, University of Reading (hereafter JC 118/2),
    PRHA, University of Reading.

12 Greene to Scott, 4 July 1969, NAA: A425, 72/4378.

13 Scott to Greene, 25 July 1969, ibid.

14 Bryan to Sloan, 10 September 1969, ibid.

15 Greene to Scott, 26 September 1969, ibid.

16 Dutton to Greene, 4 July 1969, JC 118/2, PRHA, University of Reading.

17 Harrap to Greene, 17 July 1969, ibid.

18 Sayers to Greene, 26 August 1969, ibid.

19 Greene to Sayers, 12 September 1969, ibid.

20 McDonald to Gorton, 17 June 1969, NAA: A425, 72/4378.

21 Glaskin to Customs, 31 July 1969, ibid.

22 Peacock to Scott, 14 August 1969, ibid.

23 Bayes to Scott, 20 September 1969, ibid.

24 McElhone to Scott, 7 October 1969, ibid.

25 C.S. Gleeson to Scott, 13 October 1969, ibid.

26 Burt to Scott, 15 October 1969, ibid.

27 'Portnoy to gatecrash: Greene's complaint', *Sunday Observer*, 26 October
    1969, p. 6.

28 Murphy, 'Radio script: censorship', July 1967, FLG–7–69, <http://
    lionelmurphy.anu.edu.au/Lionel%20Murphy%20speeches/LKM%203.
    html>, accessed 21 April 2019.

29 Ian Fitchett, 'Policy would end most censorship', *SMH*, 31 July 1969, p. 8.

30 Gough Whitlam, 1969 election policy speech, delivered at Sydney
    Town Hall, 1 October 1969, <https://electionspeeches.moadoph.gov.au/
    speeches/1969-gough-whitlam>, accessed 21 April 2019.

31 Hasluck, 'Events following the election of October 25, 1969', NAA:
    M1767, 3.

32 Evan Williams, 'This guy Chipp, now…', *SMH,* 11 March 1970, p. 2.

33   Harrap to Greene, 19 November 1969, JC 118/2, PRHA, University of
      Reading.
34   Greene to Chipp, 1 December 1969, NAA: A425, 72/4378.
35   Chipp to Greene, 31 December 1969, ibid.
36   Greene to Chipp, 13 January 1970, ibid.
37   Williams to Greene, 24 November 1969, JC 118/2, PRHA, University of
      Reading.
38   Warnock to McCutcheon, December 1969, ibid.
39   Stucley to Lynch, 14 October 1969; Wallman to Chipp, 29 January 1970,
      NAA: A425, 72/4378.
40   Greene to Rutherford, 15 April 1970, JC 118/2, PRHA, University of
      Reading.
41   Greene to O'Neil, 23 December 1969, ibid.
42   Harrap to Greene, 20 January 1970, ibid.
43   Stonier to Greene, 3 June 1970, ibid.
44   Evan Williams, 'Mr Chipp's little show', *SMH*, 15 April 1970, p. 2.
45   'Dirty b**k s**tion', *Arena*, 2 March 1970, pp. 16–18.
46   'MLA objects to book extract', *SMH*, 11 March 1970, p. 6.
47   'Shock therapy', *Arena*, 17 March 1970, pp. 2, 18.
48   Dyason to Chipp, 27 May 1970, NAA: A425, 72/4378.
49   O'Moffat to Chipp, 10 July 1970, ibid.
50   Richards to Mills, 5 August 1970, ibid.
51   Michie to Chipp, 19 July 1970, ibid.
52   Chipp to Michie, 23 July 1970, ibid.

Chapter 7: Straws in the wind

1   John Hooker, 'Penguin boss fell in love with sea', *Australian*,
     23 September 1994, p. 23.
2   A.W. Sheppard would write, in 1962, that whereas Australia and
     New Zealand together published around 1,000 books per year, Britain
     published around 18,000, and the US around 12,000. Moreover,
     according to P.R. Stephensen, Australia imported around a quarter of
     total British book production — around £18 million worth of books —
     each year during the 1960s, with obvious effects on Australian reading
     culture. As Stephensen put it: 'The minds of Australians are being
     conditioned 90 per cent by imported books.' See Sheppard, 'Australians
     are best-sellers', *Sunday Mirror*, 26 August 1962; Stephensen, 'Aust.
     writers and local publishers', *SMH*, 18 July 1962, p. 2.

3   'Penguin's former chief takes on another challenge', *Age*, 8 May 1976,
    p. 18; author's interview with Hilary McPhee, 6 March 2019; Munro and
    Sheahan-Bright (eds), 2006, pp. 3–52.

4   'Penguin's former chief takes on another challenge', *Age*, 8 May 1976, p. 18.

5   Froelich would later remark that, next to John Hooker (who had called
    him this), anyone would appear conservative.

6   Author's interview with Peter Froelich, 13 December 2018.

7   Dutton, 1996, p. 268.

8   Author's interview with Hilary McPhee, 6 March 2019.

9   Dutton, 1996, p. 96.

10 Meredith Michie, then married to Michie, recalled Hooker arriving at
    their home one night uninvited, 'personable but intense', and armed with
    pages of ideas for a new Australian non-fiction list for Penguin. She was
    not certain whether Michie had offered Hooker a job yet, or whether his
    appearance pre-empted that. 'They hit it off and animatedly exchanged
    ideas over a bottle of red(s),' she said later. (Author's correspondence with
    Meredith Michie, 8 July 2019.)

11 Stuart Sayers, 'The business of words absorbs John Hooker', *Age*,
    3 November 1973, p. 15.

12 Jill Rivers, 'A serious man in the sauce', *Age*, 20 October 1984, 'Saturday
    Extra' supplement, p. 11.

13 John Hooker, 'Penguin boss fell in love with the sea', *Australian*,
    23 September 1994, p. 15.

14 Ibid.

15 Author's interview with Hilary McPhee, 6 March 2019.

16 Ibid.; McPhee, 2001, p. 92.

17 Author's interview with Bob Sessions, 16 December 2018.

18 Thomas Laquer traces the supposed medical associations of masturbation
    back to an early-eighteenth-century tract titled *Onania, or the Sin of Self-
    Pollution*, which promised to guide readers in the ethics of the flesh. See
    Laquer, 2003.

19 '"Portnoy's Complaint" appeal plan', *SMH*, 28 June 1969, p. 1.

20 Greene to Dutton, in Dutton and Harris (eds), 1970, p. 101.

21 Hooker and Dutton, telephone interview transcript, 10 September 1995,
    Papers of Geoffrey Dutton, NLA MS 7285.

22 Polling in 1969 by Roy Morgan showed 60 per cent support among the
    public for either increasing or maintaining censorship; by December
    1970, support would only have slipped by five percentage points. See 'Poll
    finds support for censor', *SMH*, 4 December 1970, p. 1.

23   Graham C. Greene, 'Telephone conversation with Mr Hooker of Penguin
      Australia 8/6/70', 10 June 1970, JC 118/2, PRHA, University of Reading.

24   Hooker to Greene, 9 June 1970, ibid.

25   Newman to Greene, 15 June 1970, ibid.

26   Greene, 'Telephone conversation with Mr Hooker dated June 16th',
      17 June 1970, ibid.

27   'Memorandum for Graham C. Greene', 22 June 1970, ibid.

28   Draft contracts, 22 June 1970; Burdock to Hooker 22 June 1970; and
      Greene to Hooker, 23 June 1970, ibid.

29   Greene to Maschler, 25 June 1970, ibid. It appears that this secrecy was
      maintained. On 14 August, Greene wrote to Michie to say that he would
      soon like to let Roth know what had been going on: 'You will remember
      that we have been keeping him in the dark so that there is less possibility
      of a leak.'

30   Hooker to Burdock, 29 June 1970, ibid.

31   Morpurgo, 1979, p. 315.

32   Hooker to Greene, 29 June 1970, JC 118/2, PRHA, University of
      Reading.

33   Author's interview with David Marr, 22 November 2018.

34   Author's interview with Reginald Barrett, 4 July 2019.

35   Bill Gummow, 'Nightmares and notoriety', *Bar News*, Winter 1996,
      p. 32. Barrett is sceptical about whether this advice originated from
      Cowper. He said later he would be surprised if Cowper would offer such
      a confident prediction, and points out that there was no love lost between
      Cowper and Gordon Barton. He adds that he always drew a distinction
      between the advice that he drafted and that Cowper prepared in response
      to the instructions from London, and the subsequent publication of
      Portnoy in Australia.

36   Gordon Barton, 'An open letter to the President of the United States of
      America', *SMH*, 22 October 1966, p. 11.

37   Richard Walsh, who became publisher at Angus & Robertson in 1972,
      argues that the commercial opportunity was a notable factor. The
      knowledge that *Portnoy's Complaint* would sell in Angus & Robertson's
      stores and boost its profits, gave an additional reason to print the book;
      author's interview with Richard Walsh, 15 May 2019.

38   Everingham, 2009, p. 186; 'Gordon Barton: typescript memoir', p. 28,
      Papers of Sam Everingham relating to Gordon Barton, NSW ML MSS
      8614, 4 (27).

39   Michie to Greene, 24 July 1970, JC 118/2, PRHA, University of Reading.

40   Author's interview with Hilary McPhee, 6 March 2019.

41   'Penguin', John Hooker, Papers of Geoffrey Dutton, NLA MS 7285.

42   Dutton, 1996, p. 111.

43   Michie to Greene, 24 July 1970, JC 118/2, PRHA, University of
      Reading.

44   R.M. Keogh, 'Minute paper', 21 July 1970, NAA: A425, 72/4378.

45   Michie to Greene, 3 August 1970, JC 118/2, PRHA, University of
      Reading.

46   Author's interview with Hilary McPhee, 6 March 2019; Di Gribble,
      'Don Chipp: larrikin, censor, and party founder', *Crikey*, 29 August 2006.

47   See Edward Quill's statement on his meeting with Aubrey Cousins,
      31 August 1970, NSW State Archives (NSWSA): NRS 906, 12/4121,
      item A69/950.

48   Chipp to Eric Willis, 4 August 1970, ibid.

Chapter 8: An endemic complaint

1   Bob Gould, interviewed by Edgar Waters, 27 November 1994, NLA
      Oral History, TRC 3185, p. 160.

2   Chris Pritchard, 'Booksellers to ignore govt warning', *SMH*, 30 August
      1970, p. 43.

3   'Publishers to defy ban on US novel', *SMH*, 29 August 1970, p. 7.

4   'Banned book goes on sale', *Canberra Times*, 31 August 1970, p. 6.

5   'Banned book on sale', *SMH*, 31 August 1970, p. 4.

6   Kingsmill to Allan, 28 August 1970, NSWSA: NRS 906, 12/4121, item
      A69/950.

7   Hooker to Greene, 2 September 1970, JC 118/2, PRHA, University of
      Reading.

8   'Portnoy shop in WA', *Daily News*, 1 September 1970, p. 2.

9   Author's interview with Paul Grainger, 30 January 2019.

10   'Vic govt to prosecute on banned novel', *SMH*, 1 September 1970, p. 12.

11   Melvin to Jackson, 28 August 1970, NSWSA: NRS 906, 12/4121, item
      A69/950.

12   Bruce Skurray to Willis, 31 August 1970 and n.a., 2 September 1970,
      ibid.

13   Kingsmill to Willis, 31 August 1970, ibid.

14   '"Open mind on book" — Willis', *Daily Mirror*, 1 September 1970.

15   'Banned novel: Vic will prosecute publisher', *SMH*, 1 September 1970,
      p. 1.

16   Dutton (1996) cites John Hooker's recollection, twenty years after the fact, to the effect that police arrived at eight o'clock; a 7 September 1970 letter from Arthur Rylah to Don Chipp states that it was at ten o'clock; Kenneth Walters stated that it was 10.45 am.

17   Michie to Greene, 3 August and 24 August 1970, JC 118/2, PRHA, University of Reading.

18   Williams to Greene, 6 September 1970, ibid.

19   McCutcheon and Barwell to Greene, 18 September 1970, ibid.

20   Reid to Comptroller-General, 'Press enquiry — Portnoy's Complaint', 1 September 1970, NAA: A425, 72/4378.

21   'Agreement denied', *Canberra Times*, 1 September 1970, p. 3.

22   Len King, interviewed by Peter Donovan, 11 November 2004, State Library of South Australia, J.D. Somerville Oral History collection, OH 715/1.

23   'Portnoy complaints', *Bulletin*, 12 September 1970, p. 27; Dunstan, 1981, p. 196; 'Portnoy in WA shop', *Daily News*, 1 September 1970, p. 2.

24   Michie to Greene, and Hooker to Greene, 2 September 1970, JC 118/2, PRHA, University of Reading.

25   Author's interview with Hilary McPhee, 6 March 2019.

26   Chipp to Rylah, 14 September 1970, NAA: A425, 72/4378.

27   R.M. Keogh, 'Minute paper', 21 July 1970, ibid.

28   Don Chipp, *CPD HoR*, vol. 69, 2 September 1970, p. 832.

29   Rylah to Chipp, 7 September 1970, NAA: A425, 72/4378.

30   'Penguin dollars back Portnoy', *Age*, 2 September 1970, p. 3.

31   'WA seller has plan to beat ban on book', *Daily News*, 2 September 1970, p. 2; 'Portnoy sells — despite raids', *Daily News*, 3 September 1970, p. 4; Max Beattie, 'Portnoy's Complaint — it hits Melbourne', *Age*, 1 September 1970, p. 3.

32   David Dale, 'Mr Portnoy's complaint: why all this fuss about a book', *SMH*, 2 September 1970, p. 14.

33   'Censorable complaint', *Age*, 2 September 1970, p. 9.

34   Bob Gould, interviewed by Edgar Waters, 27 November 1994, NLA Oral History, TRC 3185, p. 160.

35   'Portnoy complaints', *Bulletin*, 12 September 1970, p. 27.

36   Bob Gould, 'A bleak wind back to a dismal past', *Ozleft*, 3 June 2008, <https://ozleft.wordpress.com/2008/06/03/a-bleak-wind-back-to-the-dismal-past/>, accessed 16 September 2018.

37   Hooker to Greene, 8 September 1970, JC 118/2, PRHA, University of Reading.

38 McPhee, 2001, pp. 109–10. McPhee said later that this fear caused her to leave the Mont Albert house she shared with Michie while he held his press conference on 30 August (author's interview with Hilary McPhee, 6 March 2019).

39 Hooker to Greene, 8 September 1970, JC118/2, PRHA, University of Reading. All of the available written correspondence between Hooker, Michie, and Greene confirms that another print run was ordered. Peter Froelich, however, states that the second print run never occurred and that there was never any intention of doing it. In addition to the publicity the news of another print run garnered, he said, it would be of benefit to the censorship fight if the public demand for more copies remained unsated: it would help to keep the book in the headlines.

40 'Penguin will publish book on Portnoy court hearings', *Age*, 4 September 1970, p. 2.

41 Hooker to Greene, 8 September 1970, JC 118/2, PRHA, University of Reading.

42 Rigg (ed.), 1969.

43 Author's interview with Julie Rigg, 31 August 2019.

44 'Vice squad antics amuse the dean', *Daily News*, 5 September 1970, p. 2.

45 'Many paths to corruption', *Canberra Times*, 4 September 1970, p. 2.

46 'Portnoy be damned, what about aged?', *Truth*, 5 September 1970, p. 4.

47 'The Portnoy tug-of-war', *Canberra Times*, 5 September 1970, p. 12.

48 John Pringle, 'Portnoy: a cry from the heart', *SMH*, 5 September 1970, p. 19.

49 Morris to Michie, 14 September 1970, NAA: A425, 72/4378.

50 Greene to Hooker, 22 September 1970, JC 118/2, PRHA, University of Reading.

51 '"Portnoy's Complaint" has a setback', *Canberra Times*, 1 September 1970, p. 1; 'No action against Portnoy seller in ACT', *Canberra Times*, 8 September 1970, p. 1; 'Portnoy hearings adjourned', *SMH*, 9 September 1970, p. 5. Hughes has no memory of this matter being brought to his attention (author's interview with Tom Hughes, 2 December 2018).

52 'Deal on Portnoy slated', *Age*, 10 September 1970, p. 10.

53 Administrative assistant to the Undersecretary, 10 September 1970, NSWSA: NRS 906, 12/4121, item A69/950.

54 Lawson, 1995, p. 91; author's interview with David Marr, 22 November 2018.

55 Undersecretary to Willis, 21 September 1970, NSWSA: NRS 906, 12/4121, item A69/950.

56 McKay to Allen Allen & Hemsley, 29 September 1970, ibid.

57 Willis's annotations, 18 September 1970, on Undersecretary to Willis, 17 September 1970, ibid.

58 Author's interview with Reginald Barrett, 4 July 2019.

59 Rylah to Chipp, 7 September 1970, NAA: A425, 72/4378.

60 Beard to Walters, 9 September 1970, ibid.

61 Michie to Greene, 23 September 1970, JC 118/2, PRHA, University of Reading.

62 John Michie, 'Community standards — it sounds all right — but what does it mean?', *Bulletin*, 26 September 1970, pp. 47–48. Drafts of the article were substantially harder-hitting than the eventually published version. Michie noted that the postmaster-general could refuse to register publications, and that registration of publishers — required in Victoria and New South Wales — could be revoked by the attorney-general's departments should they wish.

63 Hooker to Greene, 5 October 1970, JC 118/2, PRHA, University of Reading.

Chapter 9: Literature and liberty

1 Unless otherwise noted, this account of the trial draws on the court transcript, Kenneth Phillip Walters and Penguin Books Australia, 19 October 1970–26 October 1970, clippings from *The Sydney Morning Herald*, *The Age*, and the Melbourne *Herald*, and the account provided in 'Notes from the trial of a notorious onanist', *Sunday Review*, 25 October 1970, p. 10.

2 For a useful and informative overview of the tactics adopted by prosecutors during obscenity trials, see Charles Renbar's *End of Obscenity* (1986).

3 Author's interview with Stephen Charles, 10 December 2018.

4 Michie to Greene, 9 October 1970, JC 118/2, PRHA, University of Reading.

5 Author's interview with Stephen Charles, 10 December 2018. McLaren wrote later that the defence witnesses seemed to spend more time waiting outside the court than they did inside testifying; see McLaren, 1996, p. 195.

6 Greene to Michie, 19 October 1970, JC 118/2, PRHA, University of Reading.

7 *Seven Types of Ambiguity*, published in 1930 and authored by literary critic William Empson, was instrumental to the founding of New Criticism and is predicated on mining layers of meaning, irony, ambiguity,

complexity, and difficulty in poetic works.

8   'Notes from the trial of a notorious onanist', *Sunday Review*, 25 October 1970, p. 10.

9   Michie to Greene, 28 October 1970, JC 118/2, PRHA, University of Reading.

10   Author's correspondence with Dennis Douglas, 5, 8, 11, and 12 January 2019.

11   Author's interview with Brian Kiernan, 1 August 2019.

12   Notes kept by Stephen Charles, copy in possession of the author.

13   'Notes from the trial of a notorious onanist', *Sunday Review*, 25 October 1970, p. 10.

14   Buckley, 1991, p. 35.

15   Author's interview with Jennifer Strauss, 6 December 2018.

16   Author's interview with Hilary McPhee, 6 March 2019.

17   Author's interview with Joanne Lee Dow, 10 December 2018.

18   Author's interview with Lucy Frost, 27 November 2018.

19   Author's interview with Jennifer Gribble, 5 September 2019.

20   Persuaded to appear at the trial by Geoffrey Dutton and Graham C. Greene, White joked with a friend that his evidence would hinge on the book's capacity to arouse him. Where *Lady Chatterley's Lover* had given him an erection, and thus was pornographic, he said, *Portnoy's Complaint* had failed to do so — and thus was not. See Marr, 2008, p. 465.

21   McPhee, 2001, p. 108.

22   Dutton, 1996, p. 112.

23   White to Maschler, 1 November 1970, in White, 1994, p. 368.

24   Author's interview with Brian Kiernan, 1 August 2019.

Chapter 10: Peppercorns and pyrrhic victories

1   Unless otherwise noted, this account of the sentencing hearing is drawn from a transcript of the verdict hearing in the author's possession; a copy of Ross's decision, 9 November 1970, NAA: A425, 72/4378; and notes made by Hilary McPhee on 9 November 1970 and a letter sent by McPhee to Julie Rigg, dated 13 November 1970, both of which may be found in the papers of Hilary McPhee, NLA MS Acc.13.076, Box 61.

2   Author's interview with Peter Froelich, 13 December 2019.

3   Author's interview with Stephen Charles, 6 December 2019.

4   Michie to Greene, 28 October 1970, JC 118/2, PRHA, University of Reading.

5   Author's interview with Hilary McPhee, 6 March 2019.
6   'Minutes of Penguin Books Australia Limited, Directors Meeting, 5 November 1970', p. 2, D1294/4/5/1/1, Penguin Archive, University of Bristol, UK.
7   '"Portnoy" ban battle is not yet ended', *SMH*, 10 November 1970, p. 6.
8   Michie to Greene, 10 November 1970, JC 118/2, PRHA, University of Reading.
9   Hooker to Greene, 26 November 1970, ibid.
10 'Portnoy's puzzle', *Age*, 13 November 1970, p. 9.
11 'Uninformative verdict', *Canberra Times*, 10 November 1970, p. 2. There also appears to have been some division between the Department of Customs and Excise and the Victorian Chief Secretary's office. Sending a copy of Ross's judgement to the first assistant comptroller-general, D. Reid, on 12 November, the Chief Secretary's office noted that copies of the court transcript could be purchased if the department would like them. 'If Victoria can't afford to give us any more copies,' wrote Reid, on the letter, 'we don't want any!' See Dillon to Reid, 12 November 1970, NAA: A425, 72/4378.
12 See, in particular, Neale's report, 1 June 1969, and O'Neil's report, both of which conceded the existence of literary merit in *Portnoy's Complaint*, ibid.
13 Eric Willis, annotation, 9 December 1970, on Administrative assistance to Willis, 2 December 1970, NSWSA: NRS 906, 12/4121, item A69/950.
14 This account of the committal hearing draws from 'Transcript, Central Court of Petty Sessions, 14 December 1970', NSWSA: Case file, 2464 of 1970, 10/9387.
15 Author's interview with Maureen Colman, 3 December 2018.
16 McKay to the Undersecretary, 27 October 1970, NSWSA: NRS 906, 12/4121, item A69/950.

Chapter 11: A kick in the ribs

1   Davis, in Fox, Oliver, and Layman (eds), 2017, p. 153.
2   As a longstanding member of the Communist Party of Australia (CPA), Broomhall was the subject of sustained surveillance from ASIO agents between the 1950s and (at least) the mid-1970s. See NAA: A6119, 3873, 3894, 3875, 3890, and 3891.
3   'Rush for Portnoys — sell out', *Daily News*, 8 September 1970, p. 3.

4 'Police seize 18 copies of Portnoy', *West Australian*, 11 September 1970, p. 9.

5 Note of CPA meeting, October 1970, NAA: A6119, 3891.

6 Jack Coulter, 'Two charged over Portnoy', *Daily News*, 14 September 1970, p. 2.

7 Aggregated notes of CPA meeting, 25 October 1970, NAA: A6119, 3891.

8 'Beware the ideas', *Bulletin*, 30 December 1972, pp. 8–9.

9 Author's interview with Ian Viner, 28 May 2019. He was also an unsuccessful candidate for the Liberal Party at the 1969 election; in two years' time, he would be elected to the federal parliament and would serve as a minister in the Fraser government.

10 Except where otherwise indicated, this account of the trial is drawn from the notes of evidence of N.J. Malley SM in *Police v Broomhall*, Court of Petty Sessions, Perth, charge no. 611/70.

11 Davies, 1978, p. 35.

12 Ibid.

13 Ibid., p. 34.

14 Author's interview with Ian Viner, 28 May 2019.

15 Davies, 1978, p. 35.

16 Author's interview with Ian Viner, 28 May 2019.

17 Davis, in Fox, Oliver, and Layman, 2017, p. 157.

18 Davies, 1978, p. 36.

19 Colebatch would come to regret his appearance at the trial. Author's interview with Hal Colebatch, 10 May 2019.

20 N.J. Malley, 'Reserved decision: *Police v Broomhall*', 18 January 1971, charge no. 6115/70, NAA: A425, 72/4378. See also 'Portnoy's WA win', *Tribune*, 27 January 1971, p. 3; 'Obscene, but win to Portnoy', *Sun*, 19 January 1971, p. 7; and 'Magistrate rejects Portnoy charges', *West Australian*, 19 January 1971, p. 2.

21 'Portnoy books given back', *Daily Mirror*, 12 February 1971, p. 77.

22 'Rush to buy Portnoy's', *Daily News*, 19 January 1971, p. 5.

23 Notes of meeting, 9 March 1971, NAA: A6119, 3891. Self-congratulations were still being made at the end of the year. Gandini was heard to tell a CPA meeting that 'many hundreds of dollars' in advertising had been saved thanks to the publicity the *Portnoy* trial had afforded the CPA. See Aggregate meeting, 1 December 1971, NAA: A6119, 3892.

24 Davies, 1978, p. 34. For his part, Viner was unfussed: 'You win some, you lose some.' He had thought the verdict likely. The array and number of

witnesses testifying to the literary merit of *Portnoy's Complaint* meant that the strength of the evidence in the case was against the prosecution, he said. And although he believed that Malley's reading of the act and the exemption it gave was 'literal', he believed it was a reasonable verdict on the basis of the evidence. Of course, he added, 'All judges' rulings are correct — until they're overturned.'

25   Chipp to Craig, 29 January 1971, NAA: A425, 72/4378.
26   Craig to Chipp, 19 February 1971, ibid.
27   Jerry Dolan, 'Amendments to Indecent Publications Act', 27 May 1971, Premier's Department, S1228–cons1819, item 1971/465, cabinet meeting 1 June 1971, SROWA.
28   John Tonkin, handwritten note, 'Amendments to Indecent Publications Act', 1 June 1971, Premier's Department, S1228–cons1819, item 1971/465, cabinet meeting 1 June 1971, SROWA. A survey of the *Indecent Publications Act* and its amendments, on the AustLII database, confirms that there were no amendments made to the act between 1967 and 1972.
29   'Ban off book but no rush', *SMH*, 10 January 1971, p. 46.
30   'Portnoy hearing to go on', *SMH*, 20 January 1971, p. 2.

Chapter 12: The beginning of the game

1   Keesing, 1988, pp. 206–07.
2   There is some ambiguity over Penguin's involvement in the NSW trial. David Marr recalled that the file retained by Allen Allen & Hemsley was marked Penguin, not Angus & Robertson. Others involved do not recall if this was so. It is possible that Penguin's solicitors in Victoria, Mallesons, lent material to Allen Allen & Hemsley for preparation of the NSW case. There was a longstanding, if informal, relationship at this time between Mallesons and Allens, each of which at this time largely confined its activities to its respective home state.
3   David Marr, 'How *Portnoy's Complaint* made Australia a better place', *Guardian*, 26 May 2018.
4   Meagher, 1985, p. 8.
5   Kenny and Vine-Hall to McKay, 17 September 1971, NSWSA: NRS 906, 12/4121, item A69/950.
6   Kenny and Vine-Hall to McKay, 17 September 1971, NSWSA: NRS 906, 12/4121, item A69/950.
7   'QC's defence of Portnoy', *Daily Telegraph*, 3 February 1971, p. 10;

'Detectives' denial over Portnoy', *SMH*, 3 February 1971, p. 3.

8 Unless otherwise noted, what follows is drawn from the transcript: see NSWSA: NRS 2713, 19/8516.

9 See Trudy Storey, 'Judge Goran retires on his 70th birthday', *SMH*, 24 May 1984. In the trial against Portnoy, Goran would show considerable interest in the nature of the book and seemed to be genuinely of an open mind on whether it was obscene. Much later, he would comment that a judge needed to interpret what a community wanted: 'He has to go out and speak to people he has got to make it his business to live amongst the people and keep his ears open.' He would also have considerable interest in civil liberties cases: when assigned to hear Anne Summers' appeal against a conviction for use of unseemly language on a Sydney street in 1975, Goran put the arresting officer 'through far more paces than would ordinarily occur in a simple language case', and, after ruling that Summers' reaction and language was entirely appropriate in the circumstances, dismissed the charge and called her a 'pioneer of free speech': Summers, 1999, p. 312. In the course of his career, he would serve on six royal commissions, survive a knife attack in his chambers in 1975, and become chair of the Trotters Club of New South Wales.

10 'Mr Justice W.P. Deane', *Australian Law Journal*, vol. 56, no. 8, August 1982, p. 437; Mike Steketee, 'His brilliant career', *Weekend Australian*, 26–27 August 1995, 'Focus' supplement, p. 23.

11 Garry Sturgess, 'High Court job favourite vindicates the bookies', *Age*, 26 June 1982, p. 12.

12 Author's interview with Reginald Barrett, 4 July 2019.

13 Ibid.

14 Author's interview with Malcolm Oakes, 26 June 2019.

15 Author's interview with David Marr, 22 November 2018.

Chapter 13: The subject of expert evidence

1 Deane's comments echoed the language used by Mr Justice Stable in his summing-up during the 1956 prosecution of British publisher Secker & Warburg for its publication of Stanley Kauffmann's *The Philanderer*. Stable told the jury: 'Are we to take our literary standards as being the level of something that is suitable for a fourteen-year-old schoolgirl? … Of course not. A mass of literature, great literature, from many angles is wholly unsuitable for reading by the adolescent but that does not mean that the publisher is guilty of a criminal offence for making those works

available to the general public.' See *R v Martin Secker & Warburg Ltd* [1954] 1 WLR 1138.

2   'QC's defence of Portnoy', *Daily Telegraph*, 3 February 1971, p. 10.

3   Neville, 1995, pp. 36–46.

4   Author's interview with Harry Heseltine, 1 August 2018.

5   Kenny had thought of the objection (which was based on ambiguous wording in the *Obscene and Indecent Publications Act*) before the trial. Aware that it would likely prompt an unfavourable response from the public should it succeed, he had approached the government for its view of his using it. 'I see no reason why the lawyers should not be given a free hand,' Eric Willis responded. 'The defence would not hesitate to use any loophole it can find.' See Eric Willis annotation, 28 January 1971, on Undersecretary for Justice to Willis, 26 January 1971, NSWSA: NRS 906, 12/4121, item A69/950.

6   Kenny and Vine-Hall to McKay, 17 September 1971, ibid.

7   Coleman, 1963, pp. 115–16.

8   Keesing, 1988, pp. 206–07.

9   Author's interview with Paul Grainger, 30 January 2019.

10   Author's interview with Margaret Harris, 28 November 2018.

11   Kenny and Vine-Hall to McKay, 17 September 1971, NSWSA: NRS 906, 12/4121, item A69/950.

12   Author's interview with David Marr, 22 November 2018.

13   Author's interview with Maureen Colman, 3 December 2018.

14   Ibid.

15   Author's interview with Margaret Harris, 28 November 2018.

16   Author's interview with David Marr, 22 November 2018; see also Marr, 1999, p. 181.

17   White to Dutton, 1 February 1971, in White, 1994, p. 375–76.

18   Author's interview with David Marr, 22 November 2018; see also Marr, 2008 [1991], p. 466.

19   White, quoted in Marr, 2008 [1991], p. 467.

20   Legge (ed.), 1971, p. 194.

21   Kenny and Vine-Hall to McKay, 17 September 1971, NSWSA: NRS 906, 12/4121, item A69/950.

22   Ibid.

Chapter 14: Figures in dusty light

1   Author's interview with David Marr, 22 November 2018.

2 '48 books taken off banned list', *SMH*, 12 February 1971, p. 3.

3 Michie to Greene, 15 April 1971, JC 118/2, PRHA, University of Reading.

4 Klugman and Chipp, 16 February 1971, *CPD HoR*, vol. 71, p. 17.

5 For the debate, see *CPD HoR*, vol. 71, 22 February 1971, pp. 439–69.

6 See *CPD HoR*, vol. 71, 23 February 1971, pp. 490–501.

7 'Portnoy's Complaint', *Woroni*, 22 February 1971, p. 11.

8 'Portnoy sold at ANU', *Canberra Times*, 23 February 1971, p. 7.

9 'Periodical prompts ANU Bill change', *Canberra Times*, 26 February 1971, p. 3.

10 'Portnoy is too obscene for words', *Canberra Times*, 26 March 1971, p. 3.

11 'Bond for bookseller', *Canberra Times*, 2 April 1971, p. 8.

12 'The puzzled penis', *Togatus*, vol. 4, no. 1, March 1970.

13 Author's interview with Charles Wooley, 8 February 2019.

14 Ibid.

15 'Portnoy trial', *Canberra Times*, 11 March 1971, p. 8.

16 Author's interview with John Reid, 12 December 2018.

17 Author's interview with Sir Max Bingham, 14 February 2019.

18 This draws on 'Transcript of Police v Fullers Bookshop', 10 March 1971, copy in the author's possession.

19 'Police v Fuller's Bookshop Pty Ltd', magistrate's ruling, copy in the author's possession.

20 Transcript of Reid's committal hearing, 10 March 1971, copy in the author's possession.

21 The Crown subsequently suggested that, as the charge against Fullers and Pearce had been dismissed, it was unreasonable to proceed against Reid. Most doubted it.

22 'Portnoy to go to higher court', *Canberra Times*, 18 March 1971, p. 15.

23 Penguin's appeal, O/R 6665.

24 Michie to Greene, 15 April 1971, JC 118/2, PRHA, University of Reading.

25 'No government relaxation on Portnoy's Complaint', *Canberra Times*, 17 February 1971, p. 8.

26 Eric Willis annotation, 17 February 1971, Senior clerk to Willis, 16 February 1971, NSWSA: NRS 906, 12/4121, item A69/950.

27 P.J. Kenny to Undersecretary of Justice, 'Advice on no bill application', 17 May 1971, NSWSA: Case file, 2464 of 1970, 10/9387.

28 'Portnoy's Complaint', 18 February 1971, NSWSA: NRS 906, 12/4121, item A69/950.

29   'A fresh trial for Portnoy', *Canberra Times*, 2 March 1971, p. 1.

30   Michie to Greene, 15 April 1971, JC 118/2, PRHA, University of Reading.

31   Allen Allen & Hemsley to K.M. McCaw, 11 May 1971, NSWSA: Case file, 2464 of 1970, 10/9387.

32   Barton to Willis, 14 May 1971, NSWSA: NRS 906, 12/4121, item A69/950.

33   Eric Willis annotation, 17 May 1971, on Barton to Willis, 14 May 1971, ibid.

34   P.J. Kenny to Undersecretary of Justice, 'Advice on no bill application', 17 May 1971, NSWSA: Case file, 2464 of 1970, 10/9387.

35   Undersecretary of Justice to Allen Allen & Hemsley, 17 May 1971, ibid.

Chapter 15: A cloistered and untried virtue

1   Unless otherwise noted, what follows of the trial is drawn from the transcript; see NSWSA: NRS 2713, 19/8516.

2   Author's interview with Malcolm Oakes, 26 June 2019. It is worth noting that at this time women had to register to even be considered for jury duty.

3   Author's interview with Margaret Harris, 28 November 2018.

4   'Judge Phillip Lyburn Head QC MBE', *Australian Law Journal*, vol. 63, p. 578.

5   'Booksellers in court over Portnoy', *SMH*, 19 May 1971, p. 10.

6   Ibid.

7   Author's correspondence with Malcolm Oakes, 9 July 2019.

8   Author's interview with Maureen Colman, 3 December 2018.

9   There is evidence to suggest that this stung Kenny: 'The presence in the *Act* of these provisions [of the tendency to deprave and corrupt],' he wrote later, 'enabled Counsel for the accused in the second trial to repeat the jibe he had made in the first trial that the effect of the Act was to require the standard of reading matter in the community to be determined by regard to what was suitable for persons sixteen years of age.' See Kenny and Vine-Hall to McKay, 17 September 1971, NSWSA: NRS 906, 12/4121, item A69/950.

10   Author's interview with Malcolm Oakes, 26 June 2019.

Chapter 16: Paper tigers

1   'Govt drops book charge', *SMH*, 29 May 1971.

2   Eric Willis, annotation, 7 June 1971, on correspondence with the undersecretary, 4 June 1971, NSWSA: NRS 906, 12/4121, item A69/950.

3   Chipp statement, 16 June 1971, NAA: A425, 72/4378.

4   Customs office Canberra, 17 June 1971, ibid. Labor MP Richard Klugman, who had asked Chipp when he was going to admit defeat after the inconclusive verdict of the first NSW trial, telegrammed him thus: 'Congratulations on finally adopting the course I suggested in my question on February 16. I hope it will not take so long in future.' See 'Chipp and Portnoy', *Review*, 20 June 1971, p. 1043.

5   'Customs (prohibited imports) regulations', n.d., ibid.

6   Author's interview with Peter Froelich, 13 December 2018.

7   Author's interview with Hilary McPhee, 6 March 2019.

8   Greene to Hooker, 4 June 1971, JC 118/2, PRHA, University of Reading.

9   Hooker to Greene, 8 June 1971, ibid.

10   Minutes of Penguin Books Australia Limited, Directors' Meeting, 31 July 1971, p. 1, D1294/4/5/1/1, Penguin Archive, University of Bristol, UK.

11   John Hooker insisted on being present for that destruction: McLaren, 1996, p. 195.

12   'State will be a laughing stock', *Mercury*, 22 June 1971, p. 12.

13   Beard to O'Connor, Bingham statement, 24 June 1971, NAA: A425, 72/4378.

14   Author's interview with Max Bingham, 14 February 2019.

15   Lyons to Harrap, 24 August 1971, JC 118/2, PRHA, University of Reading.

16   O'Connor to the Comptroller-General, 24 June 1971, NAA: A425, 72/4378.

17   McDonald to Harrap, 21 September 1971, JC 118/2, PRHA, University of Reading.

18   Undersecretary, Premier's Department, to Harrap, 28 September 1971, ibid.

19   Evans and Ferrier (eds), 2004, p. 11.

20   'First Australian *Portnoy* ban', *Courier-Mail*, 5 May 1972, p. 3. See also — for a slanted version — 'Brisbane magistrate and that Portnoy', *Tribune*, 23 May 1972, p. 8.

21   Sutton, 1973. Queensland would maintain its ban on the book for some time yet. In May 1973, a Brisbane antiquarian bookseller was fined $20 for selling the book. He was under the impression that it was by then

legal to do so. 'I feel very much like a schoolboy being reprimanded for a breach of discipline,' he said afterwards. See 'Portnoy cost $20', *SMH*, 16 May 1973, p. 9.

22 Hansen and Jensen, 1971, p. 9.

23 Chipp and Larkin, 1978, p. 127.

24 Cabinet notebook, 'Sir John Bunting, 21 March 1972–20 June 1972', NAA: A11099, 1/123.

25 Cabinet minute no. 898, 'Little Red School Book — without submission', 18 April 1972, NAA: A5909, 898.

26 Walsh, in Munro and Sheahan-Bright (eds), 2006, pp. 57–63.

27 'Police buy book', *Canberra Times*, 30 November 1972, p. 9.

28 'Latest challenge to censor has mass appeal', *SMH*, 29 November 1972, p. 7.

29 Author's interview with Richard Walsh, 15 May 2019.

30 'A censorship bill that went wrong', *Canberra Times*, 26 December 1972, p. 2.

31 *CPD HoR*, vol. 85, 21 August 1973, p. 122.

32 Day, 1996, p. 441.

Chapter 17: Stories of Australian censorship

1 John Hooker and Geoffrey Dutton phone conversation transcript, 10 September 1995, Papers of Geoffrey Dutton, NLA 7285.

2 Moore, 2012, p. 289.

3 Author's interview with Richard Walsh, 15 May 2019.

4 *Twentieth Annual Report*, Literature Board of Review, 1 July 1973–30 June 1974, p. 2.

5 The initial bill, the *Obscene and Indecent Publications Bill*, sought to assimilate *obscenity* and *indecency* in order to overcome problems presented in the prosecutions of Wendy Bacon and Angus & Robertson. That bill removed the defences for literary and artistic merit, and the provisions for trial by jury in obscenity cases. But this final measure — justified on the grounds that jury trials caused an expense and commitment of time that was unnecessary and inefficient for the 'cheap, salacious' publications then commonly the subject of prosecution — provoked considerable opposition, and the bill lapsed. Some of its changes had been suggested by Kenny and Vine-Hall in the aftermath of the second *Portnoy* trial in NSW. They had suggested doing away with the term *obscenity* on the grounds that the Hicklin test was no

longer compelling for many jurors, and that *indecency* served the Crown's purposes well enough; rephrasing the definition of *indecent* to include the transgression of accepted community standards of decency; quantifying literary merit as *substantial*; and reversing the onus of proof on whether the manner of sale of a work is justified. See Kenny and Vine-Hall to McKay, 17 September 1971, NSWSA: NRS 906, 12/4121, item A69/950.

6   Coleman, 1994, p. 146; Bacon and Coleman, 1975, Turner (ed.), p. 62. Robert Manne (1993, pp. 47–49) makes a similar argument about censorship as expression of disapproval.

7   Griffith, *New South Wales Parliamentary Debates*, 12 March 1975, pp. 4564–70.

8   Keesing, 1988, p. 204.

9   Peter Cowan, interviewed by Stuart Reid, October 1991–August 1992, NLA Oral History, TRC 2897, pp. 9–10.

10   Dutton, in Dutton and Harris (eds.), 1970, p. 6.

11   Bedford, 2016, p. 57.

12   Sullivan, 1997, p. 137.

13   The Queensland Literature Board of Review conceded in 1971 that 'modern trends in publication indicate that the term "literary merit" is fast becoming as difficult to define as the concept of obscenity'. See *Seventeenth Annual Report*, Literature Board of Review, 1 July 1970–30 June 1971, p. 2.

14   Author's interview with Wendy Bacon, 26 June 2019.

15   Roth, 2016 [1975], p. 16.

16   Tom Molloy, 'I do not think art has got anything to do with the Vice Squad', *SMH*, 15 April 1982, p. 1.

17   Author's interview with Julie Rigg, 31 August 2019.

18   Peter Coleman, 'Living in a book world of double standards', *Bulletin*, 12 September 1970, p. 23.

19   Greene to Michie, 17 November 1970, JC 118/2, PRHA, University of Reading.

Bibliography

ARTICLES

Dennis Altman, 1970, 'How I fought the censors and (partly) won', *Meanjin*, vol. 29, June, pp. 236–39.

Wendy Bacon, 2011, 'Being free by acting free', *Overland*, vol. 202, Autumn.

William Macmahon Ball, 1935, 'Australian censorship', *Australian Quarterly*, vol. 7, no. 26, June, pp. 9–14.

Joel Barnes, 2014, 'The right to read: the Book Censorship Abolition League, 1934–37', *Labour History*, no. 107, November, pp. 75–93.

Dennis Bryans, 2011, 'The trials of Robert Close', *Script & Print*, vol. 35, no. 4, pp. 197–218.

Lloyd Davies, 1978, 'The complaint against Portnoy', *Artlook*, vol. 4, no. 2, March, pp. 33–37.

Roger Douglas, 2002, 'Saving Australia from sedition: Customs, the Attorney-General's Department, and the administration of peacetime political censorship', *Federal Law Review*, vol. 30, pp. 135–75.

Lawson Glassop, 1960, 'The *We Were the Rats* case', *Overland*, no. 19, December, p. 38.

Albert Goldman, 1969, '*Portnoy's Complaint* by Philip Roth looms as a wild blue shocker and the American novel of the sixties', *Life*, no. 58, 7 February, pp. 52–57.

J.A. Iliffe, 1956, 'The Australian "obscene publications" legislation of 1953–55', *Sydney Law Review*, vol. 2, no. 1, pp. 134–39.

Colm Kiernan, 1976, 'Arthur A. Calwell's clashes with the Australian press, 1943–1945', *University of Wollongong Historical Journal*, vol. 2, no. 1, pp. 74–111.

H.J. Kleinschmidt, 1967, 'The angry act: the role of aggression in creativity', *American Imago*, vol. 26, iss. 1, Spring, pp. 98–128.

Robert Manne, 'A case for censorship', *Quadrant*, September 1993, pp. 47–50.

Roddy Meagher, 1985, 'Ave atque vale', *Bar News*, Winter, p. 8.

Nicole Moore, 2016, 'Zola to Roth: Literature in the dock in Australia', *Buch Macht Geschichte: Beiträge zur verlags-und Medienforschung*, P.F. Blume (ed.), De Gruyter, Berlin, pp. 311–28.

A.A. Phillips, 1969, 'Confessions of an escaped censor', *Meanjin*, no. 4, December, pp. 508–13.

Philip Roth, 1967a, 'A Jewish patient begins his analysis', *Esquire*, vol. 67, no. 4, April, pp. 104, 107, 191–93.

— 1967b, 'Whacking off', *Partisan Review*, vol. 34, no. 3, Summer, pp. 385–98.

REPORTS

1904 New South Wales Royal Commission on the Decline of the Birth-Rate and on the Mortality of Infants in New South Wales Report, vol. 1, William Applegate Gullick, Sydney.

THESES

Dominic Bowes, 2012, 'Exposing Indecency: censorship and Sydney's alternative presses, 1963–1973', Honours thesis, University of Sydney.

Stephen Payne, 1980, 'Aspects of Commonwealth Literary Censorship in Australia, 1929–1941', Masters thesis, Australian National University.

BOOKS

n.a., 1965, *The Case of Lady Chatterley's Lover*, Horwitz Publications, Sydney.

James Atlas, 2019, *Remembering Roth*, Audible, New York.

Wendy Bacon and Peter Coleman, 1975, *Censorship*, Ann Turner (ed.), Heinemann Educational, South Yarra.

Sybille Bedford, 2016, *Would You Let Your Wife Read This Book?: the trial of Lady Chatterley's Lover*, Daunt Books, London.

Jeffrey Berman, 1980, *The Talking Cure: literary representations of psychoanalysis*, New York University Press, New York.

Frank Bongiorno, 2012, *The Sex Lives of Australians: a history*, Black Inc., Collingwood.

Ken Buckley, 1970, *Offensive and Obscene: a civil liberties casebook*, Ure Smith, Sydney.

— 2008, *Buckley's!: an autobiography*, A&A Publishing, Australia.

Vincent Buckley, 1991, *Last Poems*, McPhee Gribble, Melbourne.

Anthony Burgess, 1984, *Ninety-Nine Novels*, Allison & Busby, London.

Dorothy Campbell and Scott Campbell, 2007, *The Liberating of Lady Chatterley and Other True Stories: a history of the New South Wales Council for Civil Liberties*, Southwood Press, Marrickville.

Bennett Cerf, 1977, *At Random: the reminiscences of Bennett Cerf*, Random House, New York.

Don Chipp and John Larkin, 1978, *The Third Man*, Rigby, Adelaide.

Robert Close, 1977, *Of Salt and Earth: an autobiography*, Thomas Nelsons, Melbourne.

David Clune and Ken Turner, 2006, *The Premiers of New South Wales, Volume 2, 1901–2005*, Federation Press, Annandale.

Peter Coleman, 1963, *Obscenity, Blasphemy, Sedition: censorship in Australia*, Jacaranda Press, Brisbane.

— 1994, *Memoirs of a Slow Learner*, Angus & Robertson, Pymble.

Alan Cooper, 1996, *Philip Roth and the Jews*, State University of New York Press, Albany.

Zelman Cowen, 1971, *From the Trial of Lady Chatterley to the Trial of Oz: some footnotes on a decade, particularly with reference to literary censorship*, Third Annual Housden Lecture, Carey Grammar School, Kew, supplement to the Australian School Librarian, December.

Tanya Dalziell and Paul Genoni, 2013, *Telling Stories: Australian life and literature 1935–2012*, Monash University Publishing, Clayton.

Lloyd Davies, 1986, *In Defence of My Family: the inside story of the Hewett libel cases*, Peppy Gully Press, Peppermint Grove.

David Day, 1996, *Contraband and Controversy: the customs history of Australia from 1901*, AGPS, Canberra.

Don Dunstan, 1981, *Felicia: the political memoirs of Don Dunstan*, MacMillan, South Melbourne.

Keith Dunstan, 1968, *Wowsers: being an account of the prudery exhibited by certain outstanding men and women in such matters as drinking, smoking, prostitution, censorship, and gambling*, Cassell, North Melbourne.

Gil Duthie, 1984, *I Had 50,000 Bosses: memoirs of a Labor backbencher, 1946–1975*, Angus & Robertson, Sydney.

Geoffrey Dutton, 1984, *Snow on the Saltbush: the Australian literary experience*, Viking, Ringwood.

— 1994, *Out in the Open: an autobiography*, University of Queensland Press, St Lucia.

— 1996, *A Rare Bird: Penguin Books in Australia 1946–96*, Penguin, Ringwood.

Jason D. Ensor, 2013, *Angus & Robertson and the British Trade in Australian books, 1930–1970: the getting of bookselling wisdom*, Anthem Press, London.

Raymond Evans and Carole Ferrier (eds), 2004, *Radical Brisbane: an unruly history*, Vulgar Press, Carlton North.

Sam Everingham, 2009, *Gordon Barton: Australia's maverick entrepreneur*, Allen & Unwin, Crows Nest.

Charlie Fox, Bobbie Oliver, and Lenore Layman (eds), 2017, *Radical Perth, Militant Fremantle*, Black Swan Press/Curtin University, Perth.

Robert Garran, 1958, *Prosper the Commonwealth*, Angus & Robertson, Sydney.

Robin Gerster and Jan Bassett, 1991, *Seizures of Youth: the 1960s and Australia*, Hyland House, South Yarra.

Robert Gott and Richard Linden, 1994, *Cut It Out: censorship in Australia*, CIS Publishers, Carlton.

James Hall and Sandra Hall, 1970, *Australian Censorship: the XYZ of love*, Dai Nippon Printing Co., Hong Kong.

Steve Hare (ed.), 1994, *Penguin Portrait: Allen Lane and the Penguin editors 1935–1970*, Penguin, London.

Frank Hardy, 1961, *The Hard Way*, T. Werner Laurie, London.

Paul Hasluck, 1997, *The Chance of Politics*, Text, Melbourne.

Søren Hensen and Jesper Jensen, 1971, *The Little Red Schoolbook*, trans. Berit Thornberry, Stage One, London.

Michael Heyward, 1993, *The Ern Malley Affair*, University of Queensland Press, St Lucia.

Michael S. Howard, *Jonathan Cape, Publisher*, Jonathan Cape, London.

Jean-Claude van Itallie, 1968, *America Hurrah*, Pocket Books, New York.

Judith Jones and Guinevera Nance, 1978, *Philip Roth*, Frederick Ungar Publishing Co., New York.

Prue Joske and Louise Hoffman, n.d., *Inside Perth's Bookshops*, Second Back Row Press, Sydney.

Nancy Keesing, 1988, *Riding the Elephant*, Allen & Unwin, Sydney.

Ai Kobayashi, 2013, *W. Macmahon Ball: politics for the people*, Australian Scholarly Publishing, North Melbourne.

Dominick LaCapra, 1982, *Madame Bovary on Trial*, Cornell University
    Press, Ithaca.
Thomas W. Laquer, 2003, *Solitary Sex: a cultural history of masturbation*,
    Zone Books, New York.
Valerie Lawson, 1995, *The Allens Affair: how one man shook the
    foundations of a leading Australian law firm*, Macmillan, Sydney.
J.S. Legge (ed.), 1971, *Who's Who*, Herald & Weekly Times, Melbourne.
Jeremy Lewis, 2010, *Shades of Greene: one generation of an English family*,
    Jonathan Cape, London.
Wm. Roger Louis (ed.), 2008, *Penultimate Adventures with Britannia:
    personalities, politics, and culture in Britain*, I.B. Tauris, London.
Martyn Lyons and John Arnold (eds), 2001, *A History of the Book
    in Australia 1891–1945: a national culture in a colonised market*,
    University of Queensland Press, St Lucia.
David Marr, 2008 [1991], *Patrick White: a life*, Random House, North
    Sydney.
— 1999, *The High Price of Heaven*, Allen & Unwin, St Leonards.
A.W. Martin, 1993, *Robert Menzies: a life*, vol. 1, Melbourne University
    Press, Carlton.
— 1999, *Robert Menzies: a life*, vol. 2, Melbourne University Press,
    Carlton.
John McDaniel, 1974, *The Fiction of Philip Roth*, Haddonfield House,
    New Jersey.
John McLaren, 1996, *Writing in Hope and Fear: literature as politics in
    postwar Australia*, Cambridge University Press, Melbourne.
Hilary McPhee, 2001, *Other People's Words*, Picador, Sydney.
Nicole Moore, 2012, *The Censor's Library*, University of Queensland
    Press, St Lucia.
Frank Moorhouse, 2007 [1980], *Days of Wine and Rage*, Vintage, Sydney.
J.E. Morpurgo, 1979, *Allen Lane: king penguin*, Hutchison, London.
Paul W. Mosher and Jeffrey Berman, 2015, *Confidentiality and Its
    Discontents: dilemmas of privacy in psychotherapy*, Fordham University
    Press, New York.
Barry Muir, 1973, *Bolte from Bamganie*, Hill of Content, Melbourne.

Craig Munro and Robyn Sheahan-Bright (eds), 2006, *Paper Empires: a history of the book in Australia 1946–2005*, University of Queensland Press, St Lucia.

Richard Neville, 1995, *Hippie Hippie Shake*, Bloomsbury, London.

Bruce Oswald and Jim Waddell (eds), 2014, *Justice in Arms: military lawyers in the Australian Army's first hundred years*, Big Sky Publishing, Newport.

Robert Page, 1970, *Australian Bookselling*, Hill of Content, Melbourne.

Brian Penton, 1947, *Censored! Being a true account of a notable fight for your right to read and know, with some comment on the plague of censorship in general*, Shakespeare Head Press, Sydney.

Claudia Roth Pierpont, 2014 [2013], *Roth Unbound: a writer and his books*, Jonathan Cape, London.

Charles Renbar, 1968, *The End of Obscenity: the trials of Lady Chatterley, Tropic of Cancer, and Fanny Hill*, Random House, New York.

Julie Rigg (ed.), 1969, *In Her Own Right: women of Australia*, Thomas Nelson, Sydney.

Julie Rigg and Julie Copeland (eds), 1985, *Coming Out!: women's voices, women's lives*, Nelson in association with the ABC, Melbourne.

Geoffrey Robertson, 1979, *Obscenity: an account of censorship law and their enforcement in England and Wales*, Weidenfeld and Nicolson, London.

— 1999, *The Justice Game*, Vintage, London.

— 2019, *Rather His Own Man*, Vintage, North Sydney.

Bernard F. Rodgers, Jr, 1978, *Philip Roth*, G.K. Hall & Co., Boston.

C.H. Rolph, 1969, *Books in the Dock*, Andre Deutsch, London.

— (ed.), 1990, *The Trial of Lady Chatterley's Lover*, Penguin, London.

Philip Roth, 2005 [1969], *Portnoy's Complaint*, Vintage, New York.

— 2016 [1975], *Reading Myself and Others*, Vintage, New York.

— 2016 [1988], *The Facts: a novelist's autobiography*, Vintage, New York.

Derek Parker Royal (ed.), 2005, *Philip Roth: new perspectives on an American author*, Praeger Publishers, Westport.

John Sendy, 1983, *Melbourne's Radical Bookshops*, International Bookshop Pty Ltd, Melbourne.

Norman Sherry, 2005, *The Life of Graham Greene, Volume Three, 1955–1991*, Pimlico, London.

Jeff Sparrow, 2012, *Money Shot: a journey into porn and censorship*, Scribe, Melbourne.

Barbara Sullivan, 1997, *The Politics of Sex: prostitution and pornography in Australia since 1945*, Cambridge University Press, Melbourne.

Anne Summers, 1999, *Ducks on the Pond: an autobiography, 1945–1976*, Viking, Ringwood.

Bill Sutton, 1973, *The Good Looking Bookseller and the Ugly Society: a talk*, Communist Arts Society, Brisbane.

Robert P. Vine-Hall (ed.), 1967, *Bignold's Police Offences and Vagrancy Acts*, ninth edition, Law Book Company Ltd, Sydney.

Patrick White, 1994, *Letters*, ed. David Marr, Random House, Milsons Point.

W.E. Williams, 1973, *Allen Lane: a personal portrait*, Bodley Head, London.

H.N.P. Wollaston, 1904, *Customs Law and Regulations, with Notes and References*, William Brooks & Co., Sydney.

Angela Woollacott, 2019, *Don Dunstan: the visionary politician who changed Australia*, Allen & Unwin, Sydney.

Hugo Young, 1976, *The Crossman Affair*, Jonathan Cape, London.

ARCHIVAL PAPERS
New South Wales State Archives

Court Reporting, Office Transcripts, February 1971 and May 1971, *Regina vs. Angus & Robertson*, NRS 2713, 19/8516.

Summons Court Proceedings, 14 December 1970, Summons Papers, NRS 3427, 13/6063.

Case File, Angus & Robertson Ltd., 2464 of 1970, Shelf Location 10/9387.

Register of Prosecutions under the *Obscene and Indecent Publications Act 1901*, NRS 1257, 12/4142.3.

Chief Secretary's Special Bundles, 1967–1982, Files Relating to
Indecent Articles and Classified Publications, NRS 906, 12/4121,
item A69/950.

Papers Relating to Aspects of Legislation Including Censorship, NRS
1116, 12/4322.3 (Part A), and 12/4323.1 (Part B).

State Records Office of Western Australia
Premiers Department, s1228–cons1819, item 1971/465, cabinet
meeting 1 June 1971: 'Amendments to Indecent Publications Act',
27 May 1971.

National Library of Australia
Papers of Geoffrey Dutton, NLA MS 7285.
Papers of Hilary McPhee, NLA MS 13.076.
Papers of A.W. Sheppard, NLA MS 8029.
Papers of Thomas White, NLA MS 9148.

State Library of New South Wales
Papers of Sam Everingham relating to Gordon Barton, ML MSS 8614.
Papers of Angus & Robertson, ML MSS 3269.

National Archives of Australia
'Correspondence and newspaper articles relating to prohibited
publication *Portnoy's Complaint*', NAA: A425, 72/4378.

'Broomhall, Joan Volume 5' and 'Broomhall, Joan Volume 6, NAA:
A6119, 3891 and 3892.

'Commonwealth of Australia records about importation of prohibited
publications and letters about censorship, Office of Film and
Literature Classification', NAA: C4480, 23.

'Decisions, with comments, on literature forwarded by the Customs
Department to the Literature Censorship Board', NAA: A3023,
folder 1945/1947.

'Reviews submitted to Dr LH Allen, Appeal Censor and Chairman, Commonwealth Literary Censorship Board', NAA: C4419, whole series.

'Hutchinson & Co. (Publishers) Ltd. Literature for decision "L" Lolita', NAA: B13, 1964/5367.

'Representations and press cuttings — Re: application by ANU for "Lolita"', NAA: A425, 1964/5354.

'Publication — "Lady Chatterley's Lover" — Part 1', NAA: A425, 1964/8571.

'"Lady Chatterley's Lover" by DH Lawrence — Release in Australia', NAA: A4940, C3263.

'Censorship decision — "The Trial of Lady Chatterley" — edited by CH ROLPH', NAA: D596, 1961/2081

'Kenneth Donald BUCKLEY — Volume 1', NAA: A6119, 479 Reference Copy.

Paul Hasluck, 'Events following the election of October 25, 1969', NAA: M1767, 3.

Cabinet submission no. 768, 'Literature censorship — publication in Australia of prohibited book "The Trial of Lady Chatterley"', May 1965, NAA: A5827, Volume 23/Agendum 768.

Cabinet notebook, 'Notetaker EJ Bunting — Notes of meetings 6 February 1961–3 May 1961', NAA: A11099, 1/50.

Cabinet notebook, 'Notetaker EJ Bunting, notes of meetings 1 September 1964–7 October 1964', NAA: A11099, 1/69.

Cabinet notebook, 'EJ Bunting — Notes of meetings 5 May 1965–26 May 1965', NAA: A11099, 1/73.

Cabinet notebook, 'Sir John Bunting, 21 March 1972–20 June 1972', NAA: A11099, 1/123.

'Single authority on literature censorship', 27 August 1964, NAA: A5827, VOLUME 12/AGENDUM 394.

Cabinet minute no. 898, 'Little Red School Book — without submission', 18 April 1972, NAA: A5909, 898.

University of Bristol

'Pages of minutes of Penguin Books Australia Limited Directors Meetings', DM1294/4/5/1/1, Penguin Archive, University of Bristol.

University of Reading

'Correspondence relating to the publication of Portnoy's Complaint by Philip Milton Roth (1933–)', JC 118/1, Penguin Random House Archive.

'Correspondence relating to the export to Australia of Portnoy's Complaint by Philip Milton Roth (1933–)', JC 118/2. Penguin Random House Archive.

Oral Histories

Kenneth Anderson, interviewed by Mel Pratt, 1977, NLA Oral History, TRC 121/90.

Ken Buckley, interviewed by Ann Turner, 1994, NLA Oral History, TRC 3018.

Don Chipp, interviewed by Bernadette Schedvin, 14 May–12 October 1987, NLA Oral History TRC 4900/73.

Peter Cowan, interviewed by Stuart Reid, October 1991–August 1992, NLA Oral History, TRC 2897.

Geoffrey Dutton, interviewed by Suzanne Lunney, 11 June 1974, NLA Oral History, TRC 472.

Geoffrey Dutton, interviewed by Bob Brissenden, 13 November 1986, NLA Oral History, TRC 2120.

Bob Gould, interviewed by Edgar Waters, 27 November 1994, NLA Oral History, TRC 3185.

Denham Henty, interviewed by Suzanne Lunney, 1974, NLA Oral History, TRC 309.

Len King, interviewed by Peter Donovan, 10 November 2014, J.D. Somerville Oral History Collection, State Library of South Australia, OH 715/1.

Frederick Osborne, interviewed by Ron Hurst, 11 June 1985–21 January 1991, NLA Oral History, TRC 4900/108.

Malcolm Scott, interviewed by John Ferrell, 1986–87, NLA Oral History, TRC 4900/76.

A.W. Sheppard, interviewed by Ann Turner, 1991, NLA Oral History, TRC 2725.

AUTHOR'S INTERVIEWS AND CORRESPONDENCE

Author's interview with Wendy Bacon, 26 June 2019.

Author's interview with Reginald Barrett, 4 July 2019.

Author's interview with Sir Max Bingham, 14 February 2019.

Author's interview with Stephen Charles, 6 December 2018.

Author's interview with Hal G.P. Colebatch, 10 May 2019.

Author's interview with Maureen Colman, 3 December 2018.

Author's correspondence with Dennis Douglas, 5, 8, 11, and 12 January 2019.

Author's interview with Leon Fink, 5 March 2019.

Author's interview with Peter Froelich, 13 December 2018.

Author's interview with Lucy Frost, 27 November 2018.

Author's interview with Paul Grainger, 30 January 2019.

Author's interview with Jennifer Gribble, 5 September 2019.

Author's correspondence with Peter Grose, 11 June 2019.

Author's interview with Margaret Harris, 28 November 2018.

Author's interview with Harry Heseltine, 1 August 2018.

Author's interview with Tom Hughes, 2 December 2018.

Author's interview with Brian Kiernan, 1 August 2019.

Author's interview with Joanne Lee Dow, 10 December 2018.

Author's interview with David Marr, 22 November 2018.

Author's interview with Joan Masterman, 5 February 2019.

Author's interview with Hilary McPhee, 6 March 2019.

Author's correspondence with Meredith Michie, 8 July 2019.

Author's interview with Malcolm Oakes, 26 June 2019, and correspondence 9 July 2019.

Author's interview with John Reid, 12 December 2018.

Author's interview with Julie Rigg, 31 August 2019.

Author's interview with Bob Sessions, 16 December 2018.

Author's interview with Brian Stonier, 24 April 2019.

Author's interview with Jennifer Strauss, 6 December 2018.

Author's interview with Ian Viner, 28 May 2019.

Author's interview with David Walsh, 12 February 2019.

Author's interview with Richard Walsh, 15 May 2019.

Author's interview with Charles Waterstreet, 4 March 2019.

Author's interview with Charles Wooley, 8 February 2019.

Index